Maurice Francis Egan

The life around us

a collection of stories

Maurice Francis Egan

The life around us
a collection of stories

ISBN/EAN: 9783741135231

Manufactured in Europe, USA, Canada, Australia, Japa

Cover: Foto ©Andreas Hilbeck / pixelio.de

Manufactured and distributed by brebook publishing software (www.brebook.com)

Maurice Francis Egan

The life around us

THE LIFE AROUND US:

A COLLECTION OF STORIES.

BY

MAURICE FRANCIS EGAN,
AUTHOR OF "SONGS AND SONNETS," "PRELUDES," ETC., ETC.

FR. PUSTET & CO.:
NEW YORK AND CINCINNATI.

TO

EDWARD ROTH, A.M.,

THIS

COLLECTION OF STORIES IS AFFECTIONATELY
DEDICATED

BY

A WRITER WHO OWES WHAT IS BEST IN IT TO HIS CORDIAL
ENCOURAGEMENT.

A CONFIDENTIAL CHAT WITH THE READER.

THE stories in this collection were written at various times during the last ten years. They were printed in *The Catholic Record*, an excellent magazine, since suspended; *The Catholic World;* the New York *Freeman's Journal*, and other periodicals of high character. They are as various as the years in which they were written. The author's only object was to utilize the experience in story-writing gained by years of constant anonymous contributions to secular publications, in a series of stories made by a Catholic for Catholics.

He regrets that, except in one story—"A Measureless Ill"—he has not come up to his own standard.

He regrets, too, that it is impossible for him to supply a conclusion to every story that would satisfy all his past and future readers. He feels the "long felt want" of a patent adaptable ending that would fit any story without being incongruous.

He has been warned that the good Sisters (from many of whom he has received requests to make this collection) would not like the stories that end with marriages. An accomplished and saintly religious to whom he half-humorously repeated this warning, said quite gravely,

"Nuns do not object to other people marrying, if they have the vocation and are worthy to make happy homes." This answer is all the author can give to the critics who object to marriage in "The Life Around Us." He points with pride to the fact that he has exercised a self-denial unusual with Catholic story writers--none of his characters having married cousins within the prohibited degrees.

Another critic shook his head. "The love-making in the stories is too tame. Young people will not read stories unless there is plenty of love-making in them." The author admits that he is a homœopathist in the matter of love-making. He has made a very little go a great way.

A learned priest, who wrote that he always reads a good story when he finds it, complained that "Lilies among Thorns" had as many deaths at the end as the last scene of *Hamlet*, and that "A Rosebud" and "Philista" are too tragical. But all complete stories must end with death. The author has been told at least twenty times that Bernard Devir should not be separated from his devoted mother—that it was wrong to seem to punish her for her pious and laudable desire; that Jean Marquette should have been ordained a priest with his friend Ned Barnes; that Tita should not have been permitted to marry John Nelson; that it should be made clear whether the child in "A Measureless Ill" was baptized or not; that Priscilla ought not to have made a marriage which must prove unfortunate, owing to the prejudices of her friends; that the Rosebud should have gone to a convent; that Inez should not have gone to a convent; that the miserable heroine of "Philista" should have become a nun, in order to expiate her apostasy.

To this last suggestion the author objects with all his strength. In the usual romance, religious are represented as either having been disappointed in love or as accepting a life of gloom in reparation for sin,

"In that dim sepulchre of loveless death,"

as a recent versifier, very ignorant of conventual life, expresses it. The author would rather never touch a pen than give even the slightest weight of fiction to such a degrading and absurd opinion. He might have put the heroine of "Philista"—who thus far has excited more interest than all his other characters—into a house with a brown-stone front without violating nature and art. But he would not, without violating both, send her to a convent. The truth is, that the real person from whom he drew Alice O'Brien is now outwardly a very contented being, received by all the "best" families in Philista and comfortably endowed with this world's goods.

To the question, "Did Miss Catherwood become a Catholic?" he can only answer that, if she did, it was in spite of some very bad examples.

MAURICE FRANCIS EGAN.

EASTER, 1885.

CONTENTS.

	PAGE
A Tragi-Comedy,	1
Lilies among Thorns,	31
Philista,	63
A Descendant of the Puritans,	93
A Virginia Comedy,	123
A Rosebud,	139
Trifles,	157
A Measureless Ill,	193
John Nelson's Marriage,	202
Among the "Olive Branches,"—The Story of a New York Boy,	216
At the Gate of Death,	239
The Financial Crash,	259
A Story of To-day,	279
The Lisles,	297
Inez,	318
"A Sorrow's Crown of Sorrow,"	338
Rose,	358
The Jaws of Death,	379
Carmel,	390

A TRAGI-COMEDY.

I.

IT was a very great effort. The orchestra had just finished Beethoven's "Hope" when Bernard Devir stepped forward, with a bow he had practiced for several weeks at intervals, and unrolled a manuscript. His collar was high and uncomfortable, and the rose in the buttonhole of his shining black coat made him feel the stiffness that always afflicts the male sex when over-decorated.

' His father and mother, in the third row of benches from the platform, felt that the eyes of the assembly were upon them. They sat very straight, and Mr. Devir, as a relief for his nervousness, smoothed his new silk hat with his handkerchief. The room was warm; there was a flutter of fans, a scent of June roses from the nosegays; not a breath of air was stirring; a man, utterly without a soul, on the back bench, had snored during John Dempsey's impassioned parallel (thirty-six pages of foolscap) between Mohammed and Arius. Even His Grace, who sat in an arm-chair on the platform, surrounded by several of the reverend clergy, had been observed to hold his hand before his mouth during the lengthy but eloquent essay on "Grattan as a Patriot," and while Dick Weldon was making a beautiful apostrophe of five pages to the Italian republics in his "Examination of the

Genius of Machiavelli," something like a look of gentle melancholy was seen to steal across the face of His Grace, which deepened as Dick rustled twenty more leaves, written on both sides. Everybody, except the dignified personages on the platform, looked eagerly at Bernard Devir when he appeared. His father thought it was the halo of genius on his son's brow that attracted this attention; his mother thought it was his personal beauty: how nice he looked in his high collar, with his hair plastered in a hyacinthine half-circle on his forehead, and a thin, reddish down visible on his upper lip in a certain light—how superior to that sallow-faced South American who had preceded him, in broken English, with a paper on "Arctic Expeditions"! Mrs. Devir waved her palm-leaf fan and felt that she was indeed blessed. She did not know that this noticeable eagerness was due to the fact that the audience was trying, with all its failing mental strength, to guess how many pages were bound up in the valedictorian's manuscript.

It was a fine effort. He opened with a quotation which prepared his auditors for something entirely original. "*Timeo Danaos et dona ferentes*," he said, and then he began an examination of "Free Thought and its Relations to the Poetry of the Renaissance in Italy."

> "Rheni pacator," he exclaimed, "et Istri
> Omnis in hoc uno variis discordia cessit
> Ordinibus; lætatur eques, plauditque senator,
> Votoque patricio certant plebeia favori."

These words sent a thrill through the hearts of the father and mother of the valedictorian. With one accord they turned their eyes toward His Grace to see how they affected him. He was engaged in wiping his forehead with a purple silk handkerchief. Mrs. Devir wondered how anybody could think of such a trivial thing at this awful moment.

The valedictorian descended into English. He cast long, lingering glances into the past; he prophesied of the future; he talked to Mr. Gladstone in a way that no man with any respect for himself ought to stand; he fearlessly told Prince Bismarck what he thought of him; he raised Erin from her prostrate state and told her how she ought to behave herself; he quoted "Let Erin remember the Days of Old." This brought out a volume of applause, and the first violin, suddenly awakened and fancying that the end had come, played the opening bar of the waltz in the "Merry War."

The valedictorian went on, however; he gave a sketch of Darwin, and then, soaring upward, told why Raphael had included Dante among the theologians of the church in a famous picture; he castigated the pagan spirit of the Renaissance with fury, and, coming down to modern life, gave Swinburne a blow that almost moved his mother to remonstrate.

"Sure, Terence," she whispered to her husband, "he's very, very hard on that one."

"Whoever he is, he deserves it," answered that good man. "Barney knows what he's talking about."

"But I think he's making very free with the pope."

It became plain even to Mrs. Devir that her son was attacking Alexander Pope, and not Pope Alexander. The rolling of a cart outside obliged the orator to pause, and for an instant nearly everybody felt as if gentle dew had fallen from heaven. He dropped Pope and grappled with Lorenzo the Magnificent. Six pages were turned, while all watched him in silent suspense. Suddenly, with lowered voice, he addressed his classmates as "dear companions of his scholastic pursuits," and when he got to "you, right reverend prelate, and reverend clergy, whose presence here, etc., etc.," the first violin laid his bow on the strings; but when he said, "If in the dim vista of the future, hidden from us by wisest dispensation, we meet together, perhaps crowned by Fame and made the elect of her temple, with tear-dimmed eyes we shall look back on the roseate, studious, and tranquil hours spent in the sylvan shades of our Alma—" the first violin could restrain himself no longer; the strains of the "Merry War" rang out, and a weak, small voice was heard to murmur, "Deo gratias!" The breeze seemed to stir up suddenly; tired nature was at once restored; the man on the back bench awoke for the fifth time, to find happiness all around him. His Grace smiled most benevolently, shook hands with Bernard, and said kind things to everybody. All the graduates, adorned with medals and loaded with gilded books, were presented to him. All was joy, congratulations, wilted roses, perspiration, and expectation of luncheon.

There were no happier people in the crowd than the Devirs. Mrs. Devir put on her well-kept broché shawl, which Bernard held for her, and fastened the big round cameo brooch with ceremony at her throat. It was the happiest moment of her life, for His Grace had just said to Bernard, "It was a fine effort." Bernard kissed her, and gave the precious manuscript, tied with blue ribbons, into her keeping.

Jack Dempsey, now B.A., elbowed his way through the crowd and shook Bernard's hand, noticing, with a pang—for he was an orphan—the proud, tender look in the eyes of Bernard's mother.

"That composition of yours knocked us all cold," said Jack Dempsey heartily; he wanted to say something complimentary. Mrs. Devir started. Was this the young orator who had a short time ago grandiloquently discoursed on Grattan—a scholar who wore a medal and who could quote Latin? "We needed cooling," continued the unconscious Jack. "I am glad I'm done with the whole business."

Mrs. Devir's horrified attention was drawn from the free-and-easy young Bachelor of Arts to a slight, pretty girl who came toward them, bearing a big nosegay with the regulation lily overtopping it. She smiled, showing two rows of dazzling teeth.

"Mother sent this for Bernard," she said, "but I couldn't get it to him."

"Thank you, Marie," said Mrs. Devir a trifle stiffly. Bernard was out of college now, and intended for the highest vocation in life, and the mother was anxious to guard him from all possible danger.

"They are too late now, Monsieur Bernard."

"Pas du tout, mademoiselle," said Bernard, with a slight blush and a bow. "I will take a rose and keep it, and you will keep the rest."

"D'ye mind that, now?" murmured Mr. Devir, nudging his wife. "There's more learned in college than Latin."

Mrs. Devir did mind it. Even her son's readiness in French did not reconcile her to it. Jack Dempsey was not slow to claim a rose too, which Marie Regnier gave him with a pretty blush.

"She's a bold piece!"

Mr. Devir did not hear this; an acquaintance of his from the same place in Ireland was pouring into his ear encomiums on Bernard's "effort."

Marie Regnier, with a parting smile which included the whole group, retired very modestly, and Mrs. Devir, relieved, took Bernard's arm to walk to the station.

By this time Bernard had said good-bye to half a hundred people, and the precious manuscript had been given to a reporter, who had no intention of having it printed, but who did not want it to fall into the hands of a rival. This tribute of the Press to Genius was very grateful to Mrs. Devir. The next morning, when she seized the early newsman at half-past four and found only six lines of it in the *Herald* (and all the Latin left out!), she felt that the art of printing was a delusion and a snare.

Jack Dempsey's eyes had rested with longing and sympathy on Mrs. Devir as she stood so proudly at her son's side; it was beautiful to see her, but she was by no means beautiful. She was a thin, worn-looking woman, with faded blue eyes, and features sharpened by care and hard work. There were two deep, upright lines on her forehead, and her hands, encased in large mitts, were wrinkled and knotted at the joints. She wore a gala bonnet decorated with two small blue cabbages and a bunch of cherries, a rusty black silk gown which had been packed away carefully after each family festival and holiday for many years, and her cherished red broché shawl of the palm-leaf pattern.

Her husband was wrinkled and stooped, too. He had a keen blue eye and a stern mouth; a fringe of white whiskers ran all around under his chin; his broadcloth frock-coat hung uneasily on him, and his trousers, also broadcloth, were rather white and baggy at the knees—naturally, since he had knelt in them at Mass for more Sundays than any pair of trousers not embalmed carefully every Monday morning until the following Sunday can endure.

"Go forth, young men," the eloquent person who had delivered the address to the graduates had said—"go forth; use the gift of tongues your Alma Mater has given you to enlighten them that sit in darkness. You will adopt professions, and perhaps rise to eminence in those professions; but in the midst of opulence, adulation, if Fame should herald one of you as the poet of the age, the Virgil of our time; if one of you should gain the highest prizes of statesmanship; if one of you should scale the heights of military glory, which, unfortunately, leads but to the grave—remember the Alma Mater that cherished your high aspirations, guided your steps aside from the 'primrose path of dalliance,' and will ever crown your highest ideals with her blessing, until you are at last dazzled by that fierce, white light which beats around the Throne. Vale et ave!"

And so they went forth. A stranger, hearing all that had been said, might have imagined the world was longing to crown them with bays or to put them on triumphal shields, or that they had been furnished such an equipment as princes and barons in olden days gave the young servitors of their household when the time for the conferring of knighthood had come. It seemed strange to go out into the sunny, every-day atmosphere and find that the world was not standing still. The railroad conductor collected tickets from Bernard Devir and Jack Dempsey without any apparent consciousness he touched hands that had penned the essay on "Grattan as a Patriot," and that fine effort, "Free Thought and its Relations to the Poetry of the Renaissance in Italy." But for one woman the world was transformed. Mrs. Devir had suffered and toiled. One by one her children had passed away. For this one—the pride and hope of her soul—she had worked like a slave. To see him serving the altar was the desire of her life. To-day it seemed very near to her. If she might be permitted to live to see her son say his first Mass, she could, with all her heart, join in the prayer of the holy Simeon.

It was the happiest day of her life. Jack Dempsey, careless, free-and-easy Jack, looked at her wrinkled hands and sighed. What a glory it was to have a mother! He laughed and joked, kissed his hand out of the car-window right and left; but, for all that, he missed none of the tender, prideful glances that the worn, tired woman cast upon her son. Jack, in his heart, felt sad; it seemed to him that a mother's love is born to suffer —of all earthly things the nearest to heaven, yet of all earthly things most pathetic in its disappointments.

"He's a gay blade," said Mr. Devir.

"There's no thought about him at all," answered Mrs. Devir as Jack Dempsey bade them good-bye. "They say his uncle wants to make a priest of him. He'll never do it!"

II.

That essay on "The Relations of Free Thought to the Poetry of the Italian Renaissance" was the result of many days of toil and many nights of anxiety—of early rising on cold winter mornings and late working on sultry summer evenings. It was like one of those gorgeous blooms that show on prickly and ugly cactus plants. The rough plant endures, in those regions where it flourishes, storms of dust and thousands of scorching rays from the sun; but when the flower, yellow and vermilion, appears, it doubtless forgets the dust and the sun. The toil and the trouble of producing that essay had not fallen upon Bernard. He had known where to find the material for it, and he had put it together. The bricks (to drop into metaphors) were the traditional property of college orators; he had only supplied the mortar. The real work of forcing the flamboyant exotic had been done by his father and mother.

To bring forth the flower—which was supposed to represent the result of four years of college culture—Mr. and Mrs. Devir had gone to market before dawn and stood behind the little grocery-shop near the Bowery for many weary years. It was one of Mrs. Devir's boasts that during this time they had never had a bottle of whisky in their establishment. Customers who would not buy unless they were "treated to a sip" behind the screen might go elsewhere. The "old man" was more lenient, but his wife was firm.

Bernard had been kept at school, and "held up his head with the rest there." His clothes had been as good as those of Jack Dempsey, whose uncle was a great Wall Street millionaire. Spending-money had not been grudged to him, and he had been advised to entertain his friends at a down-town restaurant on the unfrequent holidays when he had leave of absence from college. Mrs. Devir flattered herself that she was a woman of the world; she said that the ways of Bernard's friends were not her ways, and she wouldn't shame the boy by having him bring his friends, with their Latin, and their Greek, and their French, into the back-room of a grocery-shop.

Bernard would not have cared, if there had been a billiard-table in that little back-room; it would have been jammed on holidays with the young persons of culture whom Mrs. Devir would have delighted to honor. His quarterly bills for tuition and books had been promptly met; his subscriptions to the various college schemes had always been "decent." Sometimes it required sharp pinching to do all this and avoid drawing on the sum deposited in the "Emigrant's." And Mr. Devir was strongly tempted to introduce the black bottle behind the screen for such of his female customers as were afflicted with "goneness" or "sudden palpitations," with a view of increasing sales; but Mrs. Devir, true to her principles, would not hear of it.

Bernard had been graduated with honor. His parents felt that they had given him what was to be his fortune —an education. They had never had much learning; Mr. Devir could write his own name, and Mrs. Devir could make her mark. They both had an unbounded reverence for "education"—that wonderful gift which was "more than a mint of money to any poor boy"; they had been coining their lives into the education which had culminated on Commencement Day in that fine effort, "The Relations of Free Thought to the Poetry of the Italian Renaissance."

This education was to be the key with which he was to open the treasures of the world. His parents rated it at the value of the sacrifices they had made. His mother had resolved that he should be a priest, and his father, in the beginning more worldly and hoping to see him in the Assembly some day, like Dennis Rooney's son, had finally come to regard it as settled that Bernard should, when the time came, go up for examination for the seminary.

In the meantime there was a vacation before him. He had worked hard; his mother felt that he, with his stores of Greek and Latin and his wonderful accomplishments, ought not to be confined to the grocery-store or its little back-room.

"He'd look nice rolling up his sleeve and diving into the brine-barrel for mackerel!" she whispered to her husband as she watched Bernard, who was talking to a classmate in the seat before them, "or selling a bunch of garlic to one of the Eyetalians."

"It's no worse than his father did before him," responded her husband.

Mrs. Devir looked at him as an æsthete of the most intense cult sometimes gazes at a hopeless Philistine. She felt that there are some things which a man ought to know without having them told to him; and, as most women do some time or other, whatever the cynics may say, she showed her sense of the impregnable stupidity of her better-half by silence. This is a medium, by the way, very expressive in the hands of women, because it is so seldom used.

She arranged, in her mind, that Bernard should not spend much time in the store, which was no place for him. He should go to some aristocratic sea-side resort, if she had to draw something from the "Emigrant's Industrial." It would not do to have him wasting his time in the store. The father and she were used to the little place and to the ways of the neighborhood. But how could Bernard, in his frock-coat and white shirt, endure them? No; he must go, as it were, from the college to the seminary without any interregnum of the store.

Before they had reached home Mrs. Devir had settled it all with her husband. It was decided that Bernard should start on the next day for Far Rockaway. There, as Mrs. Devir said, he would "meet the society of his equals" and recuperate after his studies.

Mr. Devir shook his head dubiously. His vanity was somewhat wounded by the open preference his wife showed for his son; he had worked for him like a slave, but not that he might be placed so far above him. Now, Mrs. Devir, being a woman, had no vanity of her own; all her qualities, all her foibles, seemed to be absorbed in Bernard.

III.

Far Rockaway is a very lively sea-side place in the summer. There are cottages and hotels, and much music in the morning and evening. All the popular airs are played on all sorts of pianos by the accomplished young ladies that frequent the place in time of *villeggiatura*. There is lawn-tennis, sailing, bathing, and fishing. Dancing, too, is a favorite amusement.

Bernard Devir met Jack Dempsey in this festive town, and they had a good time. Bernard indulged in all the amusements of the place, which would have included a flirtation with the most forward of the three Misses Clarke, the belles from Syracuse; but their mother, hearing that he was a "student," put an end to that with virtuous indignation.

There was little time for thought; and Bernard gave

small consideration to his future until one day, when he and Jack Dempsey were out sailing, Jack said:

"Are you going up for the examination?"

"I suppose so," Bernard answered carelessly. "Those fellows in that boat have an immense load of blue-fish— I suppose so; the old folk want me to."

Jack was silent for a moment. Bernard, watching the fortunate man in the bow of the other boat haul in another fish, forgot the subject.

"Well, Bernard," continued Jack, "if that is the way you feel about it you'd better give the idea up. I'm not much of a preacher; but I'll say to you I'd rather cut off my right hand than go into that seminary in that way."

Jack's face flushed. Bernard smiled.

"You're awfully in earnest." And then, with a touch of seriousness himself, "What can I do? I can construe Virgil a little; but I haven't any money to keep me while I grind at law or medicine. You know I am a thoughtless fellow, Jack—*I* know I am—but I have come to the conclusion that I can't have the old people working for me any longer."

"I'd go into the grocery-store first."

Bernard laughed. The suggestion was too absurd.

During the few days that followed Bernard did think; and, more, he prayed. He was glad when the last day of his vacation at Far Rockaway came.

Supper was waiting in the little back-room of the grocery-store when he arrived at home. He went behind the counter and kissed his father, to the admiration of several waiting customers. He found his mother in her seat at the neatly-spread table. The soft light of the glittering kerosene lamp showed her how brown he had become. She clasped him to her in fond pride, and called to her husband to leave the store in charge of the "boy."

Bernard was waited upon like a young prince who had honored an humble roof by his presence. His father even offered him a cigar out of the best box, apologizing for it. The parents listened with pleasure to all Bernard had to say.

"They'll never make a priest out of that Jack Dempsey," said his mother, as that young man's name was mentioned.

"There's more chance for him than for me, mother. He feels that he has a vocation, while I—I can't go in for the examination, that's all."

The silence was unbroken. Mrs. Devir set down her teacup and looked at her son. Mr. Devir took his pipe out of his mouth.

"What did you say, Barney?" she asked tremulously.

"I'm not worthy to be a priest, mother, and I can't try."

"Not worthy!" cried Mrs. Devir. "You're joking! And you, with all your beautiful education and all the prayers that's been said for you!"

"I can't help it, mother. God knows it almost breaks my heart to tell you the truth. But I can't think of it, mother—I can't. I know it's the best thing, the highest, the holiest thing, on this earth to be a priest of God; but it's a very hard thing to be a good priest, and I haven't the vocation, mother."

Bernard said all this rapidly. He felt as if a weight had been lifted off his heart when he had spoken.

"That Marie Reguier has bewitched the boy," cried Mrs. Devir bitterly, speaking out a hasty thought and then regretting it at once when she saw the look of pain on her son's face.

"Mother!"

Mrs. Devir could no longer lift the teacup to her lips. She covered her eyes with her toil-worn hands, and tears trickled slowly between the wrinkled and knotted fingers. Her husband toyed nervously with his pipe. The boy in the store was whistling a careless tune. The lull of twilight had fallen even on the noisy city. Bernard felt as if the whole world were reproaching him.

Where was his halo now? Where was the sunshine that a moment before had shone on him from the eyes of these two old people? His father seemed stunned; his mother, after a vain effort to restrain herself, burst into sobs.

And this was the end of it all? The end of the toiling, the hoping, the praying; the downfall of pride, which had been so great in this poor mother's heart that she would have become the humblest of the humble to gratify it!

After a time of silence, broken only by his mother's sobs and the whistling of the boy in the store, Bernard arose and took his father's hand, which lay limply on his knee. The old man seemed not to notice him; he did not turn his intent gaze from his wife. Bernard clasped the hand tighter. Surely his father, whose love would be less unreasonable than a woman's, could understand; but his father, with no eyes for anybody except the weeping mother, pushed him away.

Bernard's heart swelled. Suddenly his mother raised her head in sudden hope.

"You'll not make up your mind until you've seen Father Rodman at the church?"

"I have just come from him, mother."

Mrs. Devir's head sank again.

"You're breaking your mother's heart, you spalpeen!" cried his father, bringing his fist down upon the table. "Go up to bed! It would have been better a thousand times if I'd kept you in the store here, instead of cramming your head with Latin and Greek, of no manner of use if you're not to be priested. And I'll be ashamed of my life to face the neighbors!"

Bernard, no longer a boy, but a man, heavy of heart, crept up to bed. He did not dare to kiss his mother; she sank her head lower as he passed her. He threw himself on his knees at the side of the white-spread bed and was silent. He put his hands up toward the little picture of the Sacred Heart, which had hung there ever since he could remember; he could not pray, for all things, fraught with the tenderness of that mother whose broken voice he could hear from below, seemed to blame him.

What refuge was there for him? His father and mother had turned against him. "I will go down," he thought, in a burst of passion, "and I will tell her that I will do as she wishes; but I will wash my hands of it— the sacrilege will be upon her head."

Then another thought calmed him. "I can not," he thought, "act the part of Pontius Pilate, even for my mother."

IV.

It was generally acknowledged among the neighbors and relatives of the Devirs that the "student" was a failure. To be intended for the seminary and to refuse to enter the seminary was a deep disgrace in the eyes of these good people. Mrs. Devir had talked of her son as a future priest ever since the boy had entered college. The humiliation was bitter. She could not say, as she had said in her many afflictions, "It is the will of God." She did not believe it was the will of God; it could not be the will of God that *her* son should not serve the altar. She still attended to Bernard's wants, but in cold silence. His father kept sternly quiet, too. One Saturday, when Bernard went into the store and tried to help in the work, his father roughly told him that he had no business there.

"It's my place, father," he said. "It's my turn to work now."

"We don't want Latin and Greek here. Your mother and me have done without help so long, we don't want it now."

Bernard went up-stairs again, with bitterness in his heart. The food he ate almost choked him. He felt that he was a pauper; and, consciously or unconsciously, they made him feel it. There was little consolation in his books. He thumbed over his Cicero in the little, dark room, and copied the "Relations of Free Thought to the Poetry of the Italian Renaissance" and sent it to one of the magazines. It came back in a few days, accompanied by a slip of printed paper:

"The editor regrets that, owing to a press of manuscripts, he is obliged to return the enclosed."

He could hardly believe the evidence of his eyes. What! that "fine effort," which had been praised by everybody and applauded so cordially, returned to him, no doubt unread? His cup of humiliation was overrunning.

The friends of his earlier boyhood who sat on the disused carts left in the street at night, and sang songs, or practiced dancing steps on the corners after the day's work, nodded when he passed by. He was neither fish nor fowl in their estimation. He was invited to join the "Élite Chowder Club," which drove down to Coney Island in decorated wagons, with flaring torches and blaring horns, several times a year; and the well-written note of regret which he sent to the secretary procured him some temporary scrivening work at the time of election. That was the only work he succeeded in getting, although he answered hundreds of the newspaper advertisements. Nobody seemed to want him. He was too old to be taken as a learner of a trade. There were hundreds of young men who could construe Virgil in the same position as himself. People who could do "anything," were a drug in the market.

His best coat became white at the seams, and his trousers baggy at the knees. Mr. Devir said over and over again that *he* couldn't afford to keep a "dude." Mrs. Devir said nothing. His room was always neat and his food ready; but when it was necessary to speak to him she uttered only monosyllables.

It was a wretched life. The mother suffered as acutely as the son. It never occurred to her that she was not acting a virtuous part. It never occurred to the father that his son needed his assistance. Bernard had been richly and rarely educated. If he could not make his way in the world with this costly equipment he must be worthless. What could they—ignorant, hard-working people—do for him, except keep him in bread and butter?

The key to the Temple of Fame, of which the college orator had spoken so grandiloquently, would not open the meanest tenement. Around him he saw poor boys, who had been running of errands while he was declining *mensa*, cheerfully working, independent and prosperous.

In despair he plead for work on the wharves. He was laughed at; a stripling with white hands and soft muscles could not do a stevedore's work.

If he had not been a devout and earnest Catholic he would have sunk himself, his doubts, and his wretchedness in the East River. To be a burden on two old people; to eat the bread of idleness; to have no earthly hope! It was heart-breaking. Not only to be a burden, but to be in the eyes of all a failure and reproach! And then the utter impotence of being penniless! The bootblacks were better off than he; he could not have bought a box and brush.

Jack Dempsey had written from the seminary, preaching courage. On one of Bernard's gloomiest days, as he sat in his room scanning for the ten-hundredth time the advertisements in the newspapers, his mother, silently as usually, brought him a letter. It was short. Bernard opened it; another piece of paper fell from its folds upon the floor.

"DEAR BOY:—There is not much time allowed here for useless writing, so I will be brief. My cousin, Will Dempsey, has had a full account of you from me. He is a queer fellow, an old bachelor, you know, with plenty of 'chink.' He thinks he can make you useful down on his ranch in Texas, as he can't have me. Will you go? San Lorenzo Ranch, Medina County, Texas—make note of it. I inclose his check for expenses. I've been trying to bring this about for a long time. Hope you'll go, etc., etc."

Bernard clasped the letter and the check in his hand as a drowning man might catch at a spar. How good God was after all. His heart went up in gratitude. He telegraphed his answer to Jack as soon as he cashed the check.

Mrs. Devir took Bernard's announcement of his early

departure with apparent calmness. Mr. Devir's mouth twitched a little, and he evidently kept back some demonstration of affection, but he only said:

"Well, I can't say less than God bless you, though you've been a sore trial to me and your mother."

His mother carefully packed his valise and neglected nothing that might add to his comfort. But she would not remain alone with him; she would give him no chance for a tender word. When the time came for him to go he lingered in the doorway of the little room and whispered, "Mother." She was behind the counter waiting on Marie Regnier, who was a very thrifty seamstress in the little French colony around the corner. Bernard went out into the store. His mother turned her cheek coldly toward him. He touched it with his lips, and paused. She paid no further attention to him. And he, sad and desolate, left her.

There is no being on earth who can inflict more pain with a calm face than a good woman in the consciousness of her goodness.

Marie Regnier's eyes became misty. She understood the scene. With a sudden impulse she held out her hand, and said:

"*Au revoir*, Monsieur Bernard. I pray that the good God and his Blessed Mother may keep you safe!"

Bernard could not speak; he tried to say "good-bye." Mrs. Devir contracted her brows and darted a quick, jealous look at the girl.

She went to the door and watched him disappear. Once, when he turned back for a last look, she dodged hastily into the store. When she could see him no more she went up to her room and sobbed as if her heart would break, kissing over and over again a faded daguerreotype of a little boy. And yet she had let him go without a word of kindness. David, mourning for Absalom, probably forgot a son's transgressions. This mother mourned her son's obstinacy with bitter regret and a sense of deep injury. It was only when she saw him as a little boy that she could love him without feeling the humiliation of his failure.

Bernard had glanced back. He did not see his mother, but he saw Marie Regnier, looking very nice in the morning sunshine, waving her hand to him. It gave him some comfort, and he waved his in return; he could do no less. As he did it, Hope seemed to spread her wings over him again.

V.

Jack Dempsey's cousin was a hale, hearty Tipperary man, a good Catholic and an ardent nationalist. There are some people who think that these qualities can not be united; but they can. He had a comfortable adobe house on his ranch, which was well stocked with sheep. His family consisted of a dozen small dogs and a formidable array of revolvers. The first warned him of the approach of tramps; the second proved useful when the tramps arrived with hostile intent.

He was a bachelor of fifty-five, erect as a dart, ruddy as a winter apple, with side-whiskers as white as the wool on a sheep's back at shearing-time, and clear blue eyes that bulged out a little to show that nothing escaped them.

He received Bernard cordially. He said frankly that he liked his looks. He put him at the roughest work he could, "to take the starch out of him," and Bernard worked with all his might. It was good to get out among the mesquite, in the soft, dry air, and to know that at last he was of use in the world, although he was earning only a ranchman's wages and eating a ranchman's rations.

After a time old Will Dempsey and Bernard became friends. Bernard acquired some new tricks in the making of corn-bread and the cooking of beef that warmed the heart of old Will, who had never had much skill in the culinary line. He soon knew Bernard's story; for the two had many a long smoke and talk by the fire in the chilly time of the year. He smiled when Bernard alluded to Marie Regnier's leave-taking, and, much to Bernard's surprise, warned him solemnly that he was "very young." At this time Bernard could not see the drift of this. Old Will rarely talked of himself; he seemed to find little interest in any subject outside of Irish politics and the affairs of the ranch. Once, smiling at a letter he had gotten recently, he told Bernard an episode in his life. When he was prospecting in Mexico, or rather searching for one of those mines said to have been worked by the Indians before the coming of the Spaniards, he had had a partner named Marianno Galdez—"a greaser, but an honest man." Galdez had died of fever; after the priest had anointed him he had asked Will to look after his wife and children. "In fact," said Will, with a twinkle in his eye, "he asked me to marry her, if she'd be willing. And I think I'd have promised, only the Galdez children were twins. Somehow or other it seemed too much to ask as things were; but I promised to look after the mother and the little ones. It wasn't a hard thing to do, as I made several good strikes and kept flush. But the mother and one of the children died of the same fever, which was raging like a lion, before I could reach Laredo, where they were. A priest there wrote to me that Maria, the other one, was a handsome child, and said that he'd see after her bringing-up, if I'd pay the expenses—poor Galdez died before I made the strikes, as poor as a church mouse. Troth, I was glad to get off so easily. I don't know much Spanish, but I think Maria's letters do her credit. And here's the only photograph I have of her. I've never seen her myself: she must be about seventeen now. Some day I'll take you down to San Jacinto and introduce you, my boy."

Bernard looked at a photograph of a fat baby with black eyes. The letters were written in a large, sprawling hand, and signed "Maria" with a flourish.

"It seems that the good priest, who is a Spaniard, thinks that Maria ought to learn English, out of compliment to me, and he has hired a Frenchman, his sacristan, to teach her; and this linguist writes me a specimen letter to prove his proficiency. Just read it!"

"SAN JACINTO, *April* 6, 18—.

"RESPECTFUL SIR:—Maria José Galdez is shameful not to possess your astringent language, to thank his benefactor of his kindness ineffable. Maria demands that I to you write this epistle, to you give information of progress. Be not astonish that in a few monthes my pupil write so perfectly the English as me; we speak all the day English and with my sister, who late comes from New York, which he has not seen me since we parted a little babee at the eyes blue in Paris. Maria speak so well that the sheepses well comprehend the English, saying 'go lon',' and the sheepses 'go lon'.' The good presbyter implore to thank you a hundred thousand times. I hope my composition please you. For me, I would come to see you and bring Maria; but I am coward of the cowboys. With sentiments of the most profound respect, me,

"I am, your obedient,   É. REGNIER."

Bernard laughed. "Maria will speak English well, at this rate."

"Her husband shall teach her," said old Will. "In a year or two I intend to find her an American husband. I wish she could write English, for I can't read her Spanish letters. I'm sure she must be a very pretty girl, for her mother was just like one of those dark-eyed colleens—more power to them!—that I've seen in Waterford."

During the six months that followed this conversation, there was a great deal of talk between Will Dempsey and Bernard on the subject of Maria. It was a subject on which the elder man liked to dwell, and which rather bored the younger one. Several letters came from San Jacinto, purporting to be written in English. The rattling up of genders in these missives was appalling. Maria seemed unable to tell the difference between *he* and *she*, much to her guardian's amusement.

Two letters came from New York, both dictated by Mrs. Devir to a friend who wrote after the manner of the Polite Letter-Writer. The tone of these letters, although enriched with ornaments of style by the amanuensis, did not give much comfort to Bernard.

Will Dempsey amazed Bernard by proposing that he should assume the management of the ranch, and offering him an interest in the land and flocks. After some talk the veteran said:

"You see Jack's going to be a priest; he has a patrimony, and his uncle will leave him something, too. Now, I've nobody, except Maria Galdez, that has any claim on me. You're a good boy; you've unlearned a lot of useless things here and tried to make me comfortable. Attention! This house is a good house, and

I've spared no expense on it; but it needs a woman in it to complete it. How would you like to marry Maria and bring her here?"

Bernard was stunned.

"Couldn't you see that I've been aiming at that all along? Come, now; ride down to San Jacinto and take a look at my little twin. If she likes you, just talk to Padre David and bring her back the wife of the best fellow I know."

"But if she shouldn't like me?"

"Faint heart. Faith, if I were your age I wouldn't throw away the chance of marrying a pretty girl, pleasing a friend, and coming into a place like San Lorenzo Ranch."

Bernard's color rose. The face of Marie Regnier *would* flit across his memory.

"We must have a woman to look after matters here. *I* can't marry—I'm too old for illusions; you ought to. Is it yes or no?"

"Well, I'll go," said Bernard reluctantly. "Remember, if she doesn't like me I can't help it."

Will Dempsey chuckled. "Padre David will arrange it. Mexican girls are not so particular or so independent as your Americans of the North. She'll like you!"

Bernard did not find this assurance at all consoling. At any rate, he would humor his kind friend's caprice; so he mounted his mustang and started on a day's ride to San Jacinto.

"If she doesn't like you!" cried old Will in stentorian tones, "bring home somebody else. I won't have you here unless you marry a wife." And he chuckled over and over again, muttering against the absurdity of American sentimentalism in regard to marriage.

Bernard's ride was not an enjoyable one. He had not thought about marriage; it had occurred to him that, if he ever married, he would like to have a wife like Marie Regnier. But, in his imagination, he had always sent Marie to a convent.

What if this Miss Galdez *should* take a fancy to him? What? If? Why?—the whole proceeding was ridiculous; and yet not so ridiculous after all, since marriages after this prosaic and practical manner were very common among the Spanish-speaking people around San Lorenzo. Well, he needn't marry her, if he did not like her; and she couldn't marry him in spite of himself. He felt like a fool, and turned back. What was the use of that? Will Dempsey would only laugh at his sentimentalism. He went on, wondering whether Maria Galdez was at all like Marie Regnier or not. He considered Will's photograph of the fat little Galdez baby hideous; but ugly babies are proverbial for becoming pretty.

It was an unpleasant ride; and yet, when the oleanders in front of Padre David's house met his eyes, he was mildly expectant. He looked up and down the road before he dismounted, hoping to catch a glimpse of the young lady before she saw him.

Three people were standing in the garden. One was Padre David, gray-haired and bent, with soutane tucked up around him, reading his breviary. Bernard was anxious to attract his attention quietly. Singular as it may appear, he wanted to get permission to "brush up a little" before the Mexican beauty, who dwelt somewhere in San Jacinto, would see him. The other persons in the garden were a stout, light-haired man who had a spade, and a slim, dark youth who had a book.

The stout man caught sight of Bernard and opened the gate.

"I recognize you, monsieur," he said in French. "You are the friend of whose distinguished features M. Dempsey has been kind enough to send us a portrait. I am Émile Regnier, sacristan of the church here."

Bernard bowed. The sacristan spoke to Padre David, who came forward with a kind smile to shake hands with Bernard.

"And this young gentleman," said the sacristan, with another elaborate bow, "is Señor Maria José Galdez."

Bernard opened his mouth. The slim young man smiled and held out his hand.

"You can't—he can't—she can't—" stammered Bernard—"are you the twin?"

"The only twin," cut in the sacristan, with a bow.

"Is this Maria? I thought there was a lady—"

"This is Maria, the ward of M. Dempsey," interrupted the sacristan, looking a littled puzzled. "One will speak the English, if you prefer it. The only lady here is my sister; here she is!"

And from the clump of camellias which shaded the door of the priest's modest cottage came Marie Regnier, carrying Padre David's cup of foaming chocolate. She was brighter and prettier than ever. Her cheeks rivalled the oleander blossoms when she saw Bernard.

"Monsieur Bernard!"

Then there followed more exclamations and explanations, but Bernard was prudently silent. Marie had something to tell Bernard of his mother. It was not much: she had seen his mother at Mass once or twice; but it was pleasant for Bernard to hear.

Bernard was in no hurry to return to San Lorenzo Ranch. Padre David had many sermons on abstruse theological subjects to read to him, and the good priest, happy in having such an appreciative listener, said:

"Ah! amigo, you ought to have been a Levite; how fortunate would I have been with such an assistant! You ought to have been a priest, my boy."

Bernard shook his head. "It is not God's will, father. My father and mother—especially the dear old mother—longed with a holy and steadfast longing that I might serve the altar. It nearly broke my heart, and I am afraid it broke hers, when I found that I had no vocation. It was the saddest—"

"You had proper direction; you prayed you—"

"Yes, yes," interrupted Bernard. "My confessor knew me thoroughly, and I prayed with all my heart for light. But it was plain that I had no vocation for the highest, holiest, most difficult calling under heaven. Think what it is to be a priest! And yet, seeing how my mother had set her heart on giving me wholly to God, I was almost tempted to please her. It was the saddest day of my life when I told her it could not be!" Bernard's eyes moistened, and he paused. "O Father David! how beautiful her desire seemed to me. You don't know how she had worked for it half her life, how she had thought of it, prayed for it. But it takes more than even a good mother's will to make a priest. I would have given ten years of my life to make her happy! You see how pure, how unselfish was her ambition."

Padre David thought for a moment. Then he smiled slightly and took a pinch of snuff.

"And now the little Marie Regnier is teaching you to make chocolate in the Mexican fashion! Ah! the poor old mother. But she will live again in her grandchildren and pray that one of them may be a priest."

Bernard reddened and asked Padre David to go on

with his sermon—the one for Palm Sunday, which was short.

Bernard Devir, on his return to San Lorenzo Ranch, presented a very amiable and charming person to old Will, to whom he said:

"I have brought back a wife, according to your instructions."

Will Dempsey gradually permitted himself to be captivated by Marie; but for some time he denounced the Mexican fashion of calling "boys by girls' names." He declared he would never forgive the twin for "being a boy." Finally he relented.

VI.

The old couple talked many times, after the sharpest grief of Bernard's leaving had been blunted, of the glory of that Commencement Day. Jack Dempsey visited them occasionally, and they were very proud of these visits. He was as jolly as ever, but there was a recollection about him as of an interior but subdued brightness. Again and again Mrs. Dempsey had said, with a sigh:

"Wouldn't his mother be the happy one if she could have lived to get his blessing after his first Mass!"

One day she said to Jack: "I'm afraid the father and me were too anxious about Barney, and may be we worried him a bit. But indeed, Mr. Dempsey, it was only the will of God we wanted done, and it seemed as if he were running against it."

The bitterness of the disappointment seemed to be fading away. So soon as this mother began to feel that her son might be doing the will of God, although not having received the highest grace, she thanked God for his goodness.

When the letter came from San Jacinto, asking the blessing of the father and mother on the marriage of their son, her lip trembled; but she recovered herself.

"Sure," she said, "it was right to wish the best for Bernard; but, if he's got the second-best, let's be thankful. His wife's a good Catholic, anyhow."

"He says himself you were right," said Jack Dempsey, who had brought the letter, "to wish that he should be given to God, and he regrets that he was not worthy of the grace of a vocation to the priesthood."

"Cheer up!" chimed in Mr. Dovir, as he paused to scold the boy for leaving a bundle of brooms out in the rain. "Cheer up, acushla! Matrimony's a sacrament, and, if Barney has received it worthily, there may be a priest in the family yet!"

Mrs. Devir smiled through her tears.

"And after Mr. Dempsey here is priested we'll take a trip down to see them."

"Well, well, I will, dear," she said; "but Barney belongs to another. I could never think him to be the same boy."

LILIES AMONG THORNS.

I.

THE snow, which had begun to fall about four o'clock in the afternoon, came down swiftly, whirling in the wind and destroying itself on the lighted window-panes. It was now six o'clock. Under the track of the Elevated Railroad the roadway was comparatively clear; everywhere else the white carpet lay. People who had started out in the morning under a blue sky stamped energetically as the cold snow melted on their shoes. In spite of the closing of day, which ought to be sad; in spite of the whirling snow, through which the gas-lamps peered dimly; in spite of the blast, that pierced light coats and tried to tear away thin shawls, the time was cheerful.

To many it was cheerful because work was over; to many because it was near Christmas time.

The young women coming into South Fifth Avenue from the down-town factories and workshops, each with her novel and lunch-box clasped close to her bosom, had much to say, in loud and sprightly tones, of festivals, past, present, and to come: how one had assisted at the sociable of the Rosebud Coterie on Monday and at the assembly of the Select Six, and how another expected to appear in a new gown and compete for a prize for waltzing on the succeeding Monday. "Says I's," "says he's," and "says she's" were as frequent as dropped *h*'s in the streets of London. Young male persons on various street-corners raised their hats in mock politeness and expressed their opinions, in stage-whispers, of the passing damsels. Thereupon there was much giggling. Cheerfulness reigned, principally because it was Saturday night. South Fifth Avenue, dingy as it is, looked quite gay when well covered up with snow.

Beyond lay Washington Square—a smooth plain, a great, white sheet of yet untrodden snow, silent in the bustle around it.

In that lively French quarter of which Washington Square is the upper boundary is the *charcuterie* of L. Marquette. L. Marquette's veal-pies, sausages, arrangements of ham, elaborate and mysterious, are as well known even outside the French quarter as the *table-d'hôte* of his friend C. Martel in Bleecker street, where innumerable courses, a half-bottle of wine, and conversation on all the leading topics of the day may be had for the moderate sum of forty-five cents lawful money of the United States.

Aurore Marquette finished a moss-rose as the clock struck six, and descended from her little work-room over the back part of the shop to join her father and mother. Aurore was the daughter of "L"—otherwise Louis Camille Jacques. She made artificial flowers in the little back room, while her father and her young brother Jean managed the *charcuterie*, and her mother carried on a laundry in the basement. "Each to his talent," Madame Marquette often said.

L. Marquette always closed his shop at dusk. He had imperative engagements, he said, on Saturday nights. He had dressed to fulfil one of these engagements. He was leaving the house somewhat crestfallen, for madame, who did not approve of this early closing, had attacked him on the subject of religion.

"*Tais-toi!*" cried madame. "Thou hast no more religion than a pig."

"I am a Catholic," answered her husband reproachfully, "but of the liberal school—of the school of progress."

"Thou art too liberal with thy tongue. Va!" cried madame.

Monsieur felt these insulting words more deeply than usual. He felt himself to be a very important personage this evening, for he was about to preside over a dinner of the Cercle Voltaire at the restaurant of C. Martel, where free thought was poured out abundantly.

Madame Marquette was not very religious; like many of her class—she came of a race of Burgundian peasants —she looked on priests with a certain terror because they reminded her of death.

Aurore was different. She never missed Mass; she approached the sacraments frequently; her father paused in his abuse of religion while she was present. Madame approved of this. She believed that religion was good for young women; and of course, when one became old, very old, and had nothing else to do, one ought to be devout. That went without saying. But the laundry and the accounts of the *charcuterie* took all her time; besides, if one went to the priests, the priests were likely to come to one for something. Madame worked hard for Jean. She loved Jean; one day he should go back to Burgundy, live on the land she would buy him, and be a gentleman. So far Jean was abominably American; but, though disappointed, madame felt that this might be

3

overcome. She was very indulgent to Jean; Aurore she kept with a tight rein. She adored—in the French sense—the performances of opera-bouffe, but she would have swooned if Aurore had entered a theatre. Aurore had much less freedom than the young girls around her. Having lived in a tenement-house during a great part of her life, she knew more of life than girls of seventeen are supposed to know. She was good and pure. She had been sent to a parochial school, taught by Sisters, for two years.

After that, there being no room in the laundry for her, she was set to the moulding of caramels in the small factory of her uncle, Napoleon Champfleury, in Houston street. But again madame said, *Chacun à son métier*, and Aurore went into the artificial-flower business with success.

The Marquette household was much more comfortable than many of the households near it. The principal reason of this was that Madame Marquette owned the house she lived in, so that there was no landlord to be reckoned with, and a great deal of the combined earnings of the *charcuterie* and the laundry were put into bank by madame with a view to Jean's future aggrandizement. Madame tolerated her husband, respected Aurore, and worshipped Jean. Hard as a rock in her dealings with the world at large, she could refuse him nothing. The future, when her beloved son should be a proprietor in her native commune, adding land to land, was real to her. She thought of it, planned for it, every day of her life. She was indefatigably industrious. When other people could barely make both ends meet, Madame Marquette could make them lap over.

Her husband and she were materialists. He, echoing

his favorite Paris orators and journals, believed that liberty meant entire freedom from restraint; that the flesh and the world were to be cherished as the only existing things; that the devil was an invention of the priests. He held that religion was good for young girls and old women, but he often said, with the applause of the Cercle Voltaire, that a woman's husband should be her only confessor. And yet when the sharp point of a skewer had run into his side he had howled and yelled for a priest, and blasphemed horribly because the priest was slow in coming. When the priest did come the brave Monsieur Marquette had discovered that the wound was trivial, so he apologized, and, as it was Friday, invited "Monsieur le Curé to dine off a ravishing haricot of mutton." He was superstitious. He was sullen all day when anybody upset the salt. Once, when he found he had dined with twelve other men at the Cercle Voltaire, he went home and lay sick for a week.

Madame had her "feelings" about religion. Once, when Jean had the scarlet fever, she went to church to pray. She fasted rigorously on Good Friday, eating only tripe, although the other Fridays were nothing to her, and she crossed herself whenever she spilled the salt. She would cheerfully have sent Aurore to the Protestant Episcopal mission-school, but both Jean and Aurore had been insulted by a tract distributor who offered to give them new clothes, so they had been sent to the parochial school of St. Alphonsus.

Louis Marquette was never weary of uttering foul threats against "the enemy," the priest.

"*Tais-toi!*" cried madame. "It is true that they take our substance and give us nothing in return; but thou shalt not abuse them in thy loud voice in the shop

The Americans do not understand thee. They think thou art a fool, and some day an *Irlandais sauvage* will break thy head. To hear thee talk one would think that thou art a pagan, that thou hadst never made thy First Communion."

"I am not an animal!" answered Marquette, stung by the insinuation about the First Communion.

It seemed strange to the Americans who knew this pair and others like them, so utterly earthy and so ill-instructed, that a Catholic country could have produced them.

To eat, drink, work, sleep, to attend occasionally a *café concert* in Fourteenth street or the Bowery, to spout at the Cercle Voltaire, to be seen with madame at the annual ball of the Société Industrielle, was the life of this human being. A short, stout, bull-necked man, with a close-cropped bullet-head, white-skinned, with sharp, black eyes and plump hand, was Marquette. He generally wore a cook's cap and apron.

Madame was short in stature, blonde, not yet fifty, good-natured, but firm and a thorough woman of business. Manette and Ninon did the work of the laundry. Madame saw the customers, kept the accounts, and marked the "pieces" with red silk threads.

Aurore had the smooth, delicately pink-tinted complexion which seems to us essentially French because we always find it on the covers of the old-fashioned Paris *bon-bon* boxes. The good boy, with a stiff white rosette and a prayer-book in his hand, in these works of art, always has it. She had large, black eyes, bright and alert, a slight figure, neatly dressed. She was not permitted to wear the gilded ornaments which gave her acquaintances such fictitious glory. When Aurore was not making artificial flowers she was knitting. Aurore was a good Catholic; she had become used to her parents' manner of life, but she was not influenced by it. Although very much of a French girl, it seemed "foreign" to her.

Most of the working-girls of Aurore's acquaintance spent their days in hard work and their nights in revelry. They lived in their work-shops; spent a few hours in the tenement-houses where they dwelt; the rest was dancing and gas-light—assemblies in the winter, picnics in the summer.

Jean Marquette, Aurore's brother, was no stranger to this social revelry of which one-half the world of New York knows so little. He ran wild. Jean had no sympathy with the views of his father, who was "French," and consequently, in Jean's progressive eyes, imbecile. Aurore spoke a kind of *patois* with her father and mother; Jean rarely condescended to anything but the slang of the Bowery. Jean was a taller, slimmer edition of his sister, with a rougher skin, but with similar large, alert eyes and an indefinable air of New York "knowingness."

While the snow fell and the trains on the Elevated Railroad thundered through it, while Marquette uttered ribaldry over his *chasse-café* at C. Martel's, while the Bowery, further down, began to flare and glare, while God waited almost deserted on the altar of St. Alphonsus', while careless laughs sounded from the crowds on their way to the theatres, madame dozed in the little office of the laundry in the basement over her pint of Beaujolais, Aurore knitted, and Jean pitched a penny in a corner. A whistle, quick and sharp, sounded outside. Aurore hoped that Jean had not heard it. She knew it was the usual Saturday-night signal. It meant the gallery of a theatre with a boon companion and a night of anxiety for her. All night she would lie awake fearing that her father would discover that Jean was out, fearing, above all, that Jean would drink whisky. Aurore, who would have seen with perfect equanimity Jean drink glass after glass of claret or Burgundy, had an inexpressible horror of whisky.

The whistle was heard again. Jean raised his head.

"Ha!" he said in a dramatic whisper. "'Tis he! I must dissemble! We may be happy yet. Farewell, Aur-o-r-r-re!"

"Don't go, Jean. Stay with maman and me. Just this once! Do!"

Jean put his finger to his nose derisively. "What do you take me for? Mom's asleep and you're not much fun. See you later! Ned Barnes is waiting for me."

"Stop, Jean! Bring him in. Let me see what kind of a boy he is."

"Can't. He's boss, but he's shy. And the old lady would raise the neighborhood if I brought a boy in here. Good-bye. Wait up for me this once and let me in. I'll go to confession next week, I swear."

"Ah! Jean, you've promised before."

"Yes, I will—I will, Aurore, just to spite the old man."

"Don't say that, Jean; you don't mean it."

"*Tu paries ta douce vie!*—you bet your sweet life I do! I'm off, Aurore. I've got seventy-five cents. Wait up now, like a daisy!"

"O Jean! I will, if you promise not to drink the whisk-ee!" Aurore cried imploringly. To this Jean answered by forming his hands into the shape of a cup and drinking with much apparent gusto.

The whistler without struck up a lively melody. Madame awoke, and Jean slipped out. Madame raised her glass to her lips and looked around.

"Dame!" she said, "where's Jean?"

"Gone out, maman."

"Aurore, you should have kept him in. He is becoming like the Americans, an infidel, a spendthrift, a *vaurien*, respecting neither religion nor his parents. I shall take him back to France soon for his education. America," said madame, with a solemn shake of her head, "is a bad place for boys. They grow careless. They ought to make their First Communion and marry well. But here," sighed madame, "there is no *dot;* they can not marry well."

"I hope Jean will not drink the whisk-ee," sighed Aurore.

"Bah!" retorted madame. "The boy must have his *frédaine de jeunesse;* he must amuse himself. He came home the other night smelling of the whisk-ee, and I said, 'At whose wedding have you been?' and I scolded him well. He begins young. It is the way of the Americans; but it will be the sooner over. Thou wouldst make a little priest of him," cried madame fiercely, dropping into the *patois*, "with thy confessions and scapulars; but I want no priests here. I would strangle him if I thought he would wear a beretta. No money of mine shall ever make a priest, Aurore. Bah! Let the boy alone!"

Aurore smiled a little at the idea of Jean as a priest.

"No," said madame. "*Ni l'homme, ni femme, prêtre.* No priest shall ever handle *my money*, Aurore."

Aurore sighed and went on with her knitting. Madame turned to speak to a customer who had entered.

Jean met his friend.

Ned Barnes' hands were thrust into his pockets; he wore no overcoat, and this partly accounted for the vigor with which he whistled and danced clog-steps on the sidewalk. Ned was a rough-looking boy, for he had just come from work.

"Halloo, Johnny!" he said. "Thought you'd never come!"

"You're early. Had your supper yet?"

"No."

"So much the worse for you. Which shall it be, Niblo's or the Grand Opera House? There's a boss show at the Grand Opera."

The boys shuffled along aimlessly, making a shrill duet of the popular "Voici le Sabre," and exchanging snowballs at various corners with friends or enemies. Jean had a copious vocabulary of slang, which he used unsparingly.

"Haven't seen you out at night lately, Ned. What have you been doing? Did your mother bar the door?"

"Been studying."

"Studying?"

"Yes; Latin."

Jean gave a prolonged whistle. Ned turned up the steps of St. Alphonsus' Church.

"What's that for?" asked Jean. "Let us turn back. Why are you going in there?"

"Because I think I ought to go and you ought to come with me."

Jean hung back. "Say, Ned, don't let us go to-night. Some other night. I've got the chink and we can have a good time. Besides, I'll get blazes if I go; I have not been for an awful long time."

Ned gently pushed him up the steps. Once inside Jean said to himself that he was "dished." The boys entered a pew and knelt. Jean's heart felt like lead, and he looked longingly toward the door. Ned had thoughtfully taken possession of the end of the pew. The perennial light burning before the tabernacle seemed to Jean like an eye watching him. The dim lights and the sight of bowed forms waiting for their turn to enter the confessional made him gloomy. But the tranquil influence of the place gradually benumbed his restlessness. There was an old prayer-book lying in the pew. Jean, seeing by Ned's position that there was no chance of escape, picked it up and began to read. It happened to be one of those volumes, translated with more zeal than discretion from the French, which contain a most varied, minute, and scrupulous "examination of conscience."

"I ain't so bad, after all," he whispered to Ned. "I've never done more than half of them things." There was a little of the pharisaical in the tone in which he added: "Human respect? What's human respect? Is it a sin?"

"Mind your own sins, Johnny, and don't be looking after other people's."

"*He'll* give me h——; oh! blazes, there's another cuss-word!" Jean knelt down again and beat his breast vigorously. "Say, Ned, let's put it off for to-night. I can't remember anything. And there's an old crow just gone into the box. She'll keep the priest all night. Come!"

Ned was immovable. Jean nudged him in vain. For a time Jean listlessly watched the light before the tabernacle and the shadows of some kneeling figures, veiled in semi-gloom, waiting for a confessor who had not yet come. He found it hard to contemplate the dreadful task before him without a tremor of the nerves. He recalled several important transgressions; he said the Act of Contrition; but a phantasm of the theatre, with its Saturday-night crowds and glittering lights, arose before his eyes. A priest, from whose confessional the old woman—alluded to in expressive Bowery dialect as the "old crow"—had come, opened the door, looked over a group of kneeling women, and beckoned to the two boys. Jean shrank back. Ned pulled and pushed him. Hardly before he knew it Jean knelt in the dark box, facing the grating. The slide flew back and the priest spoke in an encouraging voice. It was all over in a few minutes.

Jean was soon kneeling near Ned in the pew.

After a while they stood on the steps and simultaneously drew a long breath.

"It's awful easy when it's over," said Jean.

"Was he hard?"

"I should smile," answered Jean. "I feel as clean as a whistle!"

Jean ran home, all thought of the theatre gone. He told Aurore, and she kissed him.

II.

Ned Barnes, after leaving Jean with a promise to meet him on Sunday afternoon, ran for some distance along South Fifth Avenue until he came to a dingy shop-window. There were ancient pistols in it, labelled with low "cash" prices, a collection of unpolished silverware, diamonds in settings more or less damaged, a shawl or two, a big Bible, a little child's frock, all marked with a price in black and white. It was a pawn-shop. The space in front of the counter was filled by anxious, draggled women and unwashed men, just from their work, exchanging tickets for necessary articles they had pawned during the week.

In one case it was a good coat; in another, pillows and sheets; in another, a woman's gown. The only luxury drawn out while Ned was there on this Saturday night was an old violin. Ned waited, jingling some coins in his pockets, until it came to his turn. He gave his ticket for a bundle which contained a blanket shawl; then he left. The crowd of eager applicants increased. Those who were waiting to redeem articles were generally sad-looking people, but not dissipated. Those who came to deposit things were wretched and dissipated. It was plain from their faces that the pittance thus gained would be spent during the night in drink.

Ned stopped at a shop to buy a salt mackerel, a loaf of bread, and a little tea.

Whistling cheerfully, he plunged into a narrow street where the snow melted on sidewalks encrusted with the dirt of many summers and winters. On the coal-box at the corner of this street three young men—two keeping in a sitting position the third, who was drunk—were singing. Two young girls waiting at the same corner joined their voices in the song, and then accepted the invitation of the young men to enter the grocery for a drink. This grocery-shop was evidently a resort for the neighborhood; people with baskets were entering, but more—especially children—carried pitchers and cans. The principal traffic of the place was not in solids.

Ned paused at the door of a tall house. His entrance was intercepted by the body of a woman, whose tin can lay empty beside her. She had evidently fallen in the act of going to get it refilled. A young man was trying to pull her into the hall. She was a middle-aged woman, the mother of the man. She resisted stupidly, trying to seize the handle of the can.

"Halloo, Barnes! Give us a hand. Mom's on another spree and I want to get her into the hall. I've got an engagement down-town and I can't afford to fool away my time here. We'll move her inside. She'll be sobered off by the time I get back."

"All right, Mack," said Ned.

Together they lifted the woman—or the semblance of a woman—into the hall. Her face was distorted and bloated; she opened her lips, and from them issued a strain of foul imprecations, mingled with the smell of stale beer.

Neither Ned nor her son noticed this. They were used to it. Mack, when the woman had been put in a sitting posture against the wall, invited Ned to join him in a "racket" at the ball of the Grand Moguls. Ned shook his head and ran through the hallway to a court in the rear of the house. This court was filled with piles of ashes and refuse, mercifully whitened by the snow. There was another house, a six-story building. Each story had what looked like a small balcony with an iron railing. Each of these fire-escapes was filled with flower-pots, cooking utensils; old pieces of carpet floated in the wind. They gave the house a very ragged appearance. In all the windows of all the six stories lights shone. The house seemed as full as a bee-hive. There was a great deal of noise, showing that the inhabitants were active.

Against the background of a bed-post a man could be

seen shaving himself in one window, stopping occasionally to refresh himself from a beer-can. Children, some of them shivering and half-dressed, were climbing the stairs, pitchers or cans in hand. It was Saturday night, and the beverage of Gambrinus flowed—the milk and honey of this miserable, unknown land. The dreadful dirt and dilapidation of this rear tenement-house were masked in the daytime by the house in front of it.

It was Ned's home. He ran up the narrow stairs with a light heart. There were sounds of laughter and of wrath; evil words and curses came from out open doors. From other rooms came savory odors and a clatter of dishes. A young girl, dressed in light silk and gauze—for few of these people were too poor to have gay clothes when occasion required—was being admired by a group of neighbors on a landing, she holding a kerosene-lamp over her head. Two women on the landing above were fighting about lighting the corridor. The place was a Babel; yet it was Ned's home, and it is the home of many like him, where lilies grow and bloom in the company of poison-bearing weeds.

Here Virtue and Vice jostle each other, meet each other on the stairs, speak to each other day after day. Here the libertine is one of the household with the pure of heart. Strangers breathing corruption and contamination live within these gates; and here Vice becomes so familiar that Virtue does not even blush in her presence. The little children learn the language of blasphemy before they can utter their own names; and to the young those things which Christians veil in mystery are as open books. Here the prayer and the curse are heard side by side, and the saint dies in the room next to the despairing sinner. It is a wonderful microcosm. And those who ought, know so little of it! The animalculæ that exist in a drop of Mediterranean water are as unknown to some of us as those people who are forced by poverty to have such strange companions.

Ned knocked at a door on the fifth floor. It was opened at once by his mother. Her face, which was pale and stamped with the imprint of many trials, brightened as she kissed him. He gave her a hearty smack in return, and stepped back into the passage to shake the snow from his shoes. She watched him with a look of the deepest affection in her dark blue eyes—those Irish eyes that are never without sadness after the first sparkle of mirth has passed out of them. She was not old, and yet she seemed old. There was no gray hair in the brown bands smoothed over her wrinkled brow, and there was a look of serenity in her face as her eyes rested on Ned, and at this moment it was plain that she was not much over fifty; but trials and privations had made her old-looking and frail.

"I've brought your shawl, mother."

"Dear boy!" she said, closing the door and filling a basin of water for him to wash with. "I can go to Mass now. How I missed that shawl!"

She wore a faded but scrupulously clean calico gown, with a little collar of the same stuff at the neck.

Ned plunged his head into the basin with a splash.

"Suppose you had not been paid to-night, Ned, what a difference it would have made to us! And Monday Christmas, too. I could not have gone to Mass in this dress; it would kill me in this weather. I wonder if the people who pay for work ever think what a difference *the time* of paying out a little money makes to the poor?"

"The people around here wouldn't have so much bee

to-night if they hadn't been paid," said Ned out of the folds of the towel.

"Poor creatures!"

She set about frying the mackerel and some potatoes at a cooking-stove. The well-trimmed and scrupulously clean kerosene-lamp lit a room which was sparsely furnished, yet cheerful. Ned had a bed in a sort of closet off the room. The floor was white; it had been scrubbed and rescrubbed. The walls were white, too; a picture of the Sacred Heart over the lounge which served for Mrs. Barnes' bed, and a scarlet geranium in the window, showing against a white shade, were the only patches of positive color. There was a patch of worn carpet in the centre of the room, and a packing-box covered with muslin, surmounted by a scrap of looking-glass. A table, two chairs, and a stool completed the furniture. Ned's face was cheerful and ruddy as he took down a few pages which had been torn from a book, and began to study them, while his mother prepared supper.

Years ago Mrs. Barnes had come from Ireland in possession of all the good which fortunate young girls get in the nuns' schools in Ireland. She was deft, industrious; she was intelligent and well instructed. She served in a family as half housemaid, half seamstress; then she married Tom Barnes. Tom Barnes was a giant of a North Carolinian, long-bearded and long-legged. He had come to New York because he knew that skilled labor commanded the highest wages there. Having nothing to do on Sundays, he wandered into Catholic churches, and in a year's time entered the Church. He saw his future wife in St. Peter's one morning at Mass. He asked the priest to introduce him. The wooing was not long a-doing. It was a very happy marriage. Tom lived in a populous neighborhood. He was open-handed and open-hearted. He was a machinist earning good wages, and there was nothing niggardly about him. He was of such a sunny temperament that he could not foresee a rainy day. When he died there was intense grief in his neighborhood. His wife's countrymen were particularly sorrow-stricken. He had been a good friend to many of them.

"Many's the job of work he's got for me," said one of them, "and if I spend my last cent I'll follow him in a coach to Calvary the morning."

And he did spend his last cent, and more too; for the family clock found its way to the pawn-shop, and was not redeemed until several months after Tom Barnes' grand funeral.

It *was* a grand funeral. The priest of the parish permitted only ten carriages at any funeral; but seventy-six, by actual count, kept around the corner. The wreaths, anchors, crosses, scythes, etc., done in flowers, had to be drawn in a separate carriage to the grave. It was generally said that Tom Barnes' friends had done their duty most handsomely.

A little more than a year had passed since this great ebullition of gratitude and admiration, and Mrs. Barnes pawned her shawl to help pay a month's rent which would not have reached the sum paid by sorrowing friends for two of the carriages in that now-forgotten cortège!

"Tal es la vida!" said the Spanish woman across the passage, who remembered the great floral display.

Ned was "general utility" in an office down-town. His mother sewed when she could see; but her eyes were not always to be depended upon. Ned's education had stopped short when his father died. He had learned to read, write, and cipher. It was intended by both his parents that he should have a great chance. And this great chance they talked of, dreamed of, but said little of it to Ned. They hoped and prayed that he might one day become a priest. How closely the mother watched him; how happy the father was when he found Ned, when a little boy, imitating the chant and swinging an imaginary censer! Nothing was said to the boy about it; but the father and mother prayed much.

Ned was a cheerful, boisterous boy, always ready for fun, never still, not particularly fond of study. He had never missed a baseball match, if he could help it; but no day had passed, since he had been taught to say it, that he had omitted his rosary. He was outwardly a rough-and-tumble fellow, ready with his tongue and his fist, but also ready to say or to do a kind thing, and never afraid to do what he thought was his duty.

The office-work, after his days at home and school, was hard. But he "pitched into it" with all his might. It was a great blow—he felt it more and more every day—to lose a hope which of late had become more and more defined. This was the hope his parents had secretly cherished—the hope of becoming a priest. He had served Mass and he knew the pronunciation of Latin. He had found, among the waste paper that fell to his share at the office, a few leaves from a Latin grammar. They contained only the declensions of "mensa" and "dominus," with other nouns and notes. But he made the most of them. These leaves were treasures to him. He pored over them every night. His mother was obliged—a delightful obligation!—to hear him recite them over and over again.

He must work. His mother was dependent on him.

Work, work, work stretched out before him until death. He could not be idle a day; the rent must be paid, food found. Should his work fail, his only friend was the pawn-shop. Yet nothing, he said over and over again, was impossible to God. His mother had guessed—what secrets of their sons' hearts do not mothers guess?—his aspiration. There was now no need of secrecy, and they talked it over often. These were happy hours, as they sat near the little cooking-stove and made this loving plan for the glory of God. What if the house shook at times with the mad and drunken revelry of the tenants around them? Here was an oasis of peace and hope.

Ned had a good appetite. His mother smiled as she filled his plate a second time; she asked him cheerful questions; but, nevertheless, this Saturday before Christmas had brought her a great disappointment. In one of the second-hand book-stores she had seen a Latin grammar. For months she had made little economies to surprise Ned with this longed-for book on Christmas morning. But Ned's employer had gone out of town the week before and forgotten to pay him his weekly five dollars. The rent came due that week, and to pay it—for the landlord never waited for very poor tenants—she had been compelled to sacrifice her little hoard and to pawn her shawl. It was a sore disappointment to her.

Ned told her how he had got Jean Marquette to go to confession. She was pleased.

"It will bring a blessing on you, Ned."

"Just think, mother, the poor fellow had not been to confession for two or three years! It's because his associations are bad."

Mrs. Barnes smiled a little. What were Ned's associations? A quarrel in the passage between a man and a boy, each calling the other unutterable names, answered her thought. The mother and son said the rosary. To-morrow was Sunday, and after that would come Christmas, so they could afford to chat long into the night.

"Mother," said Ned, "I think you'll have to take a run out. Mr. Marston gave me an extra dollar to-day, and I want you to buy yourself a Christmas present—something you don't want: a bit of lace or a ribbon. I want you to be extravagant just this once—at Christmas, you know." He pressed a silver dollar into her hand. Her eyes moistened. It was so like his father!

"What would an old woman like me do with ribbons or laces, dear?" she asked in a low voice. "Oh, dear boy! I wish you had a chance; I'd wear a calico dress all the rest of my life, and be happy to shiver with cold, if I could see you on the way to being a priest of God. If you had only a few years at school before your father died! If you were only fit to try for the seminary I'd be willing to give you to God and go—yes, I would, Ned —go into the almshouse myself."

"Hush, mother!" Ned said, with singular dignity. "Don't talk that way. There's no hope of one, and no fear, while I have my health, of the other. God knows I pray every day for 'the chance'; God knows I believe I can best do his will as a priest of God. This has grown stronger on me since father died. It seems to me I was such a young boy before that. Don't you remember what the Jesuit father at the Mass said the other day, 'Obedience is better than sacrifice'? Let us be obedient, mother, and wait."

His mother rocked herself to and fro with a sigh that was very like a sob.

"Sure, Ned, we want so little, and we want only the

good, and look at the people that work only for the devil and have so much. Why, the least part of it would be more than enough for us. It's hard to be patient, Ned, although I'm an old woman and have seen your brothers and sisters die one by one. And there's nothing like death to teach a woman patience. I don't complain of the dirt and the vileness of this place, Ned, though it's far from what I've been used to; but you—*you*, dear boy—"

She put up her fingers to her eyes and sobbed aloud.

Ned threw his arm around her neck and said: "And is it richness we want at Christmas time, mother dear? Isn't that queer at such a time, when He was born in a stable? Come, dear old mother, let's go out and buy a Christmas gift, to make you young again."

She kissed his red, rough hand and put her shawl around her. "No, Ned, I'll go alone. There's no fear that anybody will run away with *me*."

Ned humored her, and she left the room.

Would it be gone? Would some other anxious mother have seized it before she could get it? She need not have feared so; the inhabitants of that district did not thirst after Latin grammars any more than they thirsted after fountains of water.

She almost ran through the court and hall into the street, murky, snow-filled, and almost deserted now. She soon reached the book-stand. It was closed! No, there was the keeper relighting his torch, which had just gone out. It flared up again. She read the legend: "Any book in this row for fifty cents": *The Art of Cooking, Tricks with Cards, Charlotte Temple, Uncle Tom's Cabin*. It had been *there*. Where was it? Mrs. Barnes turned anxiously to the man.

"I change 'em every three days," he said; "that is, I

take out the unattractive ones." And he gave her the Andrews and Stoddard's *Latin Grammar* from a pile of "reduced—forty cents." Unattractive! How foolish the man was! Who could find a Latin grammar unattractive? She paid the money, took her change, and almost ran homeward. She noticed the sky was red in the direction of South Fifth Avenue. She heard the clangor of a steam-engine and then of another. The tenement-houses, both front and rear, were all alive. Excitement of any kind was a boon to their inhabitants, and they made the most of a fire.

"God help the poor folk this night!" murmured Mrs. Barnes as she hurried up-stairs with the precious book in her shawl. How glad and surprised Ned would be! She pushed open the door softly. The fire burned, the lamp was lit, his leaves lay on the table; but he was gone, and the horrible clangor of the fire-alarm filled the street. An undefined fear took possession of the mother.

III.

When Jean had come into the little office so unexpectedly early Madame Marquette wanted to know why.

"I've been at church, *ma mère*, scraping the skillet," said Jean, taking an old checker-board from the closet. ' Play, Aurore ?"

"Bah!" said madame, "I ignore your *banalités*. I understand not the scraping of the skillet. What is it, Aurore ?"

"Jean has confessed this evening; he will be a better boy."

Madame shrugged her shoulders. "He is good enough,"

she said. "But he might be more careful with his money. I don't want him to be a church-mouse, Aurore, like you."

"It would be better if I were more like Aurore. Say, Aurore, I saw James Connor at church. His hat was on the floor at the end of the pew. I'd have hidden it, if I could; but I hadn't time. You'd have liked to see him, wouldn't you, Aurore? I tell you, he is a craw-thumper. He prayed like a steam-engine!"

Madame frowned.

"Don't talk to your sister of that *Irlandais sauvage*. He is nothing; he is poor, and the *dot* of your sister shall not be wasted on him. And I want her," continued madame, pounding the desk emphatically with her fist—"I want her to be more civil to Pierre Roulé, who is rich, and most eloquent, your father says, at the Cercle Voltaire. He shall be her affianced. We have arranged."

"He is a mummy!" said Jean. He would probably have added something exceedingly impertinent; but he recollected himself. Aurore's face flushed and she bent her head over the checker-board.

Jean became restless. Checkers was a stupid game after the diversions he was accustomed to. It was too early to go to bed. There was nothing in the room to read, except a copy of the *Courrier* and a dog-eared novel, *Les Belles Amies du Diable*, a favorite of madame.

He yawned. "I think I'll take a walk, Aurore."

Aurore trembled. If he went out alone in the gay streets what might not happen?

"May I go, too?" she asked timidly.

"Why, certainly," he said, quite gently. At other times he would have laughed at such a proposition. Au-

rore put on her hat and cloak. She never thought of the
snow. It did not inconvenience her at all. Madame
made no opposition. She was lost in thought. She was
building her castle. Her father's farm at home arose
before her. Oh! to regain it, to possess it, to add to it;
to see Jean reign rich and powerful among the rich relatives and neighbors who had slighted her! To have him
take a wife from the proudest of them, to have them
sue for him, flatter and caress *her* son!—the ingrates, the
upstarts who had despised her! Madame had the French
peasant's mania for land, but only for the land in France,
in her native province.

If Marquette would let her sell the house—she knew
it would bring a good price—she would draw a good
round sum from the bank and start with Jean for France
in a week's time. Aurore and Marquette could stay
among the Americans for a while. But Jean was becoming spoiled; he hated to speak French; he was an American *gamin*. It must be stopped. Oh! if Marquette
would only consent to sell the house, she could buy the
old farm and add another to it at once. But Marquette
was obstinate; she knew that she could not move him on
this subject. He cared very little for French land.
Madame got angry thinking of it. She thrust out her
hand and hit the desk in a passion; the lamp, which stood
at the edge, fell over with a crash. Madame sprang to
her feet. But only the chimney had broken; the lamp
was safe; it had fallen on a heap of unwashed linen.
Madame picked it up with a strange feeling. What if it
had set fire to the house? Marquette was out, Jean and
Aurore were out, the bachelor tenant on the fourth floor
was out; the two servants of the laundry had gone to
bed, but they were within call. If—? Madame lit a

candle and laid the lamp among the clothes. The house was heavily insured. If—? The money in hand in spite of Marquette, and away with Jean to France! She examined the shutters and the door; then she replaced the lamp on the desk, lit it, and, getting the can of kerosene, poured the oil on the linen and on every inflammable object in the room. She flung her shawl around her and put on her bonnet. But she took the latter article off again; it might look as if she had premeditated. She thought of Marquette. Could he by some chance have come home earlier, letting himself in with his latch-key as usual? No; it was too early. As to Manette and Ninon, she would call them. It was all she could do without risk.

"Manette! Ninon!" she shrieked.

There was silence. And again she called.

"What, madame?" came back faintly.

"Fire!"

Madame overturned the desk. The lamp was dashed to pieces by the force of its fall. Instantly the flames leaped from the heap of clothes, like young serpents from a nest. Madame rushed into the street, the two servants following her, one of them singed a little. The house was old, the woodwork dry. With some satisfaction, yet with fear in her heart, madame saw the fire almost in the twinkling of an eye envelop all the lower part of the house. She shrieked and wrung her hands. The neighbors swarmed around her. She acted well the part of a frenzied woman. The devil seemed to have taken possession of her. Her screams were appalling: she would not leave the street, in spite of the efforts of kind neighbors to force her into a house. When the engines arrived the whole front of the Marquette house was covered by the flames, which quivered and waved in the wind like a fiery veil. At times the gilt letters, "L. Marquette," of the sign seemed to grin in derision through the fire. The firemen got to work with almost superhuman quickness.

Jean and Aurore stood near madame, stupefied by the suddenness of the calamity. Ned Barnes, who never could resist an alarm of fire, stood near them, ready to help, if possible.

Suddenly there was a sort of groan from the crowd in the street. A man had appeared on the fire-escape of the third story. It was Louis Marquette. His face—the face of a man sobered as to his mental faculties by danger, yet physically drunk and helpless—wore an awful expression of horror. It was the look of a man who saw a vision of death in the air—the look of a man in the presence of his Judge. He crouched down on the narrow platform. The flames hid him from view for an instant. Madame looked at him, and then stood up rigid and silent.

There were a hundred cries from the street, which were as nothing to Marquette. The firemen shot up their ladders. In vain! The horrified man clung to the railing of the fire-escape.

Jean had disappeared. He ran to the back of the house.

A cheer burst from the people below as his face appeared beside that of his father. Madame now seemed possessed of seven devils. She swore, she tore her hair, she tried to rush into the fire. The scene below was as horrible as the scene above.

The chief gave an order to clear a wide space around the building. It was about to fall. The firemen renewed their efforts to save the neighboring houses.

Jean was seen trying desperately to detach his father's hands from the iron railings, which he held in a maniac's grip. Was it the flames that wavered this time, or the house? People ran away and covered their faces. It was the house! It trembled, and then, amid crushing sounds and crackling smoke, fell on its own foundations; and with it sank Jean Marquette and his father to death.

A low murmur ran through the crowd of lookers-on, whose faces were for a moment made visible, as in the light of day, by the torrent of fire that swept down with the falling house.

Madame, who had been dragged away, and who was held back by strong men, struggled and tried to bite like a wild animal.

When the house fell a horrible cry, the like of which the listeners had never heard before, rang out:

"Jean," she cried, "my son, my son—I have killed him!"

Then, like a heavy weight which the men could not hold, she sank face foremost upon the trampled snow of the sidewalk.

They carried her into the nearest house, and among those that followed her was Mrs. Barnes. She had come out in search of Ned. Aurore, attracted by her kind, mild face, clung to her. Aurore felt herself to be friendless, for when she approached her mother, madame, with a convulsive motion, waved her away.

So all the dreary hours of that night, while the house smouldered and flamed at intervals, and the jets of water sent up by the steam-engines fell in icy spray, Madame Marquette lay on a bed in stony, sullen silence, watched by Aurore and Mrs. Barnes; the rest of the neighbors withdrew from the room, which at intervals was reddened by bursts of flame from the opposite side of the street. Only once madame spoke. Mrs. Barnes had said:

"Thank God! the other houses are safe at last."

"What matter?" asked madame in a harsh voice. "Jean is dead, and I have killed him."

Mrs. Barnes and Aurore looked at her with pity, and the former said:

"It's no wonder she is out of her mind."

Mrs. Barnes once or twice had been inclined to envy the Marquettes, and particularly the prospects of Jean, of which madame continually boasted to all her customers. But now—*now!* Mrs. Barnes shuddered and thought lovingly of the dear boy at home, perhaps even now bending over that cherished Latin grammar.

When the morning dawned neighbors came one by one to ask for the stricken woman. She would not speak. A doctor, who had been sent for, found her with her face turned to the wall. She tore her hand from him when he tried to feel her pulse.

Once she moved and spoke again. It was after Mrs. Barnes had left, promising to return. Aurore had tried to take her hand. She dashed it against the girl's face.

"Go!" she said, with horrible bitterness. "Go! I would it had been ten such as thou instead of my boy Jean. Go, miserable!"

Aurore shrank back, sobbing:

"O mother! O my mother!"

In the quietness of early morning Aurore heard a manly voice she knew asking for her mother. It was that of the "Irlandais sauvage," Pierre Roulé's rival, James Connor. It gave her comfort; and, worn out, she sank kneeling beside her mother's bed in sleep.

When Mrs. Barnes came, having been refreshed by the sight of Ned and his Latin grammar, and been kissed over and over again, with many rapturous exclamations appropriate to Christmas eve, having prayed very hard that morning at Mass, she stepped lightly into the room. Aurore still slept the deep sleep of weary youth, which sorrow and the presence of death itself can not break. Her head lay against the bed, which was empty.

Mrs. Barnes tapped Aurore on the shoulder. The girl started, bewildered; and then, as the horror of the night arose before her, she closed her eyes again and shivered.

"Where's Madame Marquette?"

This question was never answered. A policeman had seen her near the ruins of her house—or somebody like her. Had she wandered to the river and drowned herself? Nobody ever knew. Her bank-book with some pages torn out, and a handkerchief marked with Jean's name, were found on a dock.

Afterward an acquaintance of the late L. Marquette said he had caught a glimpse of madame hurrying toward the wharf from which a French steamer was about to start, having been delayed over Saturday. Nobody believed him, as he said this after the insurance people began to suggest suspicions of arson. But these suspicions, as well as madame's death, remained unproved. The insurance companies in time handed over to Aurore the sum for which the house was insured. Aurore was quite an heiress now. A change had come over her. She trembled at the slightest sound; her delicate color had faded; in her dreams she saw madame, with the face of a demon, smiting her on the face and crying, "Go, miserable!"

She clung to Ned's mother, and persuaded her to go to a neat little cottage in Harlem with her.

It did not take Aurore long to find out the desire of the hearts of this mother and son. Ever since Jean's death she had tried to find some way of showing her gratitude to Ned, who, under God, had saved Jean's soul. *He*, too, might have died in his sins—sins only too easily committed in the corruption around him. But Ned had saved him and he had died in the grace of God—Jean, her own dear Jean, for whom she would have given her life. Not very learned, not very much given to deep thought, not even very refined in the conventional sense of the term, Aurore had simple faith and deep gratitude. One day she went to the bank and to a lawyer. A few days later she went again, and, waiting until the mother and son were together in the cosey sitting-room, she kissed Mrs. Barnes on the forehead and put a packet and a roll of parchment on the table before her.

The packet was a roll of bills; the parchment a deed conveying a life interest in the pleasant cottage to Mrs. Barnes.

"I gave it not to you, but to God," Aurore said gravely.

After that there was no office-work for Ned, but much study; and one happy day he entered the seminary at Troy.

Later in the summer evenings, when the terror of that Saturday before Christmas had somewhat faded out of Aurore's life, James Connor, honest, faithful, and affectionate, was often seen on the porch of the cottage. And when he asked a certain question with some impatience again and again, Aurore always gave him the same answer, which was invariably followed by another question, "When *will* Ned be ordained?"

The time came at last. After it was all over, with the

joy of ecstatic love and its awful solemnity, an old woman lay in the quiet church, alone, before the high altar. Her bonnet had fallen from her head and the light from a stained window bathed her in purple and gold. She lay there in the attitude that Madame Marquette had taken in the snow years ago, with her face against the floor. Ned's mother had said her *Nunc Dimittis*.

Aurore's gift had indeed been given to God, and it was a fruitful gift. The young priest who " saved Jean's soul" has saved many others. He knows the people among whom he works. He has all the firm faith of his Irish ancestors and all the practical insight and readiness and acuteness of his American life. Authority and reason form in his mind that synthesis by which faith shall yet add a new world, not to Castile and Leon, but to Christ and Rome.

PHILISTA.

I.

IT was Sunday in Philista. Philista is a town in one of the Middle States. It contains several flourishing pottery-works, a canal, and numerous first families of intense respectability. The first families are very aristocratic and exclusive. They know who their grandfathers were; and in Philista, given a grandfather, a genealogy of radiance is easily constructed. Of late a genealogy has become so necessary a part of every well-regulated household in America that the family-trees of the Philistans are much regarded by visitors; and the old graveyard, which dates much beyond the time when Washington crossed the Delaware, has lost one or two of its tombstones, so great is the rage of our generation for memorials of its ancestors. The Stokes, of Beverly, Del., for instance—whose family congress is held in September of every year—have in their parlor, between the spinning-wheel of their alleged great-grandmother and a suit of armor bought in New York, one of the tombstones of Philista neatly framed in gold. What can be more convincing of the antiquity of a family than this? Gossip may maliciously say that the Stokes had no grandfather. But even Gossip ought to be silent in the presence of a tombstone.

It was Sunday in Philista, and it was Sunday at the

Catherwoods', which is the concentrated essence of all the Sabbatarian characteristics of the Philistan Sunday. The street was very quiet. The sunshine fell hot on the well-swept pavements; the leaves of the paper-mulberry trees rustled lazily, stirred by the ghost of a breeze. It was at that hour on Sunday when the smell of roast-beef taken from the oven has been dissipated, when the baked potatoes are cold and mangled, and the "help" in the Philistan kitchens softly clatters the dishes and murmurs, "I know a happy land," only rising to high C when she breaks anything.

It was a drowsy and wretched hour. Dinner was done; the younger Philistans had, on August Sundays, nothing to look forward to. There was not even the mild diversion of the cold-weather Sunday-school or Bible-class. All the books permitted to be read were of the kind that the young Philistan despised—"memoirs" of holy Methodists and pious Baptists, the doctrine of predestination arranged in an attractive primer for the use of childhood, and story-books about consumptive little boys who would not play on Sunday, and who died young. To add to the horrors of this time, when the sweet hope of dinner that had buoyed up the young soul through the long sermon of the morning had been lost in fruition, the parlor organs and melodeons in Jackson Street were let loose. To whistle would have been profanation; to draw a violin-bow across the strings sacrilege; to touch a piano, except to bring forth some sanctimonious tune, would have made the Sunday sunshine assume a rakish and week-day look in the eyes of the Philistans. But to manipulate the melodeon or parlor organ, of which instruments of torture each house in Jackson Street possessed one, was considered the proper thing for Sunday.

And now, to such an accompaniment, voices, young, old, and middle-aged, were humming the various vocal arrangements of Moody and Sankey. Heard through the hot air, " in the hush of the sunshine," there was something indescribably dreary in the sounds. It seemed as if all Jackson Street had taken to this dismal form of amusement because there was nothing else to do.

The elder Miss Catherwood sat at her melodeon in the little parlor murmuring " Beulah Land." The door was slightly ajar, kept so by a brick, in an embroidered cover, which was wedged between it and its frame. On weekdays the door was open; on Sundays it was thought proper to keep it ajar. The window-shutters were "bowed," and the room was in semi-gloom. The chromo of " Washington Crossing the Delaware," and the oil-painting of old Mr. Catherwood in the suit he wore in the great Federal procession in Philadelphia, were carefully covered with pink gauze to keep off the flies. On the marble-topped table near the window was a big Bible, and upon it a glass case containing a pyramid of wax fruit, supposed, out of respect for tradition, to be very natural. The wall-paper was covered with large green roses with gilt leaves, and the carpet was red and green. Tidies of worsted-work were arranged in a mathematical manner on the backs of the hair-cloth sofa and the chairs. On Saturday every atom of dust had been ruthlessly traced to its lair by the Misses Catherwood and exterminated. While Miss Catherwood sang, Miss Tamar Ann, her sister, sat in her rocking-chair and moved noiselessly to and fro.

The elder Miss Catherwood had a placid expression not unlike that of a sheep. Her face was white and wrinkled, but of a different kind of whiteness from that of the two tight, white curls which were visible on either side of her forehead. She wore a gray gown of stiff texture, and a lace collar fastened by a brooch in the form of a cross made of hair. Miss Tamar Ann resembled her sister in appearance, but her hair was only sprinkled with gray; she wore no cap; she was shorter and more alert; her eyes, black and small, were always in motion; and, to mark her juvenility, she had her gray gown distended by a hoop of the fashion that came in when the Empress Eugénie ruled the world.

Miss Catherwood's slim, long hands and low voice glided from "Beulah Land" into "Almost Persuaded." It was doleful enough. An unusually big fly perched on Miss Tamar Ann's palm-leaf fan, and, being disturbed, hummed drowsily among the green slats of the blind at the window. Miss Tamar Ann dropped her fan, ceased to rock herself, and quietly contemplated the hot brick wall across the street. There was no other occupation left for her on Sunday, except to read the Bible, as she did not "play the parlor organ."

Miss Catherwood's voice broke on one of those particularly strained notes which the adepts in Protestant devotional singing so often use.

"I was thinking," said Miss Tamar Ann, in monotone suitable for the time, "that it was a day like this when poor little Jimmie Reed was drowned. It was an awful warning to Sabbath-breakers. He *would* go to fish in the canal, and he fell in, you remember? It was on the 15th, the Sunday after I turned my black silk, and I remember thinking, 'I hope Jimmy put on his clean underclothing, for if he didn't his mother will be *so* mortified.' Dear, dear! And to think of the poor child going to perdition that way!"

Miss Catherwood had not attended to this reminiscence. Her eyes were full of tears. The dismal hymns she had been singing were very pathetic and solemn to her. They brought into her heart a yearning that almost broke it— a memory of the dead which was nothing but a memory.

"'Almost Persuaded' brings back Rosalia to me, Tamar. I have heard the Romanists pray for their dead. It would be a great relief to pray for Rosalia now, or to pray to her, if she is in the 'Beulah Land.'"

If Miss Tamar Ann had been a Catholic she would have made the sign of the cross; but she detested the sign of the cross, except as an ornament for the collar or in a patchwork quilt.

"I am surprised at you, Jane!" she said, shaking her head. "Poor Rosalia married a papist and died young; and if John O'Brien hadn't sent for a priest at the last, she'd have died a Baptist and the Catherwoods would have been spared the disgrace of seeing her buried among the Irish Catholics. *I* don't understand how she could have done it. I saw some of their crucifixions in the Belgian exhibit at the Centennial Exhibition. They were really distressing. But we've always done our duty by Alice, and sent her over among that low crowd at St. Bridget's, as we promised her father when he died. There's no denying it goes against the grain, and it's a disgrace. If Alice sticks to her religion who's going to marry her, I'd like to know? Not that I think she'll stick to it when she sees how very low everybody considers it."

"I don't know," answered Miss Catherwood. "I can't tell. I wish," she added with some fierceness, "that John O'Brien had never met our Rosalia. If she was right, Tamar, we're wrong. And if she's in heaven, we'll—but I want to see her again! I want to see her again! It wouldn't be heaven if she wasn't there!"

"Sister!"

Miss Tamar Ann's eyes actually snapped. *If!*

"For my part," she said, in a voice raised above the appropriate monotone, "I'd rather go to a place where the Good Man isn't than find there's nothing in all the Bible curses against idolaters. I declare I would!"

A faint knock sounded at the door, and it was pushed open after Miss Catherwood had said "Come in."

The gentlewomen were very much fluttered when a young man entered. He was rather tall, with brown hair close-cropped, a wide brow, full, bright blue eyes; a thick, reddish moustache covered his lips, but the chin it left visible was too finely moulded for a man's. He smiled good-humoredly at the Misses Catherwood, and fumbled with the red rose in the buttonhole of his light tweed coat. He gave Miss Catherwood his tall white hat, which she placed on the cover of the melodeon, and then he asked if he might see Miss Alice.

Miss Catherwood said, "Certainly." And then, with a little flush on her cheeks, "Shall I tell her your name?"

"Mine? Oh! I beg pardon," the young man answered, with a crispness of accent and a slight trill of the "r" that contrasted pleasantly with Miss Catherwood's rather flat enunciation. "Cornelius Blake."

Miss Catherwood and Miss Tamar Ann smiled. "You are the young gentleman Alice met at her cousin's in Philadelphia?"

"Yes," he said. "She was kind enough to ask me to come to see her, and, as I was obliged to—but here she is."

A girl not much over twenty had entered from the back room. She paused for an instant on the threshold, and glanced quickly at the visitor, as if she had heard his voice, but was not quite sure who he was. She was a slight young girl, having dark-brown hair and large, gray-blue eyes too densely fringed with lashes not to give her face what the people in Philista called a "peculiar" expression. Her face was a pure oval, and her nose—a feature which nature seems to find the most difficult to mould correctly—just escaped being Grecian by being a trifle too much "tip-tilted." It was an Irish type of face, in which a certain vigor of outline was corrected, or rather contradicted, by a delicacy of color and meagreness of flesh which are often observable in an Irish type grafted here. Her face was quiet and pleasant in expression; her complexion had a singular opaque whiteness, which, as it intensified the color of her eyes was considered by some an additional beauty, by the Misses Catherwood a sign of the heart-disease of which her mother died. She moved with the gentle air that characterized both her aunts. She smiled as she entered the room, and shook hands with the visitor. Miss Catherwood and Miss Tamar Ann at once arose to leave the room. It was one of the rules of etiquette in Philista that old people should always disappear when the young folk had visitors.

"I hope you'll invite your friend to tea, Alice," Miss Tamar Ann said.

"This is Mr. Blake—"

"Oh! yes," said Miss Tamar Ann, "we know."

"I don't want to interrupt your music," said Mr. Blake, showing a very good row of teeth to both aunts, and appealing to Miss Catherwood. "Do go on with your music. I am very fond of it."

There was an oppressive silence.

Music! The mention of the term in connection with the singing of hymns on the "Sabbath" seemed most incongruous to the sisters. Music, as music, was not for the Lord's day.

"I declare, Miss Catherwood," continued the visitor, with his brightest smile, thinking he had not said enough, "if I have an idol in this world—if I have an idol in this world," he repeated, fancying from something in Miss Tamar Ann's look that she was deaf, "it is—"

"We don't speak of idols," murmured Miss Tamar Ann, nervously drawing closer to the young man. "It might hurt Alice's feelings. She's a Romanist."

The young man lost his smile for a moment, and then laughed a little.

"So am I!" he said.

Miss Tamar Ann gazed at his fashionable suit of clothes in amazement. The Catholics in Philista were, she said afterward, "such a very different class of people."

"Well," spoke Miss Catherwood, "sister and I have some reading to do. I hope we'll see you at tea."

But in order to be polite, and perhaps to charm the Romanist with some sacred song, she played "Almost Persuaded," with a slight variation caused by the E-major key in the treble part of the melodeon having met with an accident.

"To think," complained Miss Tamar Ann, when the sisters had settled down in their bedroom to read an appropriately gloomy book, "that a nice young man like that should be obliged by the pope to end all his prayers with an invocation to the Virgin!"

"It's a good thing for young men nowadays if they pray at all," Miss Catherwood answered. "Most of them don't."

II.

Cornelius Blake was "a promising young man." His father and mother had come over from Ireland, with a little money earned by shop-keeping in Cork, before the famine. They had settled among the Philadelphians and done well. They were frugal, careful people, and their six children found themselves with a snug sum to begin life with when the old folk had passed away. Cornelius was the second of these children.

He had been called "bright." He had gone through the various grades of the public-school without much study or thought. He was looked on by his teachers as "a promising boy," and when he went into business, first as an entry clerk in a dry-goods establishment and afterward as a commercial traveller for a silk house, the adjective had clung to him. Having, like his father, been frugal, he saved a little money, to which, when his father died, he added the comfortable amount bequeathed to him. Then he threw up business and studied law in one of the multitudinous law-offices which abound in his native city. He mastered Blackstone and the other text-books put into his hands with a fatal facility that had been made second nature by the superficial training of the public-schools. He had never thought about anything in his life for more than three minutes. If he did not reach a conclusion then, he "gave it up." He had a very good opinion of himself, particularly of his mental abilities; but a great respect for the newspapers, although he made sprightly gibes at them. He considered material progress as the test of greatness, and poverty as a punishment following upon grievous sins against the spirit of American civilization. He was a Catholic; he believed all that he remembered of the Little Catechism he had studied in Sunday-school, which he had attended irregularly after he had made his First Communion. As to giving reasons for what he believed, he had literally none to give. He was a Catholic "all through," he said himself; to have heard him talk you would have thought that he had been dyed, religiously speaking, when young, and that the color was warranted to wash. He had assisted at Mass, approached the sacraments once or twice a year, partly out of a vague fear that he might die unexpectedly, and partly because his father and mother would have been struck to the heart by any known omission of his "duty." His brothers and sisters had gone their own ways; they had no influence on his life.

In his heart he had always felt that Providence had not treated him fairly in making him a Catholic—that is, in giving a mind like his into the keeping of Irish Catholic parents. His mother—poor, ignorant old soul!—had always struggled against his going to the public school.

"Mike," she had said over and over again to his father, "the faith's in us, blood and bone, heart and soul, and nothing could change us. But the children aren't like us. They're among new people, in a land of Protestants; and who's to teach them the true religion, if they don't get it in the schools? Sure, we can't; and if we could, we haven't the time."

And Cornelius had always rebelled at this. It was an "Irish" way of thinking, and he despised it; he felt grateful that his father had been too enlightened to give way to it. It made him shiver to think that if he had gone to the parochial school, mostly attended by the sons of Irish people not yet Americanized, and taught by Irish

Christian Brothers, he might never have gotten rid of the Cork brogue. His mother had had her way in the education of the girls, but the boys all went to the public schools.

"The Sunday-school's enough for them," their father had said. "Religion isn't everything in this country; and if a boy is to earn his living, it's mighty little good craw-thumping will do him."

Cornelius had come out of his succession of schools triumphantly. He knew a great deal of several things. He could " bound " any place in Europe, Asia, or Africa at a moment's notice. He could cipher with amazing rapidity and demonstrate the whole of Loomis' Geometry. He had studied physiology homœopathically. He wrote a good " business " hand. His essay on " Centrifugal and Centripetal Correlation " had taken the first prize on the day of his graduation; and his rendition of " Curfew shall not Ring To-night " had " marked him," as an observant journalist had said on the day after commencement, " a born orator."

He was "smart," and, though he had come out of school with the conviction that he was literally a master of all arts worth studying, he was by no means more of a fool than nine-tenths of his fellow-citizens. What he did not know—speaking of reading and study—he despised. He felt that he was well equipped for life; he was sure that he was equal to anybody; he resolved to be of importance in the world. He had read a stray volume of *Controversy between Rev. Mr. Hughes and Breckenbridge* and Smarius' book of *Controversy* just after a "mission," when his mind had been inflamed to a point of unusual devotion. But he had forgotten them easily. His last teacher had recommended him to read

Draper's *Conflict of Religion and Science*. He looked on that work as worthy of respect, as, indeed, he had no means of contradicting the falsehoods concerning the church it contains. He had, by dint of reading reviews and editorials in the daily press, acquired a knack of quoting Tyndall and Huxley against his Catholic acquaintances, as if he had read those popular authors. He had worried through *Daniel Deronda* and *Middlemarch*, in order to talk about them. He had never bought a book of any kind. He read newspapers unceasingly and "kept up" with the magazines. Once or twice a year he heard a sermon. But it made him tired to have the preacher tell him what he knew already.

Having hung out his sign with "P. Cornelius Blake" emblazoned on it, he discovered that there were too many lawyers in Philadelphia, and, hearing of a chance to enter a law-firm in Philista, he had emigrated.

He had a kind heart; good impulses constantly arose from it. He would have died rather than have done anything dishonest or acknowledged that his Christian name was Patrick. He wanted to be good and he wanted to be well thought of. So far the facts that he was a Catholic and had a suspicion of the brogue had not gone much against him. He had felt that he was an "outsider" when some of his friends had made social arrangements in which he had participated; but he was not sure whether this had been only a feeling of his or really a feeling of theirs. Taking him altogether, he was a man of excellent possibilities warped by the atmosphere around him. He had all the best qualities of his Irish parents, tempered and strained a little, the charming facility of the Celtic temperament, the impulsiveness and hopefulness, and a rooted dislike to the saying of unpleasant things. He was said to be "magnetic." He was only Celtic of the Irish.

III.

When the Misses Catherwood had left the parlor Alice untied the cord that kept the window-shutters " bowed " and let in a little more light. The young people showed to better advantage. Alice O'Brien, if not altogether beautiful, was a distinguished and graceful-looking girl. The Grecian knot of her dark hair, and her white gown relieved at the belt by a large bunch of bergamot blossoms, were very becoming to her.

"I never expected to see you again," she said to Cornelius, with a smile. "Let me see, it is three months since I met you at my cousin's."

"I have come here to stay—to improve my prospects. I am a lawyer, you know."

She smiled again.

"I never heard of anybody coming to Philista to improve his prospects before, but I suppose you intend to grow up with the city. Your beanstalk will not grow as rapidly as Jack's in the story. If it keeps pace with Philista in growth it will be ready for you to climb when you're seventy years of age—at least."

Cornelius felt a little piqued by her easy tone. When a young man comes from a large city into a comparatively rural town, with all the tone of progress that residence in a centre of culture gives, he expects the simple country lass to show a sense of his condescension.

"I don't know Philista at all," he said.

"That must have been the reason you came here. After all, you may find it lively—in comparison with

Philadelphia. The canal is most interesting. There's an insane asylum. The churches are always having 'cake love-feasts,' sociables, oyster-suppers, and fairs, and we had a troop of negro minstrels last week. At election time the excitement is intense. On last election day twelve men passed our windows!"

"Is there much society?"

"Much! The churches, particularly the Methodist, are circles within circles of gayety. But I'm a Catholic, so I'm barred out of that. Our own people are mostly factory-hands and that sort of thing. Positively there are not ten Catholic young men in Philista that a nice girl could marry. Not that I ever think of that. I'm a school-teacher, you know, and we neither die nor resign."

Cornelius felt more at his ease.

"They are not fond of Catholics here."

"I should think not. The first families are generally Presbyterians, who talk of Catholics as Aunt Tamar Ann talks. Those that have travelled are broader in their religious views, but they consider it socially 'low' to be a Catholic with an Irish name. It took all the influence of all the Catherwoods to get me a place as teacher in one of the schools. And I know there would have been less mourning in the best circles if my mother had married a negro instead of my dear, dear father. With your Irish look and that touch of the brogue you'll have a hard time here."

Cornelius flushed so deeply that his reddish moustache looked yellow by contrast.

"Do you really think that I talk as if I was Irish?" he asked, with an ingenuousness and anxiety that made her eyes twinkle.

"Certainly. No man, except an Irishman, could talk

with an echo of the music of the old sod in his voice." She broke off with a slight blush and a little laugh. "I wish I had it. I've the flat, semi-nasal accent of Philista, except when I speak a 'piece' or read poetry."

These young people, who had met only once before, seemed now quite well acquainted with each other. Young folks' friendships often grow as rapidly as Jack's beanstalk.

Cornelius was mortified by her opinion about his "brogue," and, although he tried to conceal it, she said:

"It is a pretty accent, not a vulgar twang. Do you sing? The choir at St. Bridget's is very bad. They want a tenor. I hope you sing."

"Not at all. If I did I don't think I could stand choir-singing and going to church twice every Sunday. Once is enough. Protestants have a much pleasanter time. They don't go, if they don't want to."

"But they want to here. Church-going, and the social revivals that spring from it, are the excitements of the town. I don't think it makes them much better; I think most of the people here would be as good as they are if there were no churches. But a 'broom-drill,' an oyster-supper, a donation-party, or a new minister sets the place talking for a month. The Catholics have not progressed that far yet. St. Bridget's had a fair; but there was such a mob there! But all the politicians went and spent money. Are you going in for politics?"

"I may," he returned, with an air as if he were undecided between the Presidency or a United States senatorship. She shook her head.

"I don't think you'd have the ghost of a chance. The feeling against Catholics here is very strong, and the Irish vote, though it's worth fishing for, would not carry you through. Besides, unless you are a Land-Leaguer the fact of your being a Catholic wouldn't carry all the Irish voters with you. I hope you'll keep out of politics."

Cornelius had come to say pretty things to this young lady and to patronize her a little. But there she sat, acting the part of monitress. She was a pretty monitress, an interesting monitress, but a man never likes a woman to teach him anything directly. If she teaches him with an appearance of ignorance he will assimilate her wisdom and use it as his own. Alice O'Brien despised tact; she despised the male sex; she would rather have proposed marriage to a man than have let him think she was his inferior.

Cornelius, listening to her, felt as if a cool breeze, laden with moisture, had touched him.

"You seem to have studied the political situation, Miss O'Brien."

"I have. Being a Catholic and half Irish, with a name that all the Catherwoods dislike, I have been a 'looker-on in Vienna.' Besides I have always wanted to be a man."

"Why? I assure you, if you were a man, the world would lose a great deal of—"

"Oh! yes, of course. Being a girl, I've no chance of doing anything better than teaching the primary class in a public-school. If I were not a Catholic I might rise to be principal of Hypatia College, for instance, where they would like to have me, if it wasn't for that. If I were a man I could, I *would*, surmount all the obstacles in the way."

Her lips were tightly shut; but no flush tinged the opaque white of her cheeks.

"But why can't I overcome these obstacles?"

"Oh!" she answered impatiently, "because you *are* a man. They're coming from Vespers at St. Bridget's," she added, pushing the shutters open. "Look at them! Servant-girls and factory-hands! Look at the clothes of the men and the bonnets of the women! And yet *we* are of those people; we can't escape them. I am a Catholic; I have stuck fast to the church in spite of all jeers."

"Why?" he interrupted maliciously.

She turned toward him with a startled look in her deeply-shaded eyes.

"Why?" she echoed. "Why?"

"Don't ask *me*," he returned. "When somebody asked me the other day why I wore a scapular I couldn't tell. It does seem like nonsense. All I know about it is that the priest put it on me one day in church, and I wear it because I've always worn it. I'm a Catholic for the same reason—I've always been one."

"A Mohammedan might say that," she replied, with a serious look in her eyes and a note of scorn in her voice.

"Or a Methodist, or a Presbyterian—yes. Have you a better reason?"

"Yes. The church is *true*—is truth itself. I believe."

"And your reasons?"

"I don't want reasons. I don't know why I believe. Nobody taught me the reasons. I have had no Catholic friends, and my aunts never liked me to see the priest much. And the Catholic books I have happened to find among the people here have been silly things in awfully bad taste and more Irish than Catholic. But I believe— I sometimes wish I did'nt; I should have a better time every way!"

"Well," he said, "you are frank. For myself, I am a

Catholic through inheritance and habit. It seems to me that America has outgrown religions—I don't call Protestantism a religion—and I have never, in all my reading" (he said this quite seriously), "found any reason why I shouldn't be abreast of the country. Men are about alike, no matter what religion they profess."

"That's a mistake," Alice O'Brien said. There was a pause. "I wish," she continued, "there were no such things as mixed marriages in the world. I am the victim of one. You think that's too strong? Ah! but you don't know. I'm separated from the people I love best. I suppose I'll be separated in the next world, too. I don't know whether I ought to pray for the souls of so many dear relatives who on earth hated the church and the Blessed Virgin with all their hearts. And yet I loved them and they loved me. Here I am—a Catholic among Protestants, like a fish out of water."

Cornelius laughed. It was an ill-timed laugh. She showed she thought so by silence. The drone of the reading in the room above broke the quiet.

"Well," he said, with a light air that seemed frivolous to her, "as we can't give reasons for the faith that is in us, what reason have we for sticking to it? Life would be much pleasanter and longer, perhaps, if religion did not demand sacrifices."

"I intend that my life shall be pleasant, and I think it will be long. I can never imagine myself dying."

"I never try to," he answered, with a laugh. At this moment the little servant-maid announced that tea was ready.

Cornelius talked a great deal. The impression he made may be judged from a snatch of dialogue which Alice happened to overhear.

"I must say," Miss Tamar Ann said, "that for a Romanist, he is very liberal."

"Yes," replied Miss Catherwood, "but just a little—limp. I like to see a man stand up for his principles."

Alice herself was divided between a vague disdain of him and a distinct liking. And he said to himself that if a man wanted a clever wife who would help him to rise in the world, he could not do better than choose Alice O'Brien.

IV.

Next Sunday Cornelius went to Mass as usual. He stood at the door and took a comprehensive look at the interior before kneeling, although the priest was at the Offertory. He did not see Alice. He scanned the silent congregation with an observant eye. His education had trained him to judge a man's pocketbook, and consequently a man's usefulness to him, by his clothes. He shook his head and called to mind the richly-dressed people whom he had passed on their way to the temple of Episcopalianism, the Church of St. Dunstan.

During Mass he thought much of the contrast. If one may hear Mass by being physically present Cornelius fulfilled the obligation; but his mind was engaged in speculating as to his future.

He was not really bad; he had no intention of doing anything dishonorable or disreputable. But during childhood and youth—the longest times of our life—he had learned that what we see with our corporeal eyes is the only thing that exists. Religion was well enough on Sundays. With the old people, particularly with old

Irish people, who were naturally behind the times, it might mean much. A young man with his way to make in the world had other things to think of. He knew many men, wearing white linen, broadcloth, and diamond studs, who were respected by everybody, and who, without any religion, were good enough for all practical purposes. He said to himself that he did not want to be any better than such successful men.

His religion had been a habit. And as he went out of church and compared the congregation of St. Bridget's with that of the Church of St. Dunstan, he asked himself why he should cling to a habit that might be a fatal bar to his success in Philista.

The Misses Catherwood learned to expect him to tea on Sunday nights regularly. They approved of him. Nobody had anything to say against him, except that he was a "Romanist," but a "liberal one," Miss Tamar Ann always hastened to add. They were getting old, and their income would cease at their death. They were glad to think that this promising young man, when he had gotten established, would preserve Alice from a career of ill-paid school-teaching.

"If she was not a Romanist they would give her the Literature and Elocution at Hypatia, with nearly two thousand a year. Mr. Longwood, the president, has told her so more than once."

"But she *is* a Romanist," tartly answered Miss Tamar Ann. "She can't save anything teaching in that primary school, so she'll have to marry—if she can."

After many walks and talks, some ice-cream-eating in the fashionable saloon in Philista, and a quarrel or two, Cornelius and Alice were "engaged."

Cornelius was not in a position to marry yet. All his

funds were invested in the law-firm. Alice had nothing, but she was the more ambitious. They had resolved to wait two years. How in the meantime could she help him to make money? She was entirely wrapped up in him, in his plans, in his future. She thought and thought about the problem of the future, until the quick, spasmodic beating of her heart reminded her that she was, as Miss Catherwood often said, "Rosalia's child."

Although Cornelius and Alice were much in love with each other, they never lost sight of the material resources they considered necessary to their position in life—which they put, as a matter of course, greatly above that of the Misses Catherwood. The ways and means of those old ladies would be unsuitable for Cornelius Blake, Esq., and his wife. The growth of the law business was slow. Alice said bitterly over and over again that girls were utterly useless, so far as the making of money went.

"Well," Miss Tamar Ann had answered more than once, "the place at Hypatia College is still open."

But Miss Catherwood had always said, "Hush!"

On All-Souls'-day Alice went to Vespers, which at St. Bridget's were sung after nightfall. Her forehead took a deep, perpendicular wrinkle upon it, and, as the choir began the "Magnificat," she half rose in the pew, as if to go. But something seemed to push her back. When the soprano voice sang the "Tantum Ergo," and the kneeling people began to prepare for the Benediction of the Most Blessed Sacrament, she hastened down the aisle, and, once in the open air, ran home.

"Præstet fides supplementum
Sensuum defectui!"

It rang in her ears; she could not get rid of it.

She threw herself on her bed, the frown still on her brow. Opposite her was the little crucifix her father had left her. It stood in the centre of the mantel. With a sudden movement, as of irritation, she arose and held it a moment at arm's length and with her head averted. The moonlight fell through the window on her white face and whiter dress, and, if it were not for the color of her hair and the dark circles around her eyes, she would have seemed a statue. With the same sudden movement she put the crucifix into a Japanese box on the mantel, locked it, and, going to the window, threw the tiny key as far as she could fling it. Her lips were white and drawn.

"It is done!" she said. "I shall live and forget."

Then she threw herself upon the bed again and covered her eyes with her arms. There was no sound but a distant whistle, which sounded like a despairing shriek from a steamboat in the river.

Cornelius Blake came back to Philista after a week's stay in Philadelphia, and found Alice in a strangely silent mood. When he was about to leave her, she said:

"On the 1st of January I shall open the classes of literature and elocution in Hypatia College."

"Good heavens!" he cried, starting, "you haven't—"

"I have. Don't let us say any more about it. You know why I have done it. My aunts seem pleased. Henceforth you will have to meet at the door of the Baptist church, if you still continue in your—present way."

He was shocked. He was glad, too; he had wanted her to do it, and she had understood his thought, though he had never spoken it to her.

She put her hand on his shoulder.

"I have given up more than *you* can appreciate, being

a man," she said bitterly; " but, oh, Neil!" she added, tenderly, "*you* will never forsake me, you will always be mine?"

"Till death," he said.

She shuddered. He laughed and said : " Somebody is walking over your grave."

She pushed him farther from her.

"If you were different, if you were not as you are, Neil, I might not have done it. You would have helped me—"

" Bosh! my dear girl. Keep up, and we'll start in life with a flourish," he said. " Good-bye, good-bye! You'll read something pleasant in the *Star* to-morrow."

His thoughts were not as light as his words. He had wanted her to do it, and she had done it. Religion was not of much value to him, he thought, as he went home through the quiet streets, but it ought to be a great deal to a woman. Of course Alice must laugh in her heart at the Baptists. She could not believe in their doctrines. But a woman ought to have some religion. He was glad that it had been done, but he wished she had not felt obliged to do it. Alice a Catholic and Alice without any religion—Alice playing at being a Baptist, that they might set up housekeeping in a handsome house in Court Terrace—were two different girls. He did not feel the same toward her. It did not make much difference what a man believed, he said, as he lighted a cigar, since life was to be lived in the pleasantest way; but a woman— but a woman—

And he shook his head; and as he struck another match a charm on his watch-chain, with Masonic emblems on it, glittered in the light. He had made " progress " too.

V.

Cornelius Blake had often been pressed to join the Masons, even by Masons themselves, although this is said to be against the rules of the Order. He had always said " no," apologetically, and, when pressed for his reasons, had said that he had reasons of his own; but he had not. He had refused because he believed that the Catholic Church forbade its members to enter a lodge. He had said angrily to himself that Catholics had no cause why they should not join the Masons; it was simply a piece of superstition to handicap themselves so, and absurd to bind themselves to keep out of an association that could be of so much use to them.

When Sherwood Archer, Cashier of the National Bank of Philista, who had been delighted with what he called Cornelius' " Irish smartness," had said that the Young Men's Reform Club wanted a candidate for the State Legislature who could catch the Irish vote, as an anti-monopolist faction had recently carried off a big slice of it in Philista, Cornelius felt the blood rush to his face with pleasure. He felt that this great man, who was Grand Tyler and everything else that was grand in Masonic circles, and consequently great socially, meant him.

" I'll pledge the Masons to you and I'll leave you to catch the Irish; but you'll have to join us. What! scrupulous? Why, dear boy, you haven't let go your mother's apron-strings yet. Bless you! you'll lose nothing with the Irish Catholics. They don't care a cent for religion in politics, but they do care an awful sight about ' patriotism.' We'll let you work that racket."

The consequence was that Cornelius Blake followed

Mr. Sherwood Archer's advice, borrowed all the money he could, and in the Philista *Star* of the day after his interview with Alice O'Brien the following paragraph occurred:

"The Young Men's Reform Club, of which Mr. Sherwood Archer is the genial President, have at length announced their 'dark horse' who will enter the race for nomination to our Legislature. This 'dark horse' is no other than the promising young lawyer, Cornelius Blake. While an enthusiastic American citizen, Mr. Blake is an Irish patriot of the old school that wore 'the collar of gold' won from the proud invader. Three cheers for Con! He is a friend of our glorious institutions and we say emphatically, 'Boom' him!"

The Catherwoods and Alice were pleased with this; but when the Philista *Eagle* was sent to them the next day they were disgusted by an editorial article headed: "Was his Front Name Patrick?" and a long "interview" with a supposed cousin of Cornelius, in which the Blake family history was more or less accurately given, and the nominee of the Young Men's Reform Club denounced as an "apostate" and an "informer."

Cornelius was inclined to rush into print and to declare that he had never missed Mass when he could help it. But the astute Archer held him back. "You've got to expect this. If you talk about Mass you'll shock the respectable element, and they'll begin to say you don't love the public-school system."

"But I do!" cried Cornelius. "I'm a public-school boy myself."

"All right!" returned Archer, with a wink: "we'll work that for all it is worth."

For the six weeks preceding the meeting of the Convention at the capital—Philista was not the capital of the State—Cornelius did little but talk and "treat the boys." He was in the hands of his friends, particularly of his friend Archer. He did not pretend to do any business, and the placard on his office-door, "At court— back in ten minutes," became yellow and dusty from long use.

The public-school "racket," as Mr. Sherwood Archer expressed it, "was worked." The *Star* even became so enthusiastic in the matter as to produce a wood-cut of an innocent-looking cherub on his way to a Grecian temple labelled "public-school," while the Pope—drawn after the model furnished by the *Pilgrim's Progress*—endeavored to force him back to a hut labelled "superstition." Cornelius did not like this, but he was in the hands of his friends. The "Honorable Cornelius Blake" danced before his eyes like a will-o'-the-wisp. What a magnificent future he with his cleverness, and Alice with her brilliancy and tact, would carve out!

It must be remembered that the *Star* and the *Eagle* were of the same party; for parties in Philista, finding themselves about to fall to pieces from rottenness, had united on a "reform" platform. They represented opposing factions. The *Eagle's* candidate was a Mr. Seth Weldon, remarkable only for having made a large fortune in the lumber trade.

The day of the Convention came. Alice was so nervous and anxious that she asked to be excused from her lectures at Hypatia. Cornelius visited her early; but, early as it was, his face was flushed and his eyes sparkled unnaturally. Miss Catherwood detected a strong smell of whisky about him. He had been out all night with the "boys."

"I have risked everything in the world on this, Alice. If I do not get the nomination I shall be a beggar. Archer promises to advance funds for the election expenses. I've spent all I had, and I'm in debt."

Alice smiled. "You must not fail, and if you do we'll begin over again. I wish I were a man! It's glorious, this excitement! It makes me forget."

Miss Catherwood had noticed a strange change in Alice of late. She was silent and preoccupied, or talkative and feverishly gay. Since she had given up the practice of her religion she had become a new and changed girl. There seemed to be no peace, no tranquillity about her. Miss Catherwood, seeing the wrinkle that came so often on her brow and the sullen look of her eyes, felt almost afraid of her.

"Don't you think," Miss Catherwood had said to Miss Tamar Ann, "that there may be more in Romanism than we know of? Alice seems to have lost something she can't find with the Baptists."

"Rubbish!" answered Miss Tamar Ann. "She's made herself, and she ought to be perfectly happy."

Miss Catherwood sighed. "I wish she hadn't done it, after all. I've been reading the little catechism she used to study, and I must say I like it more and more. I'm going over to St. Bridget's next Sunday to see what it's all like."

Miss Tamar Ann laughed.

The Convention opened. The excitement was intense. Everybody drank with everybody else. There was much buttonholing of the obstinate and knowing whispering by the wire-pullers. After three ballots no progress had been made. The two candidates had an equal number of votes. There was a recess then. The editor of the *Eagle* was seen to approach Mr. Sherwood Archer.

After the recess another name which had been courteously put in nomination and had received only two votes—that of Mr. Sherwood Archer himself—suddenly went to the top. Mr. Sherwood Archer received the nomination. It was known that both parties had sold out to him. But he made a speech so full of intense self-sacrifice on the "altar of his country" that few people, outside the Convention or the press, believed this when it was brought up against him at a later day.

Cornelius Blake did not get up to compliment the nominee, as he was expected to do. He had fallen forward in his chair, unconscious. The excitement, the heat of the summer, and immoderate drinking had made his blood boil until the fumes stifled him. An ambulance was sent for by the considerate Mr. Archer, and he was taken, talking incoherently, to St. Vincent's Hospital.

There he lay for seven weeks. The Misses Catherwood went often to see him. Alice went twice with them, but he did not know her. She wanted to take him home, for she shrank from the Sisters of Charity who nursed him; but the physicians would not allow it.

Her fear of the Sisters or of any suggestion of the Church she had abandoned—she could not be said to have abandoned the faith, for she *believed* still—had become morbid; therefore her aunts could not induce her to return to the hospital after the second visit.

Cornelius became conscious at last, and was so near death that he asked eagerly for a priest when the Sister in charge proposed it to him. And, after a long talk, some explanation and persuasion, he humbly received the last sacraments, perhaps for the only time since his First Communion with the proper dispositions.

The crisis of the fever passed and the physician gave Cornelius hope. The Sisters brought him books, which he read during the long days of convalescence. But Alice was constantly in his mind. He sent for her; she would not come, and Miss Catherwood told him the reason.

She would come back to the Church, he said to himself, and they would begin life as his father and mother had done, with true hearts and strong hands, and the God they had outraged would forgive them.

At last he was set free. How sweet was the air, how blue the sky, how hopeful everything!

Miss Catherwood met him at the door of the house with a little cry of pleasure.

"Alice has not got home yet from the college—it is near her time, though; and Tamar Ann is out, too. I'll get my shawl, if you like, and we'll go and meet her."

Cornelius agreed willingly. Miss Catherwood was anxious to be present at the meeting of the lovers. She said to herself that "Rosalia's child needed great care in moments of excitement."

Miss Catherwood and Cornelius, a shadow of his former self, went out into the quiet street. Sunset had tinged the white shutters of the uniform houses red, and mothers were calling lingering children to supper.

Very near St. Bridget's Church they met Alice. She looked very pretty and graceful. She wore her favorite white gown, a dainty little hat, and a bunch of scarlet sage in her belt. Cornelius' heart leaped.

"Alice, dear Alice!" he said.

She drew back from him, with a mingling of fear in her face and tenderness in her deeply-shaded eyes.

"We are in the street, remember," she said. "I have

heard it all. Is it true? I didn't believe it. Have you gone back? Are we separated forever?"

She spoke quickly but quietly, walking at her aunt's side.

"It is true," he answered. "You must come to me out of that—that place. We shall be poor, but at peace."

"And this after all I have done," she answered in a low tone, clasping her aunt's arm so tightly that Miss Catherwood started; "after all I have given up for you. I can't go back, Neil; nobody can go out of hell—out of hell!"

Miss Catherwood felt suddenly a heavy weight against her.

"Quick, Cornelius!" she cried.

Alice, her right hand pressed over her heart, had become white and rigid. They carried her into the vestibule of St. Bridget's. It was an August day—the Feast of the Assumption. Borne on the air came the solemn words,

> "Præstet fides supplementum,
> Sensuum defectui."

Her face was calm, except for the deep wrinkles on her brow. She shivered when Cornelius touched her.

"She wants something, Neil—she wants something. It's the same look I saw in Rosalia's eyes."

"A priest!" cried Cornelius.

The eyes lost their dumb, despairing look—or seemed to lose it—for an instant, and then closed.

"She is dead!" cried Miss Catherwood, and then, turning on Cornelius Blake with a fierceness he never forgot, she cried: "My God! how unworthy are you of what he gives you. It is you and such as you that help to blind us to the Light!"

A DESCENDANT OF THE PURITANS.

I.

PRISCILLA ARDEN lived in Butterville, Mo., a city of some eight thousand inhabitants on the line of the M. K. and T. R.R. Its products are railroad men, barrels, and, of late, "culture," by which term the members of the best society designate Art.

Priscilla was the daughter of the editor of the *Bazoo* —the Butterville *Bazoo*—which had a marked success among its "esteemed contemporaries" as a humorous "exchange" until the funny man degenerated into pathos and in despair took to railroading. Priscilla's father was also the postmaster. Her grandfather had come West from Massachusetts. She was descended from Priscilla Mullins through her grandmother, who was a Paybody. Over the parlor organ in the front room there hung a genealogical tree, carefully framed in oak, between a testimonial from his brother Knights of Pythias to Mr. Arden and a stuffed eagle on a bracket, presented to the editor of the *Bazoo* by a subscriber in liquidation of three years' subscription in arrears. Principally on account of this genealogical tree—for the expatriated New England element was small but strongly respectable in Butterville—and also in consideration of the political influence of the *Bazoo*, Priscilla's father had managed to hold his post since Lincoln's first term. His faltering in allegiance once in deference to the prejudices of the railroad men had done him no harm with the next administration. He was thin, wiry, with a white beard close cropped. His face was of that conformation which may almost be said to be a face of this decade, it is so common. It was like General Grant's before he became fat. And when the editor of the *Bazoo* offered his photograph, very artistically reproduced by the photo-engraving process, as a premium, many economical souls were induced to put their names on the list on the understanding that it would do for either Grant or Garfield.

All that was left of Priscilla's mother was her photograph, which had the place of honor over the hair-cloth sofa in the "front room." It represented a mild-looking woman with her hair puffed out at the sides, a wide lace collar, and an expensive silk gown evidently inflated by hoops. Priscilla did not remember her mother very well; her father rarely spoke of her, though he had written a two-column obituary notice, beginning:

"There is a reaper whose name is Death."

Priscilla tenderly preserved it in a scrap-book. She had little on which to nourish the memory of this mother, and, in her desire to keep it green and to get nearer to the dead, she prayed every night and morning for the soul of the sweet, mysterious being, with whom her heart longed to be in communion. The Congregational minister shook his head over this. But Priscilla, who could repeat all the International Sunday-school lessons for years back, floored him with a text. Several old neighbors bore testimony to the great qualities of the deceased wife and mother: "She wasn't stuck up," and "She did her own work; nobody ever saw anything slack about *Miss* Arden." So Priscilla took to her prayers.

The Congregationalists were not numerous in Butterville, but they were intensely respectable. Several large bond-holders of M. K. and T. stock—old inhabitants who had come West so far back as '59—were Congregationalists. Lately the Baptist minister, who had baptized Jesse James, had rather thinned the Congregationalist audience by preaching terrific sermons, assisted by a magic-lantern and a blackboard, and with the Ford brothers for several Sundays, during their engagement at the Academy of Music in Butterville, in a front pew.

Priscilla's religious views were peculiar. Her father was rather inclined to be an Ingersollian, but, as he wrote a religious column—" Lay Sermons by Whitehead "—in the *Bazoo* every Saturday, he felt the necessity of conforming to that Congregational mode of worship, wherein the belief in eternal punishment was considerably softened down. The editor of the *Bazoo*, being very advanced, dreaded eternal punishment, which he often alluded to in learned editorials as an " invention of the Inquisition."

Priscilla's religious views had of late become seriously modified. When she was fifteen she had been a "hardshell" Baptist; at nineteen, having read a course of Miss Yonge's novels, she was inclined to Ritualism, and longed to have an old English abbey or priory which she could restore to the Established Church. So scrupulous did she become that she broached the subject of turning over the deed of the house that her mother had bequeathed her to the descendant of the original Indian who had owned the plot of ground, if he could be found. The editor of the *Bazoo* was of the opinion that he could not be found, and coldly declined to advertise for him. Then Priscilla took to reading mild, soft, quietistic poems and essays about sitting with folded hands and waiting among lilies, and full of speculations about heaven. At twenty-two she had a religion of her own, as most of the girls around her who thought on serious subjects had. She read all the sermons in the New York *Herald*, the Monday edition of which reached Butterville on Wednesday, and she was rather inclined toward ethical culture; but she still sat under the Congregational minister. As Bessie Hartwicke, the new "help," had shown a talent for housekeeping when she was left to manage the house alone, Priscilla concluded to relinquish the domestic arts and cultivate Art. She took lessons in vocal music, and sang with much applause at a broom-drill given for the benefit of the Congregationalists, but repeated with even more success by the energetic Baptists, who offered a barrel of flour to the prettiest girl in the room on the night of the festival.

Priscilla had dark, serious, blue eyes, shaded by long lashes, rather heavy eyebrows for a girl, a straight nose a little long, a soft, creamy complexion, oval, rounded cheeks which flushed easily. This habit of blushing at unexpected times without reason was a source of embarrassment to Priscilla. There was one thing that caused her some embarrassment; this was a slight shade on her upper lip. Priscilla was almost a brunette. She attired herself very simply, eschewed "bangs" and bangles, and, in her plain, neat hat and tight blue suit, there was a Puritan simplicity not unworthy of a descendant of that Priscilla who had said,

"If I am not worth the wooing, I am surely not worth the winning.

She had a neat, trim figure, but the Butterville people thought she lacked "style." However, the Baptists did not vote the barrel of flour to her, and therefore they found the notice in the next morning's *Bazoo* very much less grandiloquent than the notice of the Congregationalists had been.

Priscilla, with her improved views, had set down the whole proceeding as vulgar.

II.

The sun, setting majestically into the level land which was an endless vista of prairie, cast a soft color on Priscilla's face as she sat one afternoon, paint-brush in hand, toning up the background of a panel of sunflowers and golden-rod. Tea was almost ready. There came a pleasant jingling from the kitchen. Casting a glance out of the bay-window, that was disproportionately large in comparison with the square, white house, Priscilla saw the editor of the *Bazoo* quickly approaching. She ran out into the kitchen to see that everything was right, and got back to the parlor in time to pick up the pile of "exchanges" which he had drawn out of his alpaca coat and thrown upon the floor. He fanned himself with his hat and pinched Priscilla's cheek as she kissed him.

"Hem!" he said, critically examining the panel, "those squashes are too yellow, and I don't understand that black splash in the centre—is it black or brown?"

"Father!" she cried reproachfully, "they are sunflowers."

"Oh!" he said apologetically, "I thought they couldn't be squashes. Have you dropped your music for art, Pris?"

"I feel that I haven't the intensity—that is, the power of expression, the soulfulness—that music imperatively requires. I think that I am more drawn to Art. I had a lovely letter from Miss Allison, who used to teach mental philosophy at the Academy, you know; she said—the letter is up-stairs—'Let it be your sole *cult* to draw out soulfulness, to encourage the better part.'"

"So?" returned her father, abstractedly stooping for one of his papers. "Oh! I forgot. Priest Riordan was in the office to-day correcting an error we made about morning Vespers, or evening Mass, or something. He is an honest man, pays his debts, and looks a great deal after the poor, though he's the very devil in controversy. He brought me a letter about kissing the pope's toe, written in answer to Rev. Isaiah Tomkins. It took the hair off, I *tell* you. He intends to have some extra music next Sunday, and his leading singer is sick. I told him you'd sing."

The editor of the *Bazoo* said this half-hesitatingly, as members of the male sex do when they announce that they have made social arrangements unauthorized.

"Just like you, father. But I haven't any more soul in my music."

"It seems to me you sing as well as the other girls." He noticed a slight contraction of the young lady's brow. "Much better than most of them. Have you any conscientious scruples about singing for the Romanists?"

"Oh! no," returned Priscilla. "I believe in universal brotherhood. And if I can help the culture of these poor people I am willing to do it."

"All right," said the father, as he drew on his slippers. "But I don't think they hanker after culture."

"They ought to be taught that it's the most precious

thing in life." Priscilla, in her imagination, saw herself as a second Hypatia teaching the consummateness of inanimate things to the Romanists who worshipped at St. Mark's.

"I guess they know what they want by this time. I've been inside of a Catholic church only once or twice myself, but seems to me, as somebody said the other day, 'they worship God as if he were a king.' 'Polly, put the kettle on!'"

Tea was well served. Priscilla made some remarks on the harmony of the form of the radish and its foliage.

"Didn't know radishes had 'foliage.' By the way, Phil Carlisle was married to Mary Reilly on last Sunday."

"No!" cried Priscilla, blushing with interest. "To the little Irish girl! Well, really, I shouldn't think Phil's folk would like that. The Irish are so ignorant, and I suppose she is no better than the rest. His family will think it a great come-down. She's a Catholic, too."

"Don't be so particular, young lady," said Mr. Arden, cutting the end off a cigar. "Marriage is a serious consideration, an anxious consideration, when a girl reaches *your* age." He laughed.

"Marriage," said Priscilla, solemnly turning her teacup upside down to read what fate had in store for her in the grounds, "is nothing to a woman with a mission. Miss Allison said that 'Art is the—'"

"Miss Allison's an old maid. Phil Carlisle may congratulate himself. Old Reilly isn't exactly a swell, but his daughter is a good girl, and she'll keep Phil straight. They were married at St. Mark's."

Mr. Arden lost himself in his papers, concealed by a veil of smoke, and Priscilla went to help Bessie with the dishes.

"I hear Phil Carlisle's throwed himself away on one of them Irish," said Bessie, who was of old Connecticut stock, "and gone and joined the Papishes. His folks must feel it awful."

Priscilla shook her head sympathetically; she kept to her sunflowers until the twilight was gone.

III.

When the room had become so dim that the gilt frame on her mother's photograph no longer shone, a weight of desolation fell on Priscilla's heart. The soft May breeze, chilling a little, bore in to her the scent of the lilac in the front garden. And the scent awoke in her a longing, an unrest; the moon arose out of the flat earth and silvered the network of railroad tracks that were visible from the slight elevation on which the Arden house stood.

All common things looked unreal; yet Priscilla had never been so heavily oppressed by the reality of life. The vain pretences of hollow and sham culture seemed so worthless! Could she ever paint that moonlight? Could any earthly being sing the inexpressible thought that the glorious shield hung in the heavens inspired?

That moon had looked upon the Crucifixion.

The thought, filling her mind so suddenly, made her shiver. The moon had perhaps shone through the massed clouds that hung over Calvary, and dropped a silver ray upon the thorn-crowned head borne down by the load of the sins of the world. She looked at the moon awe-struck. *This moon had seen it.* The sacrifice that her ministers had of late vaguely alluded to as the "atonement" became at that instant very real to her. There was no more half-doubt, half-vagueness for her. Here, suddenly among her little pretensions and frivolity, the grace of God had touched her.

Her father was enjoying his last cigar on the front step. He rose, and his voice interrupted her thoughts.

"Come in," he was saying. "Yes, this is Mr. Arden's house, and Miss Arden is at home. Bessie, light the gas! Priscilla, here is a gentleman to see you."

Another voice said something.

"Mr. O'Donnell, organist at St. Mark's? Glad to see you. Walk right in."

Bessie was standing on tip-toe, struggling unsteadily to light the gas, when the visitor entered and relieved her of an effort that seemed likely to elongate her considerably.

Priscilla held out her hand, after the rule set down in Butterville's unwritten books of etiquette—where sociability was the one great requirement—while her father read from the visitor's card, "Mr. Felix O'Donnell," and then said, "My daughter."

Bessie, also following the Butterville etiquette, seized his hat, as a savage seizes a scalp, and disappeared with it. Priscilla pulled down the shades, and Mr. Arden, after saying it was a fine night, remarked, also following the Butterville usage, that "two's company and three's a crowd," and took himself off to the office.

The Butterville axiom was that old people were always in the way when there were young ones "around." It was an axiom accepted without pangs and as a matter of course by the Butterville parents. Young people of opposite sexes were always constrained in "old company."

He came back in a few minutes, having forgotten his bundle of papers, and, putting his head into the door of the parlor, said:

"Don't go out, Pris. John Lowe said he would drop in to-night."

"Very well, father," Priscilla answered. "Don't you be long!"

"Oh! I guess neither of you will hanker after me," he said, with a slight wink at the visitor.

Felix O'Donnell looked at the bright-looking yet serious maiden who stood under the gas-jet, seeming so sweet and simple, and wondered why there was always a John Lowe or John Somebody Else dangling after every nice girl. He had never met this particular nice girl before, because she was not in his set. Society in Butterville was cut up by the churches into patches; the Catholics, who had multiplied and increased from a small nucleus of railroad laborers, were numerous. The Congregationalists, the Baptists, the Presbyterians, a knot of Second-Adventists, and a smaller knot of Spiritualists occupied various degrees in the social scale; but the Catholics—that is, the Irish—were cut off by an imaginary and impassable gulf. St. Bonifacius was the patron of a small chapel of the German congregation, which kept very much to itself.

Felix O'Donnell gazed at Priscilla with a little sarcasm in his mind. He was prepared to be on the defensive, and to laugh a little if Miss Arden should assume any airs.

Felix was a tall, well-built young fellow, more nervous-looking and with hollower cheeks than his father, who had come over from Cahirciveen, with bright, well-opened blue eyes, a complexion much reddened by the sun, which had left his broad forehead very white, and a frank, slightly humorous expression.

He wore a black sack-coat and gray trousers, and carried a wide-brimmed straw hat. Priscilla concluded that he was not at all "stylish." Priscilla's ideal young man was "stylish"—the hero of *The Bride of Lammermoor* in a frock-coat and straw-colored kid gloves.

Felix remarked that it was a pleasant evening, and said he had called to ask Miss Arden if she would sing on Sunday in Mozart's "Twelfth."

"Miss Donovan, the soprano, is sick," he continued. "Sunday will be a great feast in our church, you know—or rather you don't know—and Herr Stroebling, from Kansas City, is to come and play. I shall do the bass."

"But I thought you were the organist."

"I do very well for ordinary occasions," he said, with a pleasant laugh, "but Herr Stroebling is a good organist. It's a great thing to have him come."

Priscilla hesitated.

"I have sung parts of the 'Twelfth,'" she said, "adapted to English words, at various times; but you, in your church, you sing it in—" Priscilla paused. She felt sure it was in some dread and superstitious language; she had heard so.

"In Latin," said Felix.

"But I can't speak Latin."

"I can't either," said Felix. "I can pronounce it. That is all that's needed. A few lessons, and you will do very well."

"If you think I can succeed I will try."

In reply Felix drew from his pocket a roll of music and sat down at the organ. Priscilla, without any apology or affectation, began the "Kyrie Eleison." She sang in tune, but stumbled over the words. Felix consoled her by telling her it was Greek.

The lesson lasted an hour.

"A nice girl—no airs," thought Felix.

"What a soft voice!" thought Priscilla. "He is not at all 'Irish.'"

"Now, what have I been singing?" asked Priscilla when she had learned the "Gloria" tolerably well and Bessie had brought in a pitcher of ice-water.

Felix translated the words.

"What!" cried Priscilla, her reverent mind shocked, "have I been singing those beautiful words so carelessly and thoughtlessly?"

Felix was startled. *He* had sung them carelessly a hundred times. It was a lesson.

"I shall be glad to sing," said Priscilla, offering Felix the plate of apples which Bessie brought in with the solemnity of one serving baked meats at a funeral. "It is a great thing for a young man like you to raise your people up to your level, and to devote your time to elevating the standard of taste among the poor Roman Catholics. Your choir must have a hard time."

Felix was not accustomed to this point of view. He smiled when he understood her.

"We do have a hard time reaching the level of the people's devotion. *That* is very much above us."

"He is very modest," Priscilla thought. "You are a Catholic, too, of course."

"Oh! yes," answered Felix. Priscilla, following the Butterville etiquette, gave him the album of photographs.

"I am not prejudiced," she said. "I have known some very pleasant Catholics—educated ones. I met a girl in Sedalia when I was there with father. I found her very nice. You would never have guessed—"

"No?" said Felix, smiling, his politeness restraining him from finishing her sentence with a touch of sarcasm. "Will you play?"

Priscilla drummed through the overture to "Zampa" in that dismal succession of notes which only a parlor organ is capable of producing. When she ceased, the croaking of the frogs in the pond in the next lot was delightfully refreshing. Then Felix played a voluntary out of his music-book, and took his leave, promising to escort Priscilla to the choir rehearsal on the following night.

Priscilla sat with her hands folded, looking at the moon. She thought that she had never met anybody like this Mr. O'Donnell before. He was good-humored and agreeable, but there was something in his eyes that made her think he was laughing at her. Priscilla flushed at the thought. Laughing at *her!* The idea!

Mr. Arden returned with a stout, pompous-looking man having a bald head and an expression of entire satisfaction with himself. He formed an appropriate background to a huge locket attached to a gold watch-chain.

He apologized to Priscilla for not having "spent the evening" with her. He had been kept busy at the store. John Lowe was *the* prominent dry-goods merchant in Butterville. He was a celebrity; he was the pioneer of the ninety-nine-cent "inducement" which had revolutionized trade in the great West. He was not proud, but he felt his importance. His advertisement occupied, on Saturdays, a whole page in the *Bazoo;* and if he had run for mayor that journal would have supported him valiantly, though he was a Democrat.

He finished his cigar, sitting on the lower step with Mr. Arden, while Priscilla stood in the doorway looking at the shadow of the lilac-bushes on the path. It was a time for sentiment. The editor of the *Bazoo* felt that himself. He tried to find an appropriate quotation.

"On such a night Leander swam the Hellespont."

"Byron?" asked Mr. Lowe.

"No, the immortal Will. No, old boy, twelve cents a line won't do for five insertions of that criss-cross ad., with the reading-notices changed every week. Composition's going up to forty cents a thousand, and—"

A long altercation followed, during which the editor of the *Bazoo* yielded a point or two with seeming reluctance.

"Well, well," he said good-humoredly at last, "I'll go to bed. Bring me up a pitcher of ice-water, Pris, when you come. I'll leave you young people to do your courting. Good-night."

Lowe laughed. Priscilla still stood in the doorway, smiling a little at her father's joke. The other "young person" was over forty. The clock struck eleven. Lowe cast admiring glances at the serene, virginal figure on the sill of the doorway. The lilac-scent, enriched with dew, mingled with the heliotrope hidden in the dark. The trees were outlined against the silver haze in the horizon. The croak of the frogs was fitful, like a tremulous bass undertone. Lowe arose, threw away his cigar, and yawned. Priscilla was wrapped in a half-mournful reverie, oppressed by a delicious sadness.

"You had some music to-night? Hopkins said he heard the organ as he came back to the store after supper. Who was here?"

Priscilla felt unreasonably irritated by this not extraordinary question.

"A gentleman called."

Lowe played with his watch-chain.

"Oh!" he said with a laugh, "you can't make *me* jealous."

Priscilla flushed. What did he mean? It was well enough for her father to joke—

"It was a Mr. O'Donnell, the organist at St. Mark's."

"Catholic church? Yes, I know O'Donnell. He manages the express-office. Honest fellow; family awfully ignorant and Irish—regular 'Micks,' you know."

"I don't know," answered Priscilla, with a sense of offence. "He is a gentleman."

Lowe glanced at her quickly. Her face looked very pure and sweet in the moonlight. He drew nearer to her. The door was slammed suddenly, and there was a sharp report.

If Priscilla had not been a girl devoted to culture there might have been grounds for a suspicion that she had slapped Mr. Lowe. He picked up his hat and whistled. He was not accustomed to that sort of thing. He remembered that he was the pioneer of the ninety-nine-cent "inducement" in the West, and walked homeward in a calmer frame of mind.

IV.

Felix O'Donnell called at the Arden house and gravely practiced the musical parts with Priscilla. And on Sunday, which was Pentecost, Priscilla sang very well. She felt that she was not doing herself justice, since she did not understand what she was singing, and once or twice a fear—the remnants of the teaching she had known before she became a disciple of culture—entered her mind that she was engaging in idolatrous worship.

The silence, the devotion, the decorum of the crowd of assistants surprised her. There was Teddy O'Brien, the foreman of her father's printing-office—a careless, devil-may-care individual, and a commonplace one, on weekdays. Yet to-day, kneeling, touched by the glory of some great mystery, he looked transfigured. To Priscilla it seemed that he saw God or his angels on the altar. There was Mrs. Malley, their next-door neighbor, a hard-working woman who had "put away" a snug sum of money during the war by selling pies to the defenders of the Union. A good-hearted but very vulgar woman was Mrs. Malley, who never forgot that she was "independent rich," and who was at constant warfare with Bessie—a person, in fact, without interest to the cultured mind. Here was she, evidently forgetting her many-hued and well-kept cashmere shawl, and the fruit-orchard on her bonnet, in dumb, ecstatic devotion before this Mystery. Looking around, Priscilla saw many that she knew. They were persons whom she considered to be in the lower walks of life—persons whom she was accustomed to look down upon. Caste in Butterville was almost as well defined, though not so openly acknowledged, as in an English town.

To-day Priscilla seemed to have changed places with these people. They were somehow beyond her. They possessed something she did not possess. They saw something she did not see. A vague yearning filled her mind, and a slight impatience, too. Why was she left out?

Could that be Father Riordan, whom she had seen every day since she was a child—that figure, majestic, awful, raising the chalice in his hands? He had taken a new character, in her eyes, with his gold-embroidered robes. She could never look at his rotund form and pleasant face again with the feeling that he was much like other men, only, of course, a Romish priest. It was not the fact that his decent suit of broadcloth had been replaced by these strange, solemn vestments—which reminded her of the description of the garments of the Levites in the Old Testament—that made the difference. It was something else, indefinable, mysterious.

Priscilla did her best not to give the organist unnecessary trouble. In fact, she was the only person in the choir who did not insist on loping when the organist trotted. But nobody seemed to mind that. The sermon rather wearied Priscilla. It was an old one of Father Riordan's on his favorite theme, the Trinity. She was thirsting for some explanation of this mystery. Even her new acquaintance, Mr. O'Donnell, who seemed to be a young man like other young men, had lost himself in a strange rapture. What did it mean? What was it that transfigured these people?

When Mass was over Felix O'Donnell descended the stairs from the gallery with Priscilla.

"It is not often," he said, "that we hear a voice like yours in our church. I wish we could hear it every Sunday."

"I haven't much voice," she answered very truthfully, "but I am careful. Your service is—is strange, weird; no, those are not the words! If I was sure it was right to say so I should call it heavenly."

"It is heavenly."

There was a pause. They worked their way through the crowd to the opposite sidewalk.

"I will sing again, if Father Riordan would like me to. But I feel uneasy because I don't know what I am singing. I am sure it must be all right, since the priest pays so much respect to the Bible on the altar, but"—Priscilla laughed—"I am a conscientious heretic, you know."

Felix laughed, too.

"Would you like a translation?"

"Yes, if you will bring me one."

At this moment Mr. Arden approached, having elbowed his way through the throng on the sidewalk.

"You did well, Pris," he said, offering Felix a cigar. "The music was tip-top; reminded me of the Cincinnati festival, when you all came in together with a scream and a roar—*tout ensemble*, you know. I must say, Mr. O'Donnell, you Catholics know how to treat the Lord. You go about your service reverently. You don't try to slap him on the back, as our people do."

Mr. Arden was in great good-humor. He invited Felix to dinner. Felix declined.

"My old mother would be lonely," he said.

"Good boy!" said the editor of the *Bazoo*. "Drop in when you like."

"And," added Priscilla, with a smile, "bring me the translation."

The editor of the *Bazoo* was much impressed with the ceremonies of the Mass. He believed, with Byron,

> "Surely they are sincerest
> Who are most impressed
> With that which lies nearest."

And, through his quality of taking instantaneous and dissolving impressions, he had been enabled to make the *Bazoo* a lively paper. After dinner he read a little in Hallam's *History of the Middle Ages*, *Maria Monk's Daughter*, *Ivanhoe*, and Burton's *Anatomy of Melancholy* (for Latin quotations), and produced a two-column article, headed:

Our Roman Catholic Brethren.
What They Do and How They Do It.
Pagan Pomp Eclipsed by Papal Magnificence.
A Display That Throws the Eleusinian Mysteries in the Shade.
Eloquent and Soul-Stirring Discourse by Father Riordan, etc., etc.

The next day after this article had appeared Father Riordan entered the *Bazoo* office with ten closely-written pages of foolscap, beginning:

"Messrs. Editors: The feelings of the Catholics in this community have been shocked by a lengthy article—"

After some discussion the editor of the *Bazoo* agreed to admit the letter, provided it were cut down.

"I thought I'd please you," he said, slightly irritated. "What's wrong about the Eleusinian mysteries? They look well in print. A fellow never knows when he is treading on the corns of you Catholics."

V.

Felix escorted Priscilla to the choir rehearsals regularly. Generally, on returning, he found her father and John Lowe, who had entirely forgotten Priscilla's insult to his dignity, finishing their cigars on the front steps. Priscilla's study of the translation of the Ordinary of the Mass had satisfied her half-awakened doubts. She had found a new interest in life.

She and Felix talked little during their short walks. He spoke seldom, but he was a pleasant companion for all that. He seemed to understand her, and, if he made a half-satirical comment when her cultured raptures were overflowing, it was always good-humored. She confessed to herself that a primrose by the river's brim *was* a simple primrose to him. He had read Tom Moore, and *Evangeline*, and the *Ballad Poetry of Ireland*. He read a daily and a weekly paper. He had collected several books on rose-culture. His culture stopped short there. Withal Priscilla found it hard to patronize him. It was true he lived in the quarter of the town in which the Irish had settled. It was true that he was only slightly acquainted with the leading inhabitants. He had spent a few years at Father Riordan's school, and acquired that amazing facility in addition, subtraction, and multiplication that gave such a great superiority at the express-office. Priscilla soon discovered all this, and also that he lived with his mother, who was old. As a descendant of Priscilla Mullins, as the daughter of the editor of the *Bazoo*, as a girl who for her accomplishments and social position was much "looked up" to in Butterville, she had felt somewhat like a Queen Cophetua extending her hand in graceful politeness to an interesting beggar-man. For Felix O'Donnell was Irish, and, though very nice, still not quite—not quite, you know. "Of course one does not like to seem bigoted against the Catholics, but they are really not nice. The crowd at St. Mark's is *awful*."

This is what Faith Evans, Priscilla's bosom-friend, said one afternoon as they were walking through the plaza, planted with infant trees, which in time was to be the Butterville Public Park. Faith Evans had been delivering a remonstrance. On the preceding evening Felix, following the usage of Butterville society, had on the way from the rehearsal invited Priscilla to have ice-cream at Barker's.

Barker's was a two-story frame house at the corner of Lincoln and Liberty Streets. A huge white awning stretched before it, on which was printed in black letters, "Ice-Cream." It was filled with the *jeunesse dorée* of Butterville, of both sexes. The Willis boys, clerks in the shoe-factory, scions of an old family dating back to '52, were there with Faith Evans and several other young girls of the best society. It was hard to find room at the marble-topped tables. Faith obligingly made space for her friend and Felix; but the Willis boys, who knew the value of "family," stared, and several of the *jeunesse dorée* wondered who that "red-headed Irishman" was, though they knew very well.

Priscilla was conscious of a slight blush; she felt the atmosphere. She was defiantly attentive to Felix. She even insisted on transferring a portion of her strawberry-ice to his vanilla—a delicate attention which caused the *jeunesse dorée* to conclude, as one woman, that the couple were engaged. Hence the remonstrance from Faith Evans, a thin, tall, freckled girl wearing turbulent "bangs."

"You must remember that you are very different from *him*. His associations are no doubt of a kind repelling to refined tastes. Even a flirtation—"

"I won't hear any more of this," Priscilla interrupted. "I don't know what you mean, Faith. I am sure he is as good as Jim Willis."

Faith laughed; and her revenge came to her.

It was at twilight. Crossing the street just in front of them was an old woman, bent and shrivelled. She wore a small three-cornered shawl and a white frilled cap. She was clean, neat, and very pleasant to look upon; but as Faith at once remarked, "So awfully Irish! Suppose *she* were some relative of your O'Donnell."

The old woman had a basket on one arm. Just as she

reached the express-office Felix O'Donnell came out and kissed her. Then he took the basket and said:

"So you've come at last, mother! I've been waiting for half an hour in the doorway here. We'll have a long ride in the moonlight. But what's the basket for?"

"Sure I thought you'd be after wanting something to eat, as you wouldn't lose time coming to supper."

Felix caught sight of the girls and nodded pleasantly. Faith laughed, as the son helped his mother to mount the omnibus which carried passengers through a stretch of pleasant country out to a park much resorted to by the inhabitants of Butterville in summer.

Faith had had her revenge. She admitted to herself that Felix looked almost handsome in his gray business suit.

"He is a good son, no doubt," she added aloud. "Imagine, though, a mother-in-law in *that* cap!"

Faith laughed again.

Priscilla was shocked. His family must be very low people. Had the thing that Faith had warned her against ever entered her mind? She dared not answer. Had he meant anything? Had she encouraged him? Perhaps she had. Well, there should be an end of it now. A girl must respect her position in life. *She* would not be laughed at and looked down upon by anybody.

All this may seem absurd to people whose horizon is wider than Priscilla's was; it may also seem absurd that a young woman who could seriously think in this manner could at the same time have reasoned so deeply and prayed so earnestly as to have come to the conclusion that she ought not to be isolated from the devout group that had filled her soul with awe on the morning of Pentecost.

She had told Father Riordan she could not sing the "O Salutaris Hostia" at the offertory, though she had no difficulty about the "Ave Maria." He had spoken to her of that august Sacrifice in the presence of which every knee and heart bowed. She went home, saying to herself that she could not sing again unless she believed. The following Sunday she did not go to the choir. On the next Sunday she appeared, a little quieter, perhaps, but it was noticed that her voice was unusually expressive. On Monday she went to the Benedictine father who served the chapel of St. Bonifacius.

She would have gone to Father Riordan had not pride prevented her. Faith Evans' words awakened a sentiment of resentment in her mind. If people were thinking what they had no right to think, if Felix O'Donnell was presuming what he had no right to presume, the news that she had entered the Church would only confirm the opinions of one and encourage those of the other; so she stole to St. Bonifacius' early in the mornings, and one morning she was received into the Fold.

Her father had made no objection. "I don't want any fuss made about it," he had said. "I don't want paragraphs to get into the papers about it, and have that Cleveland *Leader* fellow call me a slave of Rome. You ought to follow your conscience, of course. I was once almost a Mormon myself. *I* won't interfere. Besides, what with Beecherism and the dearth of ministers, there will soon be no Congregationalism left. Then you'll be 'left,' my dear. And Romanism would be very decent, if it wasn't for the Irish. Go your way, Pris." And he kissed her.

VI.

In the meantime Felix O'Donnell had to admit, in moments when he paused in his work to look into the busy street, that he was becoming interested in Priscilla.

The social gulf that was so wide to her eyes did not appear to his at all. But the difference in religion was to him an insuperable barrier.

"If I had committed myself," he thought, "if she had a right to expect me to speak out, I should speak out at once." He almost wished he had. As it was, he felt that he had better nip his growing regard for Priscilla in the bud. He had great confidence in himself.

He was as polite as ever. He helped Priscilla with her music of evenings after the rehearsals, but Mr. Arden and John Lowe were always on the front step within hearing of every word.

Priscilla had determined that her religion should not interfere with her duty to her position. She talked seldom of culture, and this made her more charming in the eyes of Felix.

These evenings were very pleasant to both of them. But Felix was so sure of his own secret and of himself that he enjoyed them with a clear conscience. As to Priscilla, she felt a glow of virtue. Here was a young man rushing to his doom in spite of all her danger-signals. She was cold, reserved. She might have flirted with him, then have declared herself fancy-free and sent him off lamenting. Confidentially she told Faith Evans of her noble attitude. The astute Faith laughed incredulously. Priscilla expected a declaration every time she met Felix. She had done her best to ward it off; yet she was beginning to be slightly anxious about it.

Another proposal did come, however, or at least the prelude to it was made. The editor of the *Bazoo* announced one evening, after he had read all his exchanges, that John Lowe was a bashful man, and that he was "a long time coming to the point."

"I tell you, Pris, he's dead gone on you; but you're so hifaluting, with your culture and that sort of thing, that he doesn't dare to say a word to you."

Priscilla smiled as she thought of the scene at the door.

"I told him all about your being a Romanist, and he said he thought one religion was as good as another. If you could stand it, he could. He wants a stylish wife, a woman he can look up to; and by Jove, Pris! you're that woman."

The editor of the *Bazoo* paused. Priscilla was still smiling. Half the girls in Butterville would have jumped at an offer from the creator of the ninety-nine-cent "inducement" by which much old stock in the dry-goods line had, through the weakness of the feminine head for bargains, been turned into cash.

"Besides," continued the editor of the *Bazoo* solemnly, "I am awfully in debt. That Owl Club Mine failure was a bad thing for me. The *Bazoo* is mortgaged over head and ears to John Lowe; and now, Pris, I expect you to get me out of this hole by marrying him."

Mr. Arden spoke bluntly, yet hesitatingly. He felt that Priscilla was doing him a favor by allowing him to mention the subject. Marriage was so entirely a matter to be arranged by Priscilla herself that he considered he was interfering with an inalienable right guaranteed to every American citizen—"the pursuit of happiness."

Priscilla patted him on the cheek and kissed him. "I'll think of it, father," she said.

He looked grateful and relieved.

"Lowe will be here to-morrow night. I'm glad you're not a girl out of a story-book, hating to listen to reason. Lowe will make a good husband, and you can cultivate your taste in bric-a-brac with his money as much as you please." Then seeing that the smile had faded from her lips and that she looked thoughtful, he selected a paper from his bundle of "exchanges" and said, with fatherly kindness: "There's the Detroit *Free Press*—not much cut out of it. Brighten yourself up a little. There are worse things in the world than marriage."

Priscilla took the *Free Press* to her room. She did not find it as enlivening as her father had expected.

Should she say yes to John Lowe?

Priscilla, being a frugal American girl, knew exactly what money would buy. She neither underrated nor overrated its power. She imagined various pleasant advantages, and, by way of compensation for giving way to self-indulgence, drew a rapid sketch of a new chapel which she would persuade John Lowe to build in honor of St. Bonifacius.

But John Lowe himself?

He was an honest man, somewhat vulgar and overbearing; not—not Felix O'Donnell—

Priscilla covered her face with her hands. She was humiliated, crushed to the earth. She knew that there could be no man on earth who would be to her like Felix O'Donnell. She remembered Faith Evans' incredulous laugh. Her face became hot; tears of wounded pride filled her eyes. The people had been right; even now the Congregationalists and Baptists, missing her from church, were saying that she was coquetting with Rome for Felix O'Donnell's sake. It was very bitter, very bitter.

And her father? She was not at all afraid of what her father would say. She knew that in the matter of marriage all rights and prerogatives were a daughter's. All Butterville would despise any girl who let her father interfere in a matrimonial question.

She stayed up late. She heard her father and John Lowe talking down on the steps. She closed the window. What vile cigars John Lowe smoked! What a hateful voice he had, with his talk of per cents. Felix never— but what was he to her? "Felix" indeed! "Mrs. Felix O'Donnell!" she repeated in scorn. "That name might belong to a washerwoman!"

She awoke in the morning with a headache. She thought it all over again. The *Bazoo* mortgaged and her father in trouble. No help from anybody but John Lowe. By ten o'clock she came to the conclusion that she would sacrifice herself on the altar of filial love. At twelve she remembered that the house was her own and that she had hands with which to work. At seven o'clock, when she seated herself in the parlor with her best black gown on, indicative of sacrifice, and a spray of bleeding-hearts in her hair, she said to herself that she did not know what she would do. But in her heart she knew well enough.

She refused John Lowe. It was all over in half an hour. He took it most philosophically. He wished her joy and hoped she would be happy with the other fellow.

"I'd better take myself off," he said, with an attempt at sarcasm. "It's rehearsal night, and you may be waiting for him."

Priscilla's expression was not visible in the twilight. She made no answer. So Felix O'Donnell's intentions were plain even to this stupid John Lowe!

It was rehearsal night. Would he never come? Her heart beat at every step in the street. He had only to speak now, and she would answer as he deserved. What did she care for the world of Butterville? Faith Evans and the others might cut her, if they chose. A garret, a desert island with him, and she would be happy!

It was he at last! Bessie came in to light the gas; he unrolled his music. He looked as frank and manly as any woman could desire the man of her heart to look. He took his place at the organ. They ran through an "Ave Maria," arranged on the duet of Azucena with her son in "Trovatore," several times. After that they went to the church. Priscilla was in a dream—a delightful dream. The rose of a lifetime was blooming for her, and she had only to put out her hand to take it. This exquisite rehearsal, like a prelude to sure happiness, was all too short.

They stood under the elm at her father's gate. He paused there and remarked how lovely the night was.

It was coming! She must delay it a moment, as one delays to open a letter containing joyful news. She gave him the flowers she wore in her hair.

"I have never given you a flower before, Mr. O'Donnell. Dear me! how fragile they are. They have fallen from their stem. No, there are two!"

"Bleeding-hearts! Thank you," he said gravely. "Only two. It's a bad omen."

Priscilla laughed.

"I shall not be in the choir next Sunday, Miss Arden," he said, in a tone that had a singular constraint in it

"Mr. Stroebling will take my place. My doctor"—he hesitated—"forbids me to sing any more. My throat is slightly affected. I hope that, though we shall not rehearse together, you will not forget me."

He stopped.

Nothing more. A long pause.

"Of course not, Mr. O'Donnell."

"Good-night."

"Good-night."

He walked slowly away, thrusting the flowers away from him. He was angry with her, with himself. After such a comfortable time, such an enjoyable acquaintance, she might have said something more. Coquette! Did she think to draw him on with her flowers? "Bleeding-hearts" indeed! Some women have no hearts!

But Priscilla? Poor Priscilla, who had heroically determined to step down from her social pedestal for love's sweet sake, who had rejected the most eminent citizen of Butterville, who had offered herself, after much preparation, to the sacrificial knife and been refused; her fate was hard! She rushed up the steps, where John Lowe no longer sat, into her room, and wept aloud.

It did not end here. In truth, the story only began. Father Riordan shortly afterward alluded to Priscilla's conversion, of which many people in Butterville had heard. Felix could not believe it. He had been heartsick, angry, disgusted since he had said good-night to Priscilla. The world satisfied him not. He was as hard to please as Hamlet must have been when he rejected the wedding-hash made of the funeral baked meats. His mother—what do not mothers discover?—divined the cause, but she was silent.

Felix plied Father Riordan with questions until the good priest told him to go to the rector of St. Bonifacius'.

To make a long story short, Priscilla got her proposal.

"Well," said the editor of the *Bazoo*, after having received both congratulations and condolences, " Pris has a right to choose for herself. I've made an assignment, and I'll be pretty well off after I pay fifty cents on the dollar. O'Donnell's an honest chap—no vices. I'm going to run for the Legislature, if I have to change my politics. There's a big Irish vote in this place—don't you forget it; and Felix is a popular man!"

A VIRGINIAN COMEDY.

CHICAPICK was the flower of the flock. Chicapick, old Cæsar said, had lived all "frough de wah," having, during that long interval of terror, escaped the grasp of hungry soldiers only by reason of her evident age and toughness. She had been a spring-chicken once, sometime "'fo' de wah," Cæsar did not know when; but now she was in the sere and yellow leaf; yet she showed no intention of dying. Christmas after Christmas passed, fowls of the male and female gender died under the sharp clutch of old Cæsar's fingers; yet Chicapick, the oldest inhabitant of the poultry-roost, seemed resolved to go on forever, like Tennyson's stream. She was the Methuselah of hens.

Chicapick was "ole Miss Annabel's" pet. "Old Miss Annabel" was known to everybody, except white-wooled Cæsar, as Mrs. Dalrymple, who, silent and stately, sat in her arm-chair by the window, day after day, never unbending or smiling, except in the morning, when, by special permission, Chicapick strutted into her presence to be fed with bread and milk.

Mrs. Dalrymple lived in the past. Her mind was always busy with the old days, before the war, when the house of her husband, Judge Dalrymple, was the resort of all the talent, beauty, and blood of Virginia; when, as his wife, she was one of the most noted ladies in Paris; when, instead of the painted barn in which she and her daughter now dwelt, the Dalrymple mansion reared its head "finer and older than Mrs. Lee's house at Arlington," Mrs. Dalrymple had often said.

But the mansion had been burned, like many other mansions, and, in place of the marble halls and obedient slaves and a wide demesne, Mrs. Dalrymple had a cornfield, a cow, a few chickens, a little house in Washington, which was rented for ten dollars a month, and old Cæsar.

Old Cæsar had been Judge Dalrymple's "boy," and he was now Miss Kate's "boy"; and, if he lived to be ninety-nine, he would be somebody's "boy" to the end. He was proud of Miss Kate, for Miss Kate was the prettiest and best young lady in all Virginia; and Virginia, Virginians agree, contains all the roses of the rosebud garden of girls.

Mrs. Dalrymple was not quite so well satisfied with Kate. "To be sure, she was good enough," but then she was only a girl, and, before the war, Mrs. Dalrymple had been the proud mother of two stalwart sons; one had died in battle, the other in a Northern prison. Besides, there had been raised a barrier between mother and daughter. Kate, with her mother's permission—Mrs. Dalrymple was not a woman insensate enough to coerce conscience—had become a Catholic, and old Cæsar had followed her footsteps. Mrs. Dalrymple was an Episcopalian in theory. Had not the Rev. Arthur Wycherly, her great-grandfather, helped to plant the standard of the Church of England in Virginia? And, on that account, she felt herself pledged, in a manner, to the English creed. If it was good enough for her, why was it not sufficient for Kate? She could not understand it; consequently there was a coldness in her kindness that cost Kate many tears. Mrs. Dalrymple was an invalid—she never left her arm-chair except at night. A violent attack of rheumatism had left her powerless to walk.

Every Saturday night Cæsar went over to John Pendleton's place and asked, "with Mrs. Dalrymple's compliments," for the loan of Mr. Pendleton's gig; and when Mr. Pendleton had sent for the wheels, which had been borrowed by another neighbor, and he himself borrowed some indispensable parts of the harness, Cæsar drove the antique mare and the more antique vehicle homeward, to be ready to conduct Miss Kate over the bridge to Trinity Church on Sunday morning.

Kate's best dress was an old silk, one of her mother's reconstructed; she had not had a new bonnet for years; and these considerations, rather than self-mortification, induced her to hear the earliest Mass. She would have preferred to go to High Mass; but, with all her courage —and Kate Dalrymple had a great deal—she could not bring herself to face the congregation, in the noontime glare, in her faded gown and four-year-old hat; and so her motives in this, like the motives of all of us, whether we acknowledge it or not, were rather mixed.

Poor old Cæsar groaned and grunted, but the mare and the gig were always ready "on time"—namely, at half-past four o'clock. Kate allowed Cæsar to have his own way, and to take his own time in everything else, but on the point of early Mass her feminine will was inflexible.

One Sunday in June, Kate stands under the shed scattering corn to the chickens. Chicapick rubs her grizzled feathers against Kate's faded silk, and occasionally picks up a grain intended for the common herd, merely to show that she can condescend. Kate had been at Mass. It is nearly half-past nine o'clock; the sun shines—as only the sun does shine on Sunday—with a brightness and an intensity that seem to burn the golden eyes of the roses, and make them hang their heads.

Over the rough shed erected by Cæsar to protect the shelterless door of the barn, roses and honeysuckle cluster in bewildering profusion ; honeysuckle, with white and pink trumpets sending forth an ambrosial perfume that wafts Kate's soul far away from the burning sun, the parched soil, the smell of the rice-pudding burning—far away—somewhere, maybe among the pomegranates of the Alhambra, the orange-groves of Sicily, or those parterres of celestial flowers which the priest, speaking of a virgin-martyr, mentioned this morning. But the burning rice-pudding has claims on Kate's attention which even the imagination is bound to respect, and she rushes past her mother, dozing in the chair, to save it from destruction. Again the eager brood flutter around her, undeterred by the decorous example of Chicapick, and the sprays of red and white roses droop low to pour their odor over her brown hair.

Kate has brown hair and eyes—not those weak, light-brown eyes with no reflections in them, but eyes that catch the light like an opal. She looks at everything directly. She is tall, with a quick grace in her movements which probably comes from constant exercise rather than from nature. Her face is oval, and there is more pure color in her lips and cheeks than is common nowadays. If you had seen her grandmother Dalrymple's portrait by Sir Joshua, you would have noticed his vain attempt to catch this same pure tone of color, and also her grandmother's taper fingers, which Kate has too, but hers are not so white as her grandmother's. Her brown dress falls around her in those simple folds which ladies try so hard to "get up" nowadays. She shades her eyes with

her hands. She sees a white umbrella and a man's head
and shoulders above the low fence that skirts the cornfield.

"Who can it be? Straw hat—gray coat. It is Philip
Brown. He is coming here! What could have possessed him to come at this time? And we have nothing
for dinner but broth and rice-pudding, corn-bread and
coffee! Well, if he can put up with it, I suppose we
ought to be glad to see him."

Philip Brown advances up the road, and soon comes
within speaking-distance.

"Good-morning, Kate!"

"Good-morning, Phil!"

Rather unceremonious, but Philip Brown and Kate
Dalrymple are old friends. Philip was a ward of Judge
Dalrymple's. He was born in Connecticut, and his father,
an old college-friend of Dalrymple's, had, dying, sent
him South; he had divided his time between the Dalrymple house and a Northern college. He is about thirty;
a civil-engineer stationed in Washington; tall, with lively
blue eyes, a fresh color, and an air of careless good-nature.
He is rather matter-of-fact; he attends to his business
and his religious duties (he is a Catholic); and he is in
love with Kate, though that young woman has not
found it out yet, or, at least, she pretends she has not.

Mrs. Dalrymple tolerates him, because he was her husband's ward. She does not like him; he is a Yankee
and a plebeian. His father was not of a good family,
neither was his mother. If either of them had even
come over in the *Mayflower*, she would have some respect for him, although he is a Yankee; but neither of
them had, and his mother had actually been a servant
before old Brown married her! Now, his cousin, Philip

Brown, of Richmond, was somebody, Mrs. Dalrymple often said. His father had married a Miss Bradford, of Warwick Court-House, whose father had the best blood in Virginia—which is the best blood in the world—in his veins, whose mother was an Archer, of Queen Anne County, connected, as every one knew, with the Lees, the Carrolls— Philip Brown, of Richmond, *was* somebody, in spite of his Yankee father.

"It's only Phil," said Mrs. Dalrymple, relapsing into the doze from which she had been awakened by Philip's step on the walk.

"I stopped at the post-office," said Phil, taking off his hat and fanning himself violently. "The sun is scorching! I bring you a letter."

"A letter?" cried Kate, as he took the missive from the ribbon of his hat. "For me? It is an age since I had a letter." And she poised it in her hand, enjoying a sense of uncertainty; she had no fear of bad news—no distant friends to lose, and no unpaid bills. "A gentleman's writing—'Miss Dalrymple.' He doesn't dot the *i*, and the *l* and the *e* are both of the same size. Richmond post-mark. Who can it be?"

"Suppose you open it," he suggested; "you play with it as a cat plays with a mouse."

"How full of curiosity you men are!" She opened it; an expression, half of annoyance, half of amusement, came into her face. "It is from your cousin! 'Mr. Philip Brown, of Richmond, Va., presents his compliments to Miss Dalrymple, and begs that she will inform her mother that he will do himself the honor of calling on her to-morrow (Sunday) morning. He will remain in Washington for a few days.'"

"Oh, Phil, what shall I do?"

Phil looked at her in amazement. "Why, receive him kindly, of course. He is not a bad fellow, in his way, and your mother will be glad to hear from his mother."

"How stupid you are! I don't care what kind of a man he is! Good or bad, he has an appetite, I suppose. *There is absolutely* NOTHING *for dinner!* "

She whispered these last words with an intensity that would have done credit to Ristori.

Phil laughed, and thereby, as she expressed it, drove her nearly "wild." He, being a man, could not comprehend the whole horror of the situation.

"Oh, come now, Kate, there *must* be something?"

"There is nothing but corn-bread, coffee, rice-pudding, and mother's broth. A nice combination for Judge Dalrymple's daughter to set before—"

"A king!" murmured Phil.

Kate glared at him—"To set before a stranger. And Cæsar has gone away to Pendleton's Woods for the day, and I never killed a chicken myself!"

Phil was deeply moved by a tear that glittered in the corner of Kate's eye.

"Is that all? I'll kill the chicken, and roast it as well as you can. I often did it when I was a boy. There he is!"

A figure was visible in the road beyond the fence. Phil prepared to disappear around the corner of the house; but he stopped suddenly. Neither of them saw the situation now in an amusing light. For Kate it was almost tragical; for Phil, deeply serious.

"Kate," he said, seizing her hand, "do you like me a little?"

"The idea of asking such a thing now! Of course not, sir!"

Phil disappeared.

"What could have induced me to do it, I wonder?" he thought. "I never did it before. I know she likes me. I'll speak to Mrs. Dalrymple. What a fool I am!"

He felt like tearing his hair, but he only took off his coat and made an onslaught on the chickens.

Philip Brown, of Richmond, was unlike his cousin. He was above the average height, but lank and loose-jointed. His face was what some young ladies call "pretty." It was pink and white, with a dainty black moustache. He wore a spotless linen suit, and, though he complained of the heat, not an individual hair on his carefully-arranged head was astray.

He introduced himself to Kate, and Kate introduced him to her mother. Mrs. Dalrymple smoothed the lace at her throat, straightened herself in her chair, and became at once a model of courtesy and graceful hospitality. The young man was soon deep in a labyrinth of questions about marriages and deaths, his mother's favorite clergyman, and his own views of religious matters.

"Ah," said Mrs. Dalrymple, "it is so refreshing to find a young man like you such a firm Episcopalian! You have the true blood, sir, the true blood."

Philip Brown, of Richmond, bowed, and looked as if he would like to talk to Kate, but Mrs. Dalrymple, like the ancient mariner, held him firmly. Kate was in agony. She could plainly distinguish fearful sounds in the kitchen. She made several attempts to escape; but her mother seemed determined that she should remain in the room as long as possible.

"Don't trouble yourself about the dinner, child. I never do. I dare say we can give Mr. Brown something to eat. Where is Phil Brown?"

"Is my cousin here?" demanded the guest, while a slight cloud crossed his face. It was disagreeable to hear of a rival in the good graces of the Dalrymples.

"Yes, the Yankee is always here," responded Mrs. Dalrymple; "he's a good enough person, but plebeian; no blood, no tone."

Kate's brow flushed.

Philip Brown, of Richmond, objected to questions of a business nature on the Sabbath, but he could not help asking whether Mrs. Dalrymple owned that swampy stretch of land which ran along the Potomac, beginning at her cornfield. Mrs. Dalrymple saw no objection to answering that it was hers—all the land, except the cornfield, that she owned in the world. It was worthless, utterly worthless. If it were not, she asserted, somebody would have seized it long ago; then she turned to Kate and severely asked if they were to have no dinner that day. Kate escaped, with an anxious heart, to lay the cloth. Phil, his face flaming, came and whispered triumphantly:

"The chicken is as brown as a berry; I found the potatoes, and stuffed it with some herbs."

Kate was sorely tempted to ask what kind of herbs, but, maintaining her dignity, she only said:

"I wonder that you have the effrontery to speak to me *after what has occurred!*"

"It's all right," he said, wilfully misunderstanding her. "It's the nicest roast you ever saw. You needn't be ashamed of it."

To hide a smile that was struggling with her frown, Kate busied herself with the remnants of the Dalrymple silver.

Dinner was served. Mrs. Dalrymple made no apology, except for Cæsar's absence.

"Your father," said Mrs. Dalrymple, graciously, "was famous as a carver. May I ask if the talent has descended to his son?"

"People say it has," said the guest, smilingly, possessing himself of the carving-knife.

What was the matter with that fowl?

"Oh," thought Kate, "I must have been out of my senses to let Phil meddle with it!"

Philip Brown, of Virginia, started off gracefully—easily. The interest deepened. He grew warmer, less easy. That wing would *not* come off.

"Never mind," said Mrs. Dalrymple; "a leg will do."

The carver looked relieved. He wrestled with more ardor than before. That chicken was certainly made with steel tendons, he thought. The suspense became terrible. Mrs. Dalrymple, showing her usual good-breeding, tried to talk of indifferent matters; but she could not keep her eyes off the object of interest. Philip Brown, of Virginia, was red in the face. The perspiration stood out on his forehead.

"Let me try my muscle," proposed his cousin, with awful boldness.

"I fear that this fowl is Chicapick," thought Mrs. Dalrymple, and her fear was confirmed by Phil's next speech.

"I knew she was awfully old, but I never imagined she would turn out like this."

"It *is* Chicapick. My poor pet! The ruthless Yankee!" she thought, and, with a superb effort at self-control, she said aloud: "No chicken for *me*, sir."

"You're wise," thought the "ruthless Yankee."

After the untimely death of Chicapick, Mrs. Dalrymple refused to admit Phil to the house.

"That man," she said, "has rudely touched the finest chords of my heart. He knew how I liked Chicapick!"

Mrs. Dalrymple threatened to have hysterics whenever he appeared, and, as a consequence, Kate could not see him. This violent distaste for Phil was not wholly due to Chicapick's death. His cousin, Philip Brown, of Richmond, still sojourned in Washington, and he called every day—having the good taste, however, to choose the afternoon. The slaughter of the ancient fowl supplied the sapient mamma with an excellent pretence for keeping the field clear; for Philip Brown, of Richmond, had a large fortune, well invested in the North; his family was almost up to Mrs. Dalrymple's expectations; he was an excellent "catch" for Kate. His mother, in fact, had sent him hither as a prince who goes to seek his bride. The Browns were not wholly of the F. F. V.'s, but Kate Dalrymple was "sang pur." Had her father not been related to the Masons, of Gunston Hall, and the Cockburns, of Truro Parish? Philip Brown, of Richmond, approved of Kate. He was in no hurry to tell her so. When King Cophetua extends his sceptre, it is natural for the beggar to grasp it with grateful palms; and so Philip Brown was certain that he had only to offer himself and his money to Kate to be acepted. He had his eyes on business just now. He offered to buy Mrs. Dalrymple's swamp by the river. Mrs. Dalrymple had a horror of selling land, no matter how worthless it might be. She would rent it. Philip Brown agreed to pay her a fair rent for five years. This finished, he proposed for Kate.

"Philip Brown, of Richmond, has leased the swamp," Mrs. Dalrymple said to her daughter, after he had gone, for Kate had been busy all day in the kitchen.

"He must be crazy!"

"He is not, my dear. He intends to plant cranberries. I wish we had thought of that ourselves. Kate, you never think of anything! And, my dear, he wants to marry you."

Kate began to cry. "I don't see why a girl can't be let alone! Some Tom, Dick, or Harry is always wanting to marry—"

"Tom, Dick, or Harry!" cried Mrs. Dalrymple, in horror. "His mother is a Bradford!"

"I don't care! I don't like him! And, mother, if I must marry, I will marry only a Catholic."

Mrs. Dalrymple closed her eyes tight. "She means that Yankee," she thought; "but I will not have him for a son-in-law. I'll die first!" She reflected. Experience had taught her not to argue. "I'll send her to Miss Doolady, and, if she doesn't prefer Philip Brown, of Richmond, to a few weeks with that woman, she may have her way."

Miss Doolady was an old maid, who had been mistress of a boarding-school. She had retired from the laborious occupation of teaching the young idea to shoot; but she was still famous for her unbending severity of principle and practice. Kate had been one of her pupils, and she was rather a favorite of the old lady's. Mrs. Dalrymple regarded Miss Doolady with profound respect and great aversion. She announced that, as the rent of the swamp would make a difference in their circumstances, she had determined to visit Mrs. Bradford Brown, in Richmond. Kate would, of course, go with her, and then return immediately to Miss Doolady's in Washington. Cæsar could stay to mind "the place."

"And, Kate," said her mother, "don't let me hear of

your offending Miss Doolady's Presbyterianism with your Papist—Catholic notions."

A week later, Kate was domiciled under the gloomy shelter of Miss Doolady's roof. Miss Doolady lived by rule, as did Miss Doolady's unfortunate black maid, Miss Doolady's cat, and Miss Doolady's guest; and the rule was not the rule of three, but the more trying rule of one—Miss Doolady. Miss Doolady always wore black silk and lace mittens, and in the crackle of her silk and in the look even of the mittens there was something intensely "aggravating" to Kate, for both articles of attire seemed to have caught their wearer's habit of "laying down the law."

"It *is* horrid here," thought Kate, over and over again; "I'd rather be in the kitchen at home baking corn-bread."

But she never thought that she would rather marry Philip Brown, of Richmond. No; she was firm in her determination never to marry anybody outside of the Catholic Faith, and, perhaps, only one in that Faith. As usual, her motives were mixed, you see. Mrs. Dalrymple, by way of keeping up the punishment, sent only the briefest messages through Miss Doolady.

Mrs. Dalrymple fell sick, and pretended to become alarmed. She wrote two "last" letters, one to Philip Brown, of Richmond; the other to Miss Doolady. Philip Brown read his; he was in no hurry; Mrs. Dalrymple's fears were no doubt groundless; haste was always absurd; and, besides, he was ready to start for Mobile on business.

Miss Doolady read hers, and thus addressed Kate:

"Miss Dalrymple, your mother is ill, and she wishes you to go to her."

"I will go now, instantly!"

"No, you must have an escort. Propriety requires it.'

"I can travel alone very well. It is only to Richmond; or you can go with me. I must go, at all events!"

"You will not, I hope, disregard your mother's wishes entirely. As she remarks, no escort is as proper for a lady as her husband."

"But what has that to do with me?" demanded Kate.

"No escort would be as proper for you as your husband," said Miss Doolady. "In fact, your mamma's letter states that Mr. Philip Brown will call here, at my house, to-day, and that you shall become his wife, in order that you may travel, with propriety, in his company to your mother's bedside."

"Never!" cried Kate, with a sob, "never! It is hard when one's own mother—turns—against—her. Propriety! Nonsense!"

"You should curb your *awful* temper, Miss Dalrymple. It will lead you to destruction."

Philip Brown, of Richmond, did not call that day. Late in the afternoon the Yankee, having discovered Kate's whereabouts from Cæsar, rang Miss Doolady's bell—with some trepidation, it must be admitted.

"Are you Mr. Philip Brown?" asked the maid.

"I am," said Phil, expecting a gentle reminder that he was not wanted.

The maid grinned. "Come in, sah," she said; "we know all about it."

In a few minutes Miss Doolady had informed Phil that he was to be a happy man.

"Mrs. Dalrymple couldn't have meant me," cried Phil, overwhelmed. "I don't deserve it. Why, she hates me!"

"A sick-bed is no place for hatred," said Miss Doolady, austerely; "we forget our hatreds there. I should have been inclined to think that she meant your cousin, Brown, of Richmond, did I not know that he is at present in Mobile."

"Am I asleep?" cried Phil, pulling hard at his hair. "Am I awake?"

Miss Doolady went to tell Kate that the "intended" was awaiting her in the parlor.

"I will not see him! I am going alone to Richmond, I tell you!" cried Kate, indignantly. "He is a monster to force himself on me in this way. Send him away, Miss Doolady!"

"I can not order the gentleman from my house. The proprieties forbid it, Miss Dalrymple. Speak to him yourself."

"I *will!*" said Kate; "I'll speak to him with a vengeance!"

She paused an instant, and then ran down-stairs. She opened the parlor-door with calm dignity in her manner.

"You!"

"Of course," Phil said, calmly. "Ill be back as soon as I can. I think one has to take out a license in the district. I suppose we must obey your mother!"

"I suppose so," murmured Kate, dropping her eyelids; saying in her heart, "Dear, good mother, how I have wronged you!"

The license was issued in due time. Good Father Roccafort, of Trinity, married them, after the early Mass; and soon the happy pair were on their way to Richmond.

"Dear mother, we have come!" cried Kate. "Why, how well you look!"

"I am better, child. You!" That word was all she

said to Phil. He thought she was very cold, while he poured his gratitude and happiness into her ear. She would not openly acknowledge her defeat.

"What was your mother's name, Phil?" she asked, after a time.

"O'Toole," said Phil, promptly.

For weeks Mrs. Dalrymple searched Burke's invaluable books on Irish pedigrees. It is to be hoped that they gave her some crumbs of comfort.

But who comforted Miss Doolady under the weight of Mrs. Dalrymple's wrath?

A ROSEBUD.

I.

WHEN the "professional beauty" craze was at its height in England, and women of good repute were rushing into print with their photographs, and every shop window was graced with pictures of Mrs. Cornwallis West or Lady Lonsdale, Agnes Eliot "came out" in New York.

This "coming out" is a serious business. "The Rosebud," as she is called—this name comes more easily to English-speaking people since "French" has gone out of fashion, than "*débutante*"—is made to enter society for the first time by standing for about four hours in the afternoon, strung around with dozens of big bouquets. Some of these are sent by her father's friends, others are contributed by her father himself. The "Rosebud" who can count a great number of bouquets is happy; and so the young girl stands, smiling at the mobs of men who come and go, eat and stare. According to New York usage, these men wear frock coats or business suits, as they please. Women do not count at these "coming out" entertainments. The "Rosebud" who can count the most men is considered the most fortunate.

Agnes Eliot had been educated in a Canadian convent at the request of her mother, who had been in the later years of her life a devout Catholic. She had been baptized a Catholic; she had been well instructed in the Catholic Faith; but, at the age of twenty-one, she had married Garrett Eliot. The ceremony of marriage was performed in the Catholic church of Garrettsville; and for some months Mrs. Eliot induced her husband to assist at Mass with her; but he soon became tired of it; he preferred his cigar and his Sunday paper, and after a while she grew weary of going alone. Besides, in Garrettsville, Catholics were very unfashionable people. Positively, at St. Patrick's, the McCabe girls were the only persons who had bonnets of any style whatever; and Garrett's uncle, the founder of Garrettsville, was an earnest churchman in the Protestant-Episcopalian sense. When the rector who filled the pulpits of Garrettsville and Fielding did not come—he came every other Sunday—Mr. Garrett read the service after the manner of Mr. Booth's famous soliloquy in "Hamlet." For these reasons, Mrs. Eliot gradually withdrew from St. Patrick's, and finally sat in a front pew in the Church of the Atonement. Her conscience was chloroformed for a time. In after years, when Agnes was twelve years of age, and her husband had become richer than he had ever dreamed of being, Mrs. Eliot fell into an illness that led to death. At this time Agnes was sent to the convent in the West.

Ten years had passed, and Agnes was to "come out." Her father had worked hard; his name had been mentioned in a New York paper's list of millionaires. His house on Fifth avenue had stained glass by La Farge, Moorish and arabesqued arches after models taken from the Alhambra, a Corot, two Millets and a Velasquez, for which he had outbidden the Californian millionaires. He had the best French cook in the country, an English coachman who had left the service of an English peer, and a butler who was perfection, and who had the art of "coaching" his master in all the arts of the larder and the cellar, which Americans engaged in trade all their lives can not be expected to know. And now, having all the things which are supposed to make happiness in New York, Mr. Eliot wanted something else. He did not look forward to anything in the next world. He often said he had no time to think about it. He said he believed in a Supreme Being, and that every man who stuck to the rules of business would doubtless get along somehow after death, but he didn't know. His associations were Protestant-Episcopal, and, as that denomination was respectable, he tied to it, although he did not think the P. E.'s understood their own creed. Mr. Eliot never approved of convent education for his daughter until he went abroad; he had preferred Vassar, but, after a short sojourn in England and France, he came to the conclusion that it gave a girl a gentle and feminine air, much in vogue among the best class of English, to have her educated in a convent. Mr. Eliot, having been engaged all his life in piling up earthly treasures, was now anxious to acquire social reputation. The Fifth avenue millionaire was important on Wall street, and an acknowledged power in many ways. He gave good dinners; the President had lunched with him at Newport; but there were fields beyond. There were places where he was nobody. He knew that people said he could not tell Chateau La Rose of '52 from the same wine of the vintage of '70; he knew they said that he could not tell Corot from Millet, and that he deserved much credit as the son of a Western carpenter for having made himself a great man in Wall street. This last assertion galled him worse than anything else. He felt that abroad he was nobody but a "rich American," and at home a "self-made man." If he could have made a specialty of art or literature, he would have amused himself by playing the magnificent patron; but he knew nothing about either, and here he was, a well-preserved man of fifty-five, with an immense income, restless and unhappy. The excitement of making money was no longer a stimulant to him; he had more than he wanted. His sister, Mrs. Montgomery Weston, a widow who had lived much abroad, kept house for him. She was stout, self-possessed, with palpably painted eyebrows, bleached hair, and an acquired expression of superciliousness. She had her gowns from Worth; but she, Mr. Eliot said in his heart, was, in spite of it all, a trifle vulgar. She could spend money in a way that produced gorgeous effects; her dinner-table was a blaze of glory. Her famous effect was what she called a "symphony in red." When Mr. Eliot had young Sir Tomkyn Tomkyns to dinner, she covered the walls with scarlet gauze and tulips, at great expense, and this had given occasion for the Englishman's *bon mot*, which still rankled in Mr. Eliot's heart.

"You should have some more canvas-back," the host had said; "you are not eating anything."

"Thanks," drawled the Englishman, "I can't eat; I'm afraid of infection; the scarlet fever is in the room."

This was not very witty, but it was very insolent; and in "society" insolence passes for wit.

After this, Mr. Eliot distrusted Mrs. Montgomery Weston's symphonies and nocturnes in color. He wanted somebody to give his house the proper "tone"; so Agnes, weeping, left her beloved convent home.

"I will come back to the old nest some day," she said.

Mr. Eliot smiled at this. He felt the need, in democratic New York, of ancestors. He was resolved to attain them, not by the cheap and easy way of having them manufactured by the professional herald and the painter of family portraits, but by marrying Agnes to a man of rank. He was resolved that she should never see the convent again.

He was pleased with her. She was tall and rather thin; but she had a pure complexion, hardly rose-tinted at all, deep blue eyes and long lashes. "Irish eyes, like her mother," he said; "they looked as if they had been put in 'with a dirty finger.'" She walked well; her voice was low and soft; her motion quiet, and her manner simple and frank.

"She has an air," he said to himself. "She will do." And when he wrote his last check for the Mother Superior he was correspondingly generous.

Mother Regina sighed and shook her head, as the carriage drove away.

Agnes had never spent a vacation at home. She knew her father was rich, because the girls had said so; but she had not been permitted to wear gayer gowns than the other pupils, or jewels of any kind. She was amazed by the splendor that awaited her.

The father and daughter reached New York on a bright, cold morning. Agnes gazed with interest at the stately houses on the avenue, gilded by the sun. She surprised her father by declaring that Euclid avenue, in Cleveland, was just as handsome as *the* avenue. Mr. Eliot laughed and showed her the Cathedral. A few minutes afterward he took her by the hand and led her into a hall, resplendent with brass work and stained glass. Agnes felt herself kissed by somebody; it was Mrs. Montgomery Weston, who looked at her searchingly, and then clasped her to her bosom. Agnes' nose was pressed against some sharp jet ornaments, so she did not reciprocate the embrace very warmly. How beautiful the place was, but how cold! A vision of the convent chapel, with the Sister and the pupils kneeling before the Tabernacle, arose before her. A desperate longing filled her heart to go away—to go back to the only home she had ever known.

Her father stood near her, looking very proud of all this grandeur. Her aunt was there, too; but they seemed strangers to her. Both Mr. Eliot and his sister had been so much abroad, that neither had seen Agnes, except at rare intervals.

"I will show you to your room, my dear," Mrs. Montgomery Weston said. And Agnes, with a smile at her father, followed her aunt's rustling train up-stairs.

Agnes found herself in a charming little room, filled with subdued light and color. But there was no crucifix there—no sign of any other world than this.

II.

"She will do," said Mrs. Montgomery Weston. "She is quite too awfully unformed; but she will do—with careful attention."

"Think so?" returned her brother. "I'm glad of it. She seems to have a lot of foolish religious ideas in her head. She said she couldn't go with me to Christ Church when I told her I had a pew there."

"How queer!" said Mrs. Montgomery Weston, in a high voice, intended to be modulated after the fashionable manner. "But really, that is all nonsense. I must say, though, that some very desirable people in society are Romanists. There is really a great deal of color in that belief. Her manners seem very well, although she lacks—"

"Boldness," said Mr. Eliot, shortly.

"*Aplomb*," his sister said, in an injured tone.

"Well, the less *aplomb* she gets, the better. I don't want her to be one of those brazen creatures who dance the german night after night, like maniacs, who stare young men in the eyes, who are not afraid to smile at insinuations of doubtful meaning—"

"Robert, Robert," cried Mrs. Weston, raising her hands in horror; "such things never occur in society."

Mr. Eliot laughed, and bit the end off a cigar.

"Of course," continued Mrs. Weston, "girls are not supposed to be ignorant of everything. They read the newspapers."

Mrs. Weston looked at her brother in pity and surprise.

"Now, Robert," she said firmly, "you can't eat your cake and have it. If Agnes were going on the stage, you would not expect her to remain ignorant of a great many things that young girls are supposed not to know. Society's a big stage, and the comedies and tragedies acted on it bring knowledge. We think a great deal of manner and manners here in New York, but morals are too far away from society's ken to be of importance. If Tom, Dick, or Harry—whose father is rich—wears his dress-coat well, doesn't say rude things and outrage the proprieties, asks Agnes to waltz with him, I shall not say no. *You* may know that he frequents haunts of vice; but I am not supposed to know it."

Mr. Eliot looked serious.

"I don't like it."

"Your opinions are crude," said Mrs. Montgomery Weston. "The girl must do as the rest do—if you want her to make a good match. Sir Tomkyn Tomkyns intends, I hear, to stay at the Brunswick all winter."

Mr. Eliot's face brightened. "He is rich and his uncle is a peer. Don't spare any money, Helen; above all, don't let the girl make herself absurd by any religious scruples."

Mrs. Montgomery Weston shrugged her shoulders. "Trust me. The girl's a perfect lamb."

III.

The first difficulty between Agnes and her aunt occurred just before the "coming out." John Neville, the artist, was at this time in great vogue. He met Agnes at a quiet luncheon, given by her father for the purpose of having him mark her good points and plan some costumes for her. Mr. Eliot was determined that Agnes should enter "the race" with every advantage. John Neville was charmed.

"A peach-blossom," he said. "And, by the way, that must be her flower. She'll make it the rage all over the country in a month."

Not long afterward, Mrs. Weston displayed John Neville's costume sketches to Agnes.

"Lovely, are they not?"

"Am I to wear them?" asked Agnes doubtfully.

"Yes. Aren't you a happy girl? That robe of peach-blossom silk and swan-down is the 'coming out' gown."

Agnes' face flushed. The sketch of the gown was

very elaborate. The artist had barely outlined her head and shoulders rising from it.

"Aunt," she said, after a pause, "I will wear neither of those dresses."

"Not wear the loveliest gowns ever made? Nonsense! What do you mean?"

"I will not wear dresses that are—immodest."

Mrs. Weston gazed at her niece in amazement. "Not wear these gowns, *designed by Neville* and to be made by Madame Connelly, because they are a trifle low! Why, *I* wear gowns quite as low. Am I immodest?"

Agnes looked up, with anything but a lamb-like air.

"I will not wear them."

"I will appeal to your father."

"*I* will appeal to my father."

"You have pretty shoulders, although you don't deserve to have them, and it is sinful to cover them up."

Agnes smiled. She was afraid of her aunt no longer. At first this model of deportment and high fashion had somewhat awed her.

Mr. Eliot, when appealed to, agreed that the gowns were too low. Agnes, therefore, on the momentous afternoon of her "coming out," wore a high gown and carried ten bouquets of peach-blossoms and lilies of the valley. And on the next Saturday her portrait appeared in two weekly journals. She was the new beauty. New York had found a rival of the English beauties. In another week her photograph was in Broadway windows near that of Sullivan the prize-fighter, near that of the popular variety actresses and well-known people of the theatre. Peach-blossoms were all the rage. But they are such delicate things that the women could not keep them long.

"They are not fit for a ball-room," Mrs. Weston said.

"They are like me," answered Agnes wearily. "I am not fit for a ball-room. To stand the glare of light they ought to be artificial."

"You will not insist on a high dress to-night?"

"Yes." Agnes' cheeks reddened as she picked up a photograph from the table. It was a fine photograph.

"How could you have *dared* to do this, aunt?"

It was a photograph of Agnes as painted by Neville from one of his sketches. She was represented in one of the lowest of the low dresses. It was an artistic picture, but no vicious caricature could have given Agnes more pain.

"Aunt, aunt," she cried, tears forcing their way into her eyes. "I have no mother. *You* ought to have protected me from this!"

There was so much pathos in the girl's voice that the indomitable Mrs. Montgomery Weston almost imagined for an instant that she had a heart.

"The photographs have made a great sensation. Five thousand have already been sold. You are a greater celebrity than any girl in New York."

"I wish God had let me die before I suffered this," cried Agnes, in a tone that shocked Mrs. Weston's nerves.

"Convents are not good for girls who are to go into the world," said Mrs. Weston; but Agnes had left the room.

IV.

Could it be true? Agnes asked herself. Could it be true that this picture, in which she, a child of Mary, a client of St. Agnes, stood exposed defenceless to the gaze of the world, was for sale in the shops?

She could not believe it. Her face flushed and paled as she thought of it. What could her father, who seemed to love her, be thinking of? He seldom spoke to her, except to ask her if she had enjoyed herself; but he was very kind in his manner.

She looked at the miniature of St. Agnes given to her by the dear Mother Superior. *She*—her sweet St. Agnes—was permitted to die rather than feel the degradation of a similar exposure. Agnes recalled the moving description given by Cardinal Wiseman, in "Fabiola," of the death of this Christian martyr.

It was now that she felt the need of friends. Oh, for one half-hour with the Sisters! She felt that she *must* talk to somebody.

She went out into the street, eluding the vigilance of her aunt, who held that "rosebuds" should not stir abroad without a chaperon. At the corner she met Rosalie Lodge, the only girl acquaintance she had made. Rosalie pulled a woolly dog after her. Her hair was dragged down over her eyes, and bangles of all sizes jingled when she moved. She wore a huge bunch of yellow roses, and she kissed Agnes at least twenty times.

"I want to talk to you, Rosalie."

"What are you going to wear to-night? They say the favors for the german are to be quite too awfully swell. I'm so glad they are not going to give it this year at Delmonico's. I hate the yellow light there. And, oh, my love, what a success you have had! Sir Tomkyn Tomkyns said the other night that you were like Connie Gilchrist."

"Who is she?"

"Oh, the most lovely actress, who is turning the heads of all the young men in London."

Agnes held her head very high, and red spots showed themselves on either cheek.

"But he was awfully cut up because you refused to dance the german with him. Why, he is a nephew of Lord Crawfordshire!"

"I do not care. I never waltz with young men. I am a Catholic."

Rosalie laughed. "How prudish! Why, I know lots of Catholics that waltz. Let's go to the Vienna Bakery and lunch. I *do* so want to talk about everything."

Seated in that very pretty restaurant, with its tiny city garden and the panorama of Broadway before them, they began to chat. Agnes burst forth impetuously with the story of her wrong.

Rosalie laughed till the tears came into her eyes. Agnes' "freshness," as she termed it, made her feel that the new beauty would not try to rival her in any way, and she showed her kindly intention by not sneering at this "truly moral ingenuousness."

"You're a lucky girl, Agnes Eliot," she said, solemnly, at last. "Your father has pulled the ropes for you *splendidly*. Everybody says so. Your picture is everywhere; there was a sonnet written to you by the author of 'Pearls and Lobster Salad,' in last Sunday's *Times*, and your papa has spared no money in getting things written about you. If you have a good pair of shoulders and a decent bust, it's your duty to show them. Every girl wears her gown very low. Papa's going to work up a 'professional beauty' boom for me. There's going to be a whole column about my engagement to the Marquis de Carabas in the Sunday papers. Papa showed me the proof last night."

Agnes was speechless. Evidently Miss Lodge had no sympathy with her.

Agnes sat silent. The street was very bright with sunshine and color. The silver and gold of the caparison of horses flashed in the sun; ladies in gay costumes passed and repassed. To the girl just out of her convent school there was exhilaration in this sunlit scene. But it was made gloomy by the thought that somewhere in this glittering thoroughfare people were looking at her picture —at the picture of *her*, Agnes Eliot, represented in the garb of an actress.

The two girls wandered through the street from window to window. They were both faultlessly dressed. Agnes was exceedingly graceful and as stately as a lily. Now and then somebody turned and whispered: " That is she!" But Agnes was unconscious of this.

Suddenly, while she and Rosalie were commenting on Boughton's " Priscilla," shown in the window of a print shop, they became aware that a group of young men, cigarette in mouth and cane in hand, were deeply interested in a picture in the next window.

"What are the wretches talking about? *I* don't know any of them," said Rosalie, gazing with curiosity at the carefully attired young men. "I thought I heard them mention your name."

"By Jove!" cried one of the youths, with the English drawl. "She isn't half as good-lookin' as any of the English beauties. I don't see why they're makin' all this fuss."

"Look at that neck—look at those shoulders! She's superb, I tell you—and such a foot!" said another.

" She's hollow-chested—"

" Not at all. The line of beauty—"

"Rosalie," whispered Agnes, the red spots on her cheeks burning deeper. "Is it—is it my picture?"

Rosalie all of a sudden realized the degradation of the exhibition.

"I am afraid it is," she answered, soberly. "Let us go."

The youths had managed to spread themselves over the sidewalk in such a manner that it would have been difficult to pass them without attracting attention. Two older men had joined them.

"A deuced pretty girl," said one of these. "An actress, I suppose?"

"No," answered the other. "She's the new beauty; daughter of old Eliot, the millionaire. She has a very graceful hand and wrist."

Rosalie, by this time, was indignant. It seemed to her, artificial as society had made her, as if all modest women had been insulted in the person of Agnes.

"Let us pass—*gentlemen*," she said, in a tone full of scorn.

The group made way.

"I am alone," said Agnes, bitterly. "*Alone!* I have nobody to protect me against insults like those."

The color in her cheeks deepened. She breathed a prayer. But what girl was ever so wretched as she!—what girl ever exposed to ribald crowds—she thought of St. Agnes. If she were only safe in the convent.

Rosalie was silent. It *was* bad, she thought—that is, if anything could be bad for a girl whose father had a staff of English servants and one of the handsomest houses in the Avenue.

V.

Mrs. Montgomery Weston said she considered Agnes Eliot the most evil-tempered person she had ever met.

"You will scarcely believe me," she said to her friend, the Marchesa Villeviani, *née* Miss Hoggs, as they met in the row reserved for chaperons in the ball-room of Delmonico's, "when I tell you that Agnes would not come to-night. She tore about like a fury this afternoon because the photographers insist, in spite of our protests, in selling her picture. Her father was quite amazed. Everybody has been congratulating him on her success, for she is really the only rosebud who has been a success. She won't waltz; but I wouldn't mind that; it is rather distinguished and certainly more pleasant not to have one's clothes torn off in the german. But, do you know, Sir Tomkyn Tomkyns has asked her to have a seat on his coach."

This information was received with interest, and the conversation wandered off to the glories of the Coaching Club parade.

Agnes had again appealed to her father. He had laughed at her.

"You must get rid of these silly fancies. Everybody envies you; everybody thinks you are the happiest and most fortunate girl in town."

"Father," said Agnes, with a serious look in her deep eyes, "I would be willing at this moment to be Bridget, the chambermaid. She wears calico, she is poor, but "— Agnes' voice was choked by tears; and Mr. Eliot laughed and returned to his newspaper.

He was very well satisfied. Agnes *was* beautiful; he

had pulled the ropes "splendidly," and Sir Tomkyn Tomkyns, the club men said, was "smitten."

Although she had refused to go to the german with her aunt, she dared not refuse her father when he asked her. She entered late, leaning on his arm. Sir Tomkyn Tomkyns asked her to waltz at once; and, as usual, she refused. Nevertheless, he did not leave her while she remained in the room. It was a desperate flirtation, people said. Agnes had little need to talk. The young Englishman rattled away about himself, about America, about everything.

From that night, society considered it settled that Sir Tomkyn Tomkyns would marry Agnes Eliot.

Mr. Eliot smiled when the supposed fact was alluded to. The wedding would be in Grace Church, of course, —Sir Tomkyn's people at home were very Ritualistic, but Sir Tomkyn did not care much. One afternoon Sir Tomkyn rode up to the door and arranged matters with Mr. Eliot. Agnes had not given him an answer; she said she had not thought of marriage. But Mr. Eliot had, and he graciously accepted Sir Tomkyn's proposal.

Agnes had no positive dislike to the young Englishman. She accepted the announcement, that she was to be married, with resignation. She said to herself that she could not suffer more than she had suffered. The preparations for the wedding were begun, for Sir Tomkyn wanted to return to England in a few months. The truth was, Mr. Eliot had agreed to pay off certain very pressing mortgages on the baronet's estates, and this must be done quickly.

But an unexpected obstacle intervened. Agnes refused point-blank to go to Grace Church to be married; and two ceremonies would not satisfy her. Mrs. Weston almost tore her hair; Mr. Eliot raved. Agnes was firm. Sir Tomkyn stormed. He showed more ill-breeding than Agnes had thought him capable of.

"It would be against my conscience," she said. "I know that you are a Protestant, and, frankly, if I saw any way out of an engagement into which I have entered in obedience to my father, I should take it. But I will be married to you only by a Catholic priest."

Mrs. Weston groaned. What audacity!

"It's superstitious nonsense!" cried Mr. Eliot. "Don't mind the girl, Sir Tomkyn. I'll bundle the girl back to her convent, if she says much more!"

"I wish you would!"

But Sir Tomkyn, who believed that he was lowering himself by an alliance with this insolent American girl, was aroused. He wanted the old man's money; but he resolved to take it as a conqueror. He would tell these toadies how cheap he held them, and then make them sue for pardon.

"I like this," he said, ironically. "I like to hear a girl uttering such pious sentiments—a girl whose name is common in the mouth of every shop-boy."

"Sir Tomkyn!" cried Mr. Eliot, his face becoming purple. A moment before, he had said to himself that, in spite of the whim of a foolish girl, his most earnest wish was about to be realized. Now the blood rushed to his head; he tried to stand, but he staggered.

"I don't care much whether she is a Papist or a Turk," continued Sir Tomkyn, growing more angry, "but I won't be dictated to. It's bad enough to have to marry—well, as I am about to marry; but I swear it goes against me to hear such cant from a girl whose picture is in every shop window, the butt for every cad's jokes."

Agnes stood white and cold, facing him.

Mr. Eliot struggled to speak.

Mrs. Weston spoke, the flush on her cheek outshining the rouge:

"Remember, sir, you are about to marry the young lady who stands here."

"'About to marry!'" cried Sir Tomkyn, his bull-neck and fat face glowing with rage. "Men like me flirt with such girls. They don't often marry them."

Mr. Eliot sprang toward the Englishman.

"Father!" It was a strange sound, like a sob. Mrs. Weston screamed. A stream of blood was flowing from Agnes' mouth down over the front of her white dress. The roses she wore at her waist were no redder than this blood. Her father caught her in his arms.

"I am glad," she said, in a faint voice. "I shall die and escape danger, and perhaps sin—dear father!"

Sir Tomkyn had disappeared.

Mr. Eliot at this moment remembered only one thing: her mother had died of hemorrhages.

. . . . . .

When the peach-blossoms bloomed again under the tender blue sky of May, Agnes Eliot was to the world like one of last year's leaves. In the peaceful school the Sisters remembered her; and every year there comes a broken-down and weary-looking man to talk to the Sisters of her. It is sweet to him to find one or two people in the world who knew the sweet and beautiful soul that he tried to sacrifice on the altar of false gods.

TRIFLES.

I.

"TRIFLES LIGHT AS AIR."

PIERRE FRÈCHON invariably called the nondescript vehicle of which he was the owner "a cabriolet of the first class"; but by any other name it could not have been less uncomfortable. In dinginess, discomfort, and in the astounding variety of groans and strange noises that it contrived to emit, it certainly was "of the first class"; but Pierre generally managed *before starting* to conceal the equivocal meaning of his pet epithets.

On a certain evening in February Pierre's cabriolet jolted lazily on the road between Paimbœuf and Nantes. It contained but two passengers, both men, who grumbled unceasingly at the slowness of the cabriolet, and kept up a constant war of words with the conducteur. One of the passengers was Monsieur Jérémie Hercule Blanque, a middle-aged cloth-dealer of Bordeaux, going to Nantes on business; the other was Gaston de Francheville, who, having been visiting a friend at Paimbœuf, was now on his way to his mother's château near Nantes.

"Figure to yourself, monsieur," Blanque was saying, having ceased for an instant to exchange compliments with the driver—"figure to yourself the immense advantage of Christianizing China and the Feejee Islands!

When they had civilization they would require fashion and dress-coats. Figure to yourself the yards and yards of broadcloth *ces autres* would consume! Parbleu! c'est magnifique! the progress of civilization. I assure you, monsieur, that I consider it a blessed privilege to assist our missionaries with my mite."

"You cast bread upon the waters that it may return," Gaston de Francheville began. "Pierre," he called out to the driver, "stop! There's somebody lying in the road."

"Ma foi!" responded Pierre's drawling voice; "I see nothing."

"Are you blind? The light from the lantern falls on it—a dark object at the edge of the road."

"You are right, Monsieur le Comte," said Pierre, alighting, lantern in hand. "Ma foi! c'est une femme!"

"A woman?" echoed Gaston, jumping to the ground.

"One never knows what may happen," muttered prudent Monsieur Blanque, taking advantage of the absence of his fellow-traveller and Pierre, to transfer his watch and purse from his pocket to the leg of his left boot.

"A woman out on such a night!" And Gaston joined Pierre at the side of the road, where, with the leafless branches of an old thorn-tree waving above her like skeleton fingers, a woman lay prone on the rain-soaked ground. She was wrapped in a cloak of the stuff called waterproof, which was anything but proof against the swift-descending torrent of mingled sleet and rain. She was insensible. Between them, Gaston and Pierre carried her to the cabriolet. Her hood fell away from a fair, girlish face, framed by clustering brown hair, that under the gleams of the lantern seemed threaded with gold. Her eyelids, pale and pure as the petals of a camellia, did not tremble in the light, and there was no trace of color in the exquisite lips.

"She is dead!" cried Pierre.

Gaston kept his eyes on the fair young face, and prayed that it might not be so. They laid her carefully on a seat, obliging the merchant to vacate his place, which he did the more readily as he noticed the sparkle of a diamond on the nerveless hand that had escaped from the wet folds of her mantle. Monsieur Blanque felt much relieved in spite of himself. He had a genuine respect for wealth; he was sure that no woman who wore a diamond ring could have designs on his property.

"What will you do with her?" demanded he.

"Leave her at one of the Nantes hospitals if she does not make her wishes known before we reach the city," answered Pierre, taking out a flask of wine and forcing a portion of its contents into the girl's mouth.

The cabriolet pursued its slow course. After a while the girl shivered, and moved her head with a faint moan.

Gaston rather clumsily divested her of the wet cloak, and supplied its place with his overcoat.

"Very imprudent, young gentleman, very imprudent," put in the cloth-merchant, who, since he had heard Gaston called Monsieur le Comte, looked on him with increased interest. "Though young myself, *I* would not have done so, but youth, unaccustomed to the cloth-business, is ever imprudent. I assure you, Monsieur le Comte, that if your coat has not been sponged the dampness will greatly inj—sacr-r-r-r-re!"

A crash and a sudden shock cut short his speech. The cabriolet, with its usual deliberation, sank on one side.

"A wheel off, messieurs!" Pierre laconically announced.

"Where are we?"

"Four miles from Nantes—a quarter of a mile from the château de Francheville."

"That's fortunate," said Gaston. "Drive on to the château. They'll give you a bed there, for you'll not be able to find a wheelwright to-night."

Pierre granted an assent to this proposition, and groped about in the dark to ascertain the extent of the injury.

"I deceived myself, gentlemen," he said, when he had completed the examination. "It is not the wheel. It is a broken axle. You'll have to alight and walk to the château."

Expostulation was useless. "What would you?" demanded Pierre, calmly eying his passengers. "Can one drive on with a broken axle? I ask you that, messieurs!"

Gaston supplied himself with all the rugs and blankets he could lay hands on for sheltering the lady, and the two passengers got out on the road, while Pierre drove toward the château with his disabled vehicle, leaving them to follow as best they could.

Monsieur Blanque was only upheld from sinking under this misfortune by the consciousness that his valuables were in a comparatively safe place, and that his coat, having been sponged, would not be likely to suffer from the rain. When Gaston tendered him the hospitality of the château, he had grown nervous. "People don't give anything for nothing," reflected this profound student of bourgeois human nature. "One never knows what may happen. The château de Francheville may be a high-sounding name for a den of thieves. What if the Comte and the conducteur are in league to rob the junior member of the firm of Drap et Blanque?"

Disturbed in mind by these frightful conjectures and groaning in spirit, Monsieur Blanque toiled over the yielding soil of the road, feeling like a lamb led to slaughter.

Gaston was compelled to carry his charge. The only sign of consciousness she gave was a moan uttered at intervals.

Monsieur Blanque, who had fallen in the rear, suddenly uttered a stifled exclamation. Gaston stopped. Monsieur Blanque had stumbled upon one of the softest places in the very soft road. The sticky, yielding mud clung to his boots. He stood on his right foot, and pulled up his left; then he stood on his left and pulled up his right, and then *da capo*. Poor Monsieur Blanque!

"Sacr-r-r-r-re! help! dame!" he cried in answer to Gaston's inquiry. His struggles were as vain as they were violent. His boots had been made to accommodate his corns, and when at last he extricated himself, one of his boots remained a prey to the tenacity of the soil. His anguish was excessive when he discovered that this was his left boot—the boot that contained his money and watch.

To plunge in after it would be to renew his troubles. To ask his companions' assistance, incumbered as he was by the unconscious girl, merely to recover a boot, would seem ridiculous, and Monsieur Blanque would not bring himself to confess that the lost boot contained his valuables. In an agony of perplexity he entered the warm hall of the château.

The appearance of guests rather surprised Madame de Francheville; but she regarded hospitality as a duty to be exercised with discretion and a frugal mind. She welcomed her son and Monsieur Blanque with stately cordiality, while wondering whether the remains of the game *pâté* left from dinner could be warmed up for these hungry new-comers.

Madame de Francheville's rich pearl-colored silk and delicate point lace thoroughly impressed the cloth-merchant with a sense of the perfect respectability of his fellow-traveller.

When Madame de Francheville heard the young girl had been found on the road, she elevated her eyebrows and dropped the cold hand she had taken, but something in the girl's face seemed to change her scorn to pity, for instead of leaving her in the care of a maid, she went herself to see that a room was made comfortable.

After she had left the room, Monsieur Blanque explained his mishap, and begged that a servant might be permitted to accompany him in his search for the missing boot. Gaston proposed that a servant should go alone. The idea made the cloth-dealer tremble. Wearing a pair of Gaston's slippers, he set out, attended by old Berthe, who was "general utility" at the château.

Old Berthe took off his shoes, and wading into the slough, succeeded in finding the boot with its precious contents. Monsieur Blanque was not usually generous, but in his joy he actually gave Berthe a five-franc piece; it is only fair, however, to state that he first searched in vain for a smaller sum.

While old Berthe was rooting in the mud for the boot, Monsieur Blanque had found something else. This treasure-trove was a package wrapped in a handkerchief. With his usual caution, the cloth-dealer, unobserved by his attendant, slipped the package under his cloak. The packet had not lain long on the road, he surmised, for the handkerchief was but slightly damp. Perhaps it belonged to the Comte de Francheville or to the unknown young girl. Monsieur Blanque determined to examine it.

When he and Gaston had partaken of their luncheon—served with a display of plate and old china that infinitely increased the guest's respect for the house of Francheville—he asked to be shown to his room. Alone in the large square chamber, with a canopied bedstead and a tall wax candle, the flame of which was reflected in the highly-polished floor, he took out the packet, noticing that in one corner the handkerchief bore the initials " A. M." The packet itself was covered with thick white paper, on which was inscribed in delicate, feminine handwriting:

"In case of accident to me open this, but not until you reach Nantes. Your mother, Y. M."

Monsieur Blanque did not hesitate to tear this cover. Beneath it he found an envelope addressed to " Madame la Comtesse de Francheville."

The cloth-merchant was mean by nature, and therefore unscrupulously curious. He was sure now that the young girl had dropped the packet. It belonged neither to Gaston nor to the driver. What could this unknown girl have to do with the mistress of the château? His curiosity was intensely excited. He held the envelope between his eyes and the candle, vainly endeavoring to get an inkling of its contents. He gave the attempt up, and laying the envelope on the table, tried to compose himself to sleep. Who was this young woman? Madame de Francheville did not seem to know her. Who was the mysterious " Y. M."? He puzzled himself with numerous conjectures. He could not sleep. He rose, and again took the envelope in his hand. It bore no seal. Stifling the voice of conscience, he moistened the gummed flap of the envelope, and gradually, carefully, opened it. He read the following words, in French:

"LA COMTESSE DE FRANCHEVILLE.

"MADAME: To you, the oldest friend and neighbor of my father, I address myself. A glance at the signature appended to this letter will at once remind you of my story, for you know it well. When I became the wife of Bernard Moore, and my father, in consequence, disowned me, we—Bernard and I—sailed for America, the native land of my husband. There we lived for twenty years—years which would have been of unmixed happiness, had my father sent one forgiving word across the sea. I used to think him cruel. I know now that he was just. Four years ago Bernard died, and I was left with one daughter, Adèle. Of four children, she alone lived. The death of my husband reduced us from comparative affluence to poverty. Twice I wrote to my father. No answer came. I should have sunk into despair, madame, for the consequence of my sin was very bitter, had not the holy consolations of the Church crowned my repentance and given me resignation.

"In the latter part of last year I received, through the French Consul at New York, a letter from you. You told me that my father had forgiven me. I blessed you for those words, madame! But my joy was bitter: *his* cold, dead lips could never speak that forgiveness.

"I answered your letter and, with Adèle, started at once for Europe. The fear that you may not have received my answer causes me to write this.

"My daughter has not been informed of the motive of our voyage. I have been fearful lest there might be some mistake—fearful that my father might have willed his estate to another. The realization of this fear would be terrible to me, and crushing disappointment, I have no doubt, to Adèle. I am not avaricious, madame, but poverty has taught me the value of wealth. I have determined that Adèle shall know nothing until it is certain, beyond doubt, that I am the heiress of the Marquis de Saluces.

"Adèle will come to you with this letter. Read it privately, and if my hope be unfounded, burn this paper. Do not let Adèle know of the disappointment. Judging her nature by mine, I am sure that the knowledge would embitter her life. If it be as I fear, I implore you, by the memory of my father's friendship for you and your late husband, to provide for her in France, or send her back to New York.

"On Adèle's finger you will see the only souvenir of my father's kindness, a ring bearing his crest.

"May Mary, Immaculate Mother of the unprotected, guard her well, and reward you for aught of kindness you may do in her behalf!

"YOLANTHE MOORE,
"*née* DE SALUCES."

This strange young woman was, then, the granddaughter of the Marquis de Saluces!

Monsieur Blanque's curiosity was satisfied. How was he to restore the packet to its original appearance? How make the envelope look as if it had never been opened? These *were* questions. A new idea entered his mind. The letter he had just read plainly stated that Adèle Moore was unaware of the object that had brought her mother to France; and without this letter how was Madame de Francheville to know that the heiress of the Marquis de Saluces had arrived at the château?

During the day Monsieur Blanque had been on a collecting-tour through the neighboring country, and he had met many garrulous people and asked many questions. He had obtained some scrap of information about every family of note in the vicinity. Among other things, he had learned that the Marquis de Saluces had lately died, bequeathing his entire wealth to a daughter in America, and so Monsieur Blanque knew that Yolanthe Moore's hope was not groundless.

"Madame de Francheville will not be blind to her own interest," Monsieur Blanque reasoned. "If I give her the letter, she will marry the rich mademoiselle to Monsieur Gaston; and why should I be blind to my own interest? Why should I not gain the prize? I am not old; I am, they tell me, not positively hideous; I am, I flatter myself, of good address."

And Monsieur Blanque tried to imagine the envy of his fellow-bourgeois of Bordeaux, when it should be known that he, Jérémie Hercule Blanque, of the firm of Drap et Blanque, was the husband of the heiress de Saluces. His face flushed at the thought of the brilliant prospect before him; but it paled in an instant, and his cloud-castle faded away. The girl's name and the ring! Madame de Francheville would surely recognize them.

In feverish haste he returned to the letter, in search of something to dispel his fear. In the envelope he found a certificate of the marriage of Bernard Moore and Adèle de Saluces. There were several other papers of importance, but nothing that he wanted just now. Again he re-read every word of the letter. He found a postscript crowded on three lines at the end of the last page. He had overlooked it.

"You will deem me over-cautious, madame, when you read that I changed my name while *en route*, for a weak woman has everything to fear when travelling; besides, my means were small, and I did not wish it to be known that ladies of our name and condition were reduced to take passage in the steerage. I have assumed the middle name of my husband—Martin—that none might suspect our coming and going."

"Women are fools," remarked Monsieur Blanque, somewhat relieved, "and it is well for men."

The ring would have to take its chance of recognition. Monsieur Blanque climbed into the canopied bed, to dream that under the title of Marquis de Saluces he had been appointed Prime Minister to His Satanic Majesty, and to awake frightened by the thought that even sponging would not secure cloth against fire!

Next morning, at breakfast, Monsieur Blanque met Gaston and his mother.

Madame de Francheville was at least sixty years of age, but she seemed ten years younger. Her features were small and regular, her skin pure white and scarcely wrinkled, and the dainty puffs of snowy hair arranged above her forehead added to the beauty of her complexion. She was proud of her pride and her exquisite taste in dress. Of these two qualities she had sufficient to have stocked all the de Franchevilles since the days of Bertrand du Guesclin. She was a devoted adherent of the fallen Empire, and since the Emperor's death she had never failed, on every opportunity, to indulge in a little sentimental grief. This morning her *negligé* of white and purple was perfect, and Monsieur Blanque was fascinated by the lace at her throat and wrists. He knew the value of it. After the weather and the state of madame's health had been disposed of, he asked about the "heroine of last night's adventure," as he phrased it.

"She is not well, poor thing! She has a slight fever, and I have sent for a physician. I hope her malady is not contagious"; and madame shivered.

"Pauvre demoiselle!" said Gaston. "It is strange that she ventured out alone last night. She seemed from her appearance to be a lady. Is it not so, madame?"

"It is impossible to tell, Gaston. There is no dividing-line between the classes under this *vilain gouvernement provisoire*, and everybody is a lady; but the poor child has not the air of a common person. It was certainly improper that she should be out last night without an attendant, but then, I have reason to believe she's an

American, and one never knows what to expect from *them*—the Americans. Why, when I was in Paris—"

This one visit to Paris was the crown and glory of madame's life. Having heard every detail of it at least a score of times, Gaston was anxious to avoid the interesting subject; he was also curious about the young girl.

"Why do you think she is an American, madame?"

"Politeness, Gaston, should teach you never to interrupt a lady," returned madame, freezingly. "I was about to observe, Monsieur Blanque, that when I was in Paris some years ago, there were at Meurice's two demoiselles Américaines who rode in the Bois every afternoon. Their dress was *outré* in the extreme; their appearance very singular. It was said that their modiste had made a fortune in arranging *bizarre* toilets for them. One day, when the Emperor and Empress were riding in the Bois, one of these demoiselles stopped her horse immediately in front of the imperial carriage. The coachman, of course, reined his horses, to avoid a collision. The other demoiselle at once rode up to the side of the imperial vehicle, and, holding out her hand, said, 'I've made a wager to shake hands with Your Majesty in the Bois, and I'll do it! Donnez moi la main, vieux drôle.' What was it, Gaston?" Madame sank back in her chair, and fanned herself with her handkerchief, as if the audacious words were too much for her.

Gaston knew the anecdote by heart, and he was well prepared to take up the thread.

"Give me your hand, old fellow, here's my paw!" he laughed, giving the words in English. "And now, madame, how do you know that our young lady is of the nation of those bold demoiselles?"

"And she actually shook hands with the Emperor—

truly, Monsieur Blanque!" pursued madame, not to be diverted from her story. "The poor Emperor—*requiescat in pace!*" she continued, brushing away an imaginary tear with a handkerchief bordered with imperial violets. Having divided an instant of silence between her grief and the measuring of the exact quantity of cream she could endure in her coffee, madame at last condescended to answer her son's question. "I discovered some cards in the young woman's pocketbook as I was searching for her address—for one doesn't care to have a sick person on one's hands, you know. On the cards was written, 'Adèle Martin, New York.' I found no address."

Monsieur Blanque silently congratulated himself on the sharpness of his intellect. What should be his next move? He resolved to keep madame in a good humor at all events. He respectfully expressed ardent admiration for madame's lace, and offered to procure her some marvellous ochre-tinted Valenciennes at a remarkably low price. He called her "countess" as often as he could. Madame allowed herself to be pleased, and concluded that the cloth-merchant knew his place.

"One forgets time in the society of Madame la Comtesse," said he, rising from the table; "doubtless the cabriolet is waiting."

"The cabriolet started two hours ago," said Gaston. "Pierre's lazy conscience began this morning to reproach him for his delay, and when old Berthe had called you once, he started for Nantes."

Monsieur Blanque waxed indignant. "Three thousand devils!—pardon, Madame la Comtesse! 'Tis an unheard-of thing,—a conveyance to start without its passenger! It's incredible! I will complain to the proprietaire! I will complain to the maire! Parbleu! a thousand devils, madame—pardone, I would say, Madame la Comtesse! I will—"

"You had better take it quietly," said Gaston. "Pierre is sole owner of the cabriolet, and if you complain to anybody he will surely manage to put you in the wrong. There is nobody equal to Pierre for making excuses. Besides, he is not bound to wait until his passenger chooses to rise. It is raining now. I will order the carriage if monsieur is impatient."

Madame de Francheville entertained no thought of ordering her stately equipage merely for the convenience of a bourgeois.

"Nantes is only four miles away," she insinuated, "but I am sure Berthe will never allow the horses to be taken out on such a day. Old servants are such tyrants, monsieur! When the rain ceases the walk from here to Nantes will be quite pleasant. If monsieur wishes it, however—"

"Oh, no, madame! By no means! I like to walk. I am a lover of Nature and exercise."

"You delight me, monsieur; we have kindred tastes." Gaston had already left the room. Madame rose to follow his example.

"Will Madame la Comtesse favor me with a moment's conversation?"

Monsieur Blanque had decided on his move. Madame, stiffly bending her neck in assent, returned to her seat.

"I am an eccentric man, Madame la Comtesse. I am charitable—too charitable for my own temporal good, for this world has many bad hearts. I am also impulsive, madame, foolishly impulsive."

Madame smiled sweetly, and looked at her watch.

"When I saw that poor young girl in the rain last night, I said to myself, 'Perhaps she has no home—no friends.' I gazed into her innocent face, and my heart added, 'She has need of a protector,' and I said, 'I, Jérémie Hercule Blanque, will be that protector!'"

Monsieur Blanque placed one hand on his heart, and assumed an attitude. For the moment he really believed that he was doing something very generous and heroic.

"Eh bien!" said madame, placidly taking out her gold and ivory *bonbonnière*. "But suppose the girl requires no protector?"

"In that case, Madame la Comtesse, my good intention will be its own reward. I am unmarried. I desire a wife. My soul is an abyss of pity for this young girl. If you find that she is friendless, inform me. I will leave my address. During the two coming months I will remain at the inn of the Golden Horse, Nantes. If this girl is penniless, if she is wholly without *dot*, I care not. My fortune is sufficient for both."

Overcome by the thought of his own disinterestedness he actually wept. Madame thought it only proper to draw out her own violet-embroidered handkerchief and apply it to her eyeglass. Although the man was a bourgeois and a fool, one must be polite, you comprehend?

"I will think of your proposition, monsieur. It is a decided novelty to have an utter stranger thrown on one's hands, and to receive an offer of marriage for her from another stranger."

"You will do a good action by mentioning my offer to her, and if she is homeless—"

"She will, if she is prudent, accept it."

"It is customary to present a slight gift to the pro

motor of the marriage, and if the Valenciennes of which—"

"Very well, monsieur," said madame, haughtily. "If I have anything further to say, I will address you at the Golden Horse."

"What fools women are!" thought monsieur, as he held the door open for madame.

"Truly vulgar stupidity!" mentally commented madame, as she went to receive the physician, whose gruff voice was heard in the hall. The doctor was a short, bustling man, attired in a suit of black and white plaid, which gave him the appearance of an animated checkerboard. He refused all offers of refreshment; he was in a hurry, and he knew madame's *vin ordinaire* of old. He demanded to see his patient at once.

This patient was a tall, slight girl, apparently about nineteen, with soft, dark-blue eyes, which, from the pallor of her forehead and temples, seemed unnaturally large. A faint blush-rose tint shone in her cheeks; a thick mass of smooth, golden-brown hair was loosely drawn back from her broad, low brow and knotted at the back of her head. She wore a plain dark dress lent to her by madame's maid.

She rose from her seat at the window and made a step forward as madame and the doctor entered. Even in that slight movement there was a nameless grace that bespeaks the gentlewoman.

"I am much better," she said, in a clear, low voice, answering the query of her hostess; "indeed quite well. The *tisane* which you so kindly sent has completely restored me. With your permission, madame, I will at once start for Nantes."

"But the cabriolet—"

The flush in the girl's cheeks deepened.

"I will walk."

"No, ma'amselle, you will not!" thundered the doctor, who had taken possession of her slender wrist. "You'll not leave this room for two days! Do you hear? You want rest and quiet. You've been exciting yourself—you've been out in all sorts of weather. If you want to kill yourself, take poison; it's a quicker way than walking in the rain, but no surer."

"You speak truth, doctor," said madame; "my grandfather walked out, rain or shine, for seventy years, and then died; but if he had taken poison—"

"Your grandfather was—a gentleman," said the irritated doctor. "*I* say that ma'amselle *must* have rest and quiet. That's all! I'm off!"

The doctor wrote a prescription and made his exit.

"You must remain here, Mademoiselle Martin. I will not allow you to go," said madame, moved in spite of herself by the fragile beauty of the girl. "And now tell me how you came to be out last night. Speak freely. Regard me as your own mother."

After a slight hesitation, Adèle complied.

"The story is short, madame, but very sad. My mother and I started from New York on our way to Brittany. The voyage was pleasant. When we reached L'Orient, my mother caught a fever, and in a week's time died. She was buried four days ago." The girl's voice broke, but she bravely strove to speak. "She instructed me to continue on the road to Nantes. She gave me a packet, telling me not to open it until I should reach that city. I had but little money, madame, and I walked whenever I could. A market-woman gave me a seat in her cart part of the way, but by mistake I reached Paim bœuf instead of Nantes. I was retracing my steps last night. I had been walking all day, and I was weak. I fainted, I suppose."

"That was sad. You speak French well."

"My mother was born in France."

"And her name?"

"I do not know. She never spoke of her family. She had some great object in view when she came hither, but I can not even guess what it was. She was an invalid— very nervous and reserved, but oh! the best—the kindest—" Tears drowned the words.

"Exceedingly mysterious," commented madame to herself. "But you alluded to a packet?"

"Have you seen it, madame?" asked Adèle, eagerly. "It was wrapped in a white handkerchief. I can not find it. It must have fallen on the road, or in the cabriolet last night."

"I will send a servant to search for it."

Having recommended her guest to rest tranquil, madame left her.

Madame de Francheville did not doubt the truth of Adèle's story. A girl with such a face as hers could not tell a lie without betraying it, madame thought, as she constructed a little plan. This Mademoiselle Martin was apparently well educated and refined. Now, madame had been for some time on the lookout for a companion who could play, sing, and read to her. If Mademoiselle Martin could do all three, she could also teach English, and madame, old as she was, had a mania for languages. Having no alternative, Mademoiselle Martin would doubtless be glad to accept the position at a very low salary. This was, in madame's eyes, the crowning recommendation. She was well satisfied with her little plan.

She sent her servants in various directions to search for the missing packet. Monsieur Blanque was standing on the covered terrace waiting for the rain to abate. He chuckled as he saw the servants turning up the mud in the road. He was complacently reflecting on his own astuteness, when he felt a light touch on his shoulder. He turned round and saw Adèle—"*belle comme un ange*"—he thought.

"The *femme de chambre* has told me that you are a merchant, monsieur," she said, standing just within the long window of the salon.

"Of the firm of Drap et Blanque, Bordeaux, at your service." He bowed profoundly.

With a quick motion she drew the one ring from her finger: "I thought that you might perhaps dispose of this for me."

For an instant Monsieur Blanque's small black eyes rivalled in brightness the brilliant diamond that bore the faintly-traced crest of the de Saluces. Then, with affected indifference, he said:

"Is it valuable?"

"Oh, yes, very valuable. My mother, who gave it to me, said it was worth five thousand dollars."

"Dollars?"

"Or, in French currency, about twenty-five thousand francs. Am I not right?"

Monsieur Blanque raised his eyebrows and shrugged his shoulders.

"I'll give you a thousand francs for it."

There's no harm in that, argued Monsieur Blanque. Will not my property soon be hers, and hers mine—that is, if Madame de Francheville does not play me false?

"I will pledge it to you for that sum—"

"I am not attaché of the Mont de Pieté," he interrupted, blandly.

Adèle hesitated. She was penniless in a strange land. It was hard to sacrifice the ring, but it would be still harder to be utterly dependent on the charity of strangers.

"Take it," she said, averting her face as she gave him the ring.

He drew his purse from some hidden portion of his attire, and counted the thousand francs. She followed him into the empty salon at his request. He found pen and paper, and she signed a receipt.

He chuckled jubilantly. Assuredly success seemed all on his side. The packet first, and now the ring, had fallen in his way without any effort of his own. With the ring in his pocket, he started for Nantes in high good-humor.

The future seemed very dark to Adèle. She trembled at the thought of the journey homeward. She imagined herself landing alone at New York. There she had neither relatives nor friends, for her mother had kept her rigidly secluded from the world around her. Inexperienced and unskilled as she was, how could she earn a living?

When madame discovered that Adèle could play and sing, she made her proposal, which was gratefully accepted by the girl. There was one concession that madame required which gave her great pain. She was not allowed to wear black in her bereavement, for madame detested black. It reminded her of death, and madame did not like to be reminded of death. She did not object to a little pleasing sadness now and then—a tear over the departed, a wreath of immortelles; but she had a horror of deep grief and deep mourning. When Adèle's trunk came from L'Orient, she endeavored to improvise toilets of white and purple from her slender stock of wearing-apparel.

Often in the early morning, when the dim landscape lay in the uncertain but glowing light of dawn, Adèle stole softly down to the village church to pray for her mother's soul.

"That is better than wearing black, my child," the old curé, to whom she had told her trouble, would say when they met at the church-door after Mass.

Adèle's days passed pleasantly. While madame sewed or embroidered in the latter part of the morning, Adèle played lively galops or stirring marches. In the afternoon she read to madame in French and gave her lessons in English. In the long, quiet evenings, she sang opera airs or played Beethoven and Mozart, while Gaston, the doctor, his wife, or perhaps the curé, indulged in a game of chess with madame.

There was one subject on which madame was never weary of expatiating, and of which Adèle was heartily tired of hearing. This was the value of the adjoining estate, that had belonged to the late Marquis de Saluces.

The heiress to this great estate was in America. Madame, however, daily expected her to arrive with her daughter. This heiress had secretly married a strolling geologist—that might not be the right term, madame said; however, he was a Bohemian of some kind. This tourist, having broken his leg—it served him right!—in trying to climb a rock, in search of worthless pieces of stone, had been taken to the château of the marquis, and thus became acquainted with Mademoiselle de Saluces. On discovering the marriage, the marquis had disinherited his daughter. But when he came to die, he had forgiven her, and bequeathed all he possessed to her, by way of reparation for his long years of displeasure.

It never occurred to madame to mention the name of the "foreign adventurer," or Adèle would have discovered that he was her father. The name "Yolanthe" might have given her a clue, but madame always spoke of the heiress as Mademoiselle de Saluces.

Although Yolanthe Moore had never been wholly free from sickness, she had none the less exacted unquestioning obedience of her gentle daughter. Adèle knew that the name of Martin belonged to her father, and when her mother had desired her to assume it, she had complied, showing some surprise, but asking no questions, for experience had taught her that they would be unanswered. And now that the people at the château had got into the way of calling her Mademoiselle Martin, she did not think it necessary to tell her real name.

Madame de Francheville looked forward to Gaston's marriage with the granddaughter of the marquis as a certain thing. She had hinted at such a conclusion in her letter to Yolanthe Moore, and she awaited only the arrival of that lady in France to plunge at once into preliminaries.

"And the name of Gaston's wife will be Adèle; the same as yours, my child," madame had said.

Adèle caught herself wondering whether this young countrywoman of hers were pretty or not, and whether Gaston liked the name "Adèle."

II.

"TRIFLES MAKE THE SUM OF HUMAN LIFE."

The sad, pensive look left Adèle's face. Gradually the color of health returned to her cheeks, and she grew less slender. The tranquil, uneventful routine of life at the château rested her, and she bloomed and brightened in the pure country air. How kind, how good, God was to her! she often thought. He had made her guardian angel lead her to this haven of peace after a night of storm—a brief but terrible night.

The old-fashioned garden was the prettiest spot within the limits of the de Francheville grounds. In the latter part of May and earlier part of June it was a perfect wilderness of roses—roses of all shades, from the creamiest white to the deepest yellow, from the palest pink to the redness of blood. Besides roses, there were beds of those gorgeous tulips and carnations in which our ancestors delighted, and which remind one of the flaunting dames of Versailles in the time of Louis Quatorze.

At that pleasant time when afternoon and evening meet, this quaint garden, with its trees and boxwood clipped into strange shapes, was Adèle's favorite resort. With a cherished volume of poems—usually Longfellow or Miss Procter—she would walk up and down the broad path until the trim yew peacocks and green pyramids appeared through the darkness like sentinel spectres.

Gaston suddenly grew very fond of this garden. His coign of vantage was an arbor at the end of the broad walk. This arbor was entirely covered with ivy. It was very damp and infested by spiders. Notwithstanding these drawbacks, he seemed to derive great gratification from sitting there, and, through the network of ivy-stems, watching the unconscious Adèle.

He liked to look at her; he liked to see her smile, and when once she laughed at one of his rather weak jokes his delight was unbounded, but afterward he went off in a melancholy state of mind to wonder whether she had laughed at the joke or the joker. Gaston did not analyze his feelings. He did not even seek her company; he only gazed at her from a distance, as a man might gaze at an angel, and thought her the best and most beautiful woman in the world.

Gaston de Francheville could not have sat for a typical portrait of young France. He was rather phlegmatic than excitable. He was true-hearted and steadfast. It generally took him some time to reach a conclusion, but when that conclusion was reached he stood firm as a rock. Some people called this quality obstinacy: others, firmness; but they all agreed that it was "Gaston de Francheville's way."

A handsome young man — nothing remarkable — you would have thought, had you casually met him on a boulevard or in the Bois. He was somewhat taller than the average Frenchman, with dark brown, generally close-cropped hair, a light brown moustache, a bronzed complexion, and honest hazel eyes. He was always well dressed, as became a de Francheville.

One soft, balmy May eve, Adèle opened her "Evangeline," and, as usual, began to pace along the garden-path.

There was a slight rustling among the ivy that covered the summer-house, and a cloud of curling smoke arose. Adèle, with her back to the arbor, did not notice the sound or the smoke, but went on with her poem:

"In that delightful land which is washed by the Delaware's waters,
 Guarding in sylvan shade the name of Penn the apostle,
 Stands on the banks of its beautiful stream the city he founded.
 There all the air is balm—".

"I doubt that," murmured Adèle, who had spent a winter in the said city.

"Mademoiselle—ahem!" said a somewhat uncertain voice at her elbow.

"Mademoiselle Adèle—Martin!"

She turned quickly and saw Gaston. His sudden appearance had startled her. He seemed rather uneasy himself, and not self-possessed. He walked beside her, throwing away his half-smoked cigar. He drew another from its case in silence, lit it, and then, remembering himself, blushed and threw it away.

"Will you permit me to say a few words to you, mademoiselle?"

"Certainly."

He paused a while after she had answered.

Why this ceremony? He had spoken to her often without permission. Her heart beat quickly. Perhaps madame had need of her services no longer. "Thy will be done, O Lord!" she murmured.

"Well, then, mademoiselle—well, then—" Gaston was stricken with something akin to stage-fright. It occurred to him with terrifying suddenness that Adèle might never have considered the proposition he was about to make—that thus far he had thought of it from only one point of view. But Adèle was waiting for him to speak.

"Well, then, mademoiselle," he continued, desperately, "I want you to be my wife. I love you!"

This *was* abrupt, and Gaston knew it, but it was too late to soften it now.

Adèle started in surprise, but her heart sang a song of joy, and her face brightened.

"Have you any objection?" he asked, taking her hand.

"I have not thought yet, Monsieur Gaston," she said, turning away her face, perhaps to conceal the new light in her eyes, and she made a very slight effort to withdraw the imprisoned hand.

"Then it is settled, Adèle. Thou wilt try to love me?" he said, using the tender "*tu.*"

"But madame, your mother—"

"It is not madame that is to marry you, Adèle; it is I. She shall know of it to-night."

Although the rosebuds had not yet opened, a sweet odor, as of roses, seemed to surround Adèle. She tore her hand from Gaston's grasp, and ran up to her room. There she blushed, sighed and laughed, finally subsiding into what is technically called "a good cry."

Shortly after that little scene in the garden, madame, in rustling gray silk, point lace and pearls, sailed into the salon. The curé had been invited to dine at the château, but at the eleventh hour he had sent a regret. He was obliged to answer an unexpected sick-call.

"Sick indeed!" exclaimed madame, with asperity. 'People are continually getting sick at unreasonable times. They might exercise a little self-denial, and let the poor man eat his dinner in peace! Selfishness, selfishness, all is selfishness!"

Gaston was trying to read by the light of one wax candle perched in a chandelier high above his head. Madame, being economical, had forbidden the lighting of more than one candle until the curé's arrival.

"Ma mère," began Gaston, "I have asked Mademoiselle Adèle to be my wife, and she has promised— that is—"

"What!" demanded madame, standing still, and bending her eyes on her son in amazement.

"I have asked Mademoiselle Adèle to be my wife, and she has not refused."

Madame stood as one stricken dumb. She opened her lips and then closed them. When one loses one's temper, one loses all, was a favorite maxim of hers. In silence she took out her *bonbonnière*, and with great deliberation selected some vanilla chocolate.

"You have done a very foolish thing, Gaston," she said, in her gentlest tone. "Consider. Have you committed yourself irretrievably?"

"Have I not said, maman, that I asked Adèle to be my wife? I have told her that I love her."

"That is nothing. Twenty young men told me the same thing before I had seen your father."

"But my father would not have told you so had he not meant it, and you have often said that I am like my father."

Again madame applied herself to her *bonbonnière*. Vanilla chocolate had a soothing effect on her nerves.

"Gaston," she said, "you well know the house of de Francheville is not as rich as it was long ago, when your ancestor Gontran founded a church in Nantes which was the wonder of the surrounding country. There is only one estate in our province which could bear such a drain now, and that is the magnificent estate of the Marquis de Saluces. The heiress to that estate I expect each day to arrive in France. She has a daughter. Of this daughter I have spoken to you, Gaston. Will you throw away the chance of becoming one of the richest proprietors in France?"

"But I love Adèle, mother."

"Bah!" said madame in a tone of infinite scorn. "Give up the thought of this girl, Gaston. I will persuade her—"

"Never!" cried Gaston, aroused for once. "I'll never marry without your blessing, but I'll never sacrifice my honor to gain it!"

"But you are willing to sacrifice the honor of your family for an obscure girl!" Madame was losing her temper. The *bonbonnière* again came into use.

"The honor of our family, if true and honest love can sully it, is a false, boastful, empty name!"

There was a short silence, during which madame closed her eyes and reflected.

"I will consent to your marrying this girl on one condition. You shall go to Paris on Friday, Gaston. To-day is Wednesday. You will have one day for preparation. It is sufficient. In Paris I wish you to remain a month. If, at the end of that time, your mind is still unchanged regarding this girl, I will receive Adèle Martin as my daughter. Do you consent?"

Gaston hesitated. He hardly knew how to take this.

"I consent," he said; "I will start for Paris on Friday."

Before madame retired that evening she wrote a letter and directed it to the inn of the Golden Horse, Nantes.

All the next day Gaston was occupied with the preparations for his journey, and madame took care that Adèle should be occupied too. Work was provided for her in the mysterious recesses of madame's apartment. Gaston made several attempts to see her, but his mother's vigilance rendered them fruitless. He spoke to her once before he started, but madame was present, and so he was forced to leave the château, according to promise, without having been able to say one tender word to the "*dame de ses pensées.*"

On Saturday—Gaston had started for Paris the previous day—a letter came to madame from Monsieur Blanque, and on the same night she paid a visit to Adèle's room. The interview between this woman of the world and the girl lasted some time. Madame's voice was in unvarying monotone, but Adèle's was passionate and sob-broken.

"I do not blame you, my dear," the former was saying in answer to some outbreak of the girl's. "I do not blame *you*, for in America no distinction of rank is acknowledged, but here things are entirely different. If my poor Gaston marries you, he will be generous, but foolish; but if you consent to marry him, you will be the executioner of my dearest hopes—the destroyer of my son's future happiness."

"Madame," Adèle interrupted, in a tone that had more impatience in it than she had yet shown, "you forget that your son's happiness depends, in part at least, on his love for me."

"Poor, poor child!" murmured madame. "And you believe that because Gaston says so! When you have seen as much of the world as I have, you will be less credulous. Believe me, my child, one pretty woman is just as dear to a man as another. But when did Gaston tell you all this nonsense?"

"He never told it to me in words exactly," said Adèle, the lovely blush-rose hue growing deeper in her cheeks; "but since he spoke to me in the garden, his eyes—in a word, madame, I am sure that he loves me."

"Love! Bah! it is folly," cried madame, losing her equanimity. "Have some vanilla chocolate? No? Well, my dear," she continued, changing her tone, "I believe that Gaston thinks he loves you, and, *hélas!* he is obstinate; but remember that I have almost engaged him to the granddaughter of the Marquis de Saluces."

"And has he no voice in the matter?"

"My dear, in France parents arrange these affairs."

"It is not so at home," said Adèle, the tear-drops on her lashes sparkling in the resolute light of her eyes. "I do not care. I will not give him up!"

"You are selfish, mademoiselle," said madame, in a tone delicately modulated to express sorrow rather than anger. "But can I blame you? You are not a mother, and none but mothers know what self-sacrifice truly is. Listen to me. Gaston is comparatively poor now, for he has only one thousand francs *de rente* of his own, and when this is divided between two, he will be poorer. Neither am I rich, but I am not wholly destitute; and I tell you, mademoiselle, that when—" Madame hesitated and shivered slightly. "No matter. I will give him nothing if you become his wife. How could you two live? It is true that Gaston has studied medicine, but the idea of a de Francheville practicing that profession is absurd! He has nothing. You have nothing. Surely you will not be silly enough to marry?"

Adèle did not answer, though madame paused.

"You will not cause my son to sacrifice everything—wealth, rank, ease—for you? Will you, mademoiselle?"

Adèle's face became white, and she turned to madame imploringly.

"Answer me, mademoiselle."

"No," sobbed Adèle. "I will not see him again. I do not doubt his love, assure him of that, madame, but I doubt that mine could compensate him for all he would lose."

"A noble girl!" cried madame, turning up her eyes. "Would that I could call you daughter! But *that* is impossible. Hélas! But your sacrifice is not yet complete. You must marry another."

"Madame!"

"Yes, my child, and I have provided a bridegroom for you, a worthy man, Jérémie Hercule Blanque. You must put it out of Gaston's power to marry you, and the only way to do so is to marry somebody else. Gaston is obstinate as the rock. If you are not extremely firm, strong, and true to yourself, he will make you his wife in spite of everybody."

Adèle wished that he would, but she did not say so. It was very hard, very hard, she sobbed.

Madame talked far into the night, and at last, dizzy, wretched, and exhausted, Adèle promised to become the wife of Monsieur Blanque.

Monsieur Blanque, when he had been informed of the result of this interview, paid frequent visits to the château. He was often thrown into Adèle's way. At these times the girl greeted him with a cold bow or a few monosyllables, and then took refuge in her room.

"Mademoiselle Martin does not speak much now," said Monsieur Blanque, "but I fear that it will not be so after marriage."

Madame de Francheville had named the wedding-day. The marriage was to take place three days before Gaston was expected home from exile. A dead calm seemed to have fallen upon Adèle. The worst had come to the worst. She could not weep, and she found it hard to pray. Her visits to the church grew more frequent, and the curé did not fail to notice that she seemed sad. "Thy will be done—Thy will be done, dear Lord! But, O

Mother of Sorrows, have pity on me!" This was her prayer.

Gay Paris had now no attractions for Gaston. Three weeks of his time of probation had crawled away. Adèle was constantly in his mind. Another week, and then years of happiness!

Two days of this fourth week passed. Gaston had reached the last stage of restlessness, and when Pierre Frèchon's well-known voice was heard outside his room-door in loud conversation with the concierge, he rushed forth and warmly welcomed that individual.

"You overwhelm me, Monsieur le Comte," said Pierre, helping himself to the coffee and cognac which Gaston offered him. "I can tell you nothing about the people at de Francheville except that they are all well, and that Monsieur Blanque, whom you doubtless remember, frequently visits the château. It was only the day before yesterday that I drove him there, which event causes my visit to you. I have sold by beautiful cabriolet, monsieur."

Pierre Frèchon paused, evidently expecting that the startling information would stun Gaston.

"Indeed?"

"Yes, I am going to my brother who is in America. The day before yesterday, Friday—an unlucky day, too! *quel dommage!*—a letter came from my brother, and at once I sold my cabriolet to a man who had long wanted to buy it. Unfortunately Monsieur Blanque had left his overcoat, and a packet, which fell from the inside pocket of it, in my cabriolet. I had not time to convey them after him to the château, and so, as I was on my way to Paris, I brought them to you. Will you oblige me, Monsieur le Comte, by returning them to their owner?"

Pierre might have added that he could just as well have sent the articles to the château by the new driver of the cabriolet, had he not required some pretext for visiting Gaston, in the hope of receiving a parting "*pour boire.*" He was not disappointed. Having left Monsieur Blanque's light overcoat and the packet, he departed in great good humor. When he had gone, Gaston hastily glanced at the packet. It was addressed to his mother.

"This may be important," he thought; "it was very careless of Blanque to forget it."

The next day he took up the packet again. "It *is* important, I am sure," he said; "I had better risk everything, and take it to her at once. It is not necessary that I should see Adèle until the month has fully passed. I will leave the château as soon as I deliver the packet."

And yet, had he not cherished a hope of catching a passing glimpse of Adèle, he would not have troubled himself about that packet. How elaborately we disguise our real motives sometimes!

He packed his portmanteau, and went out to settle some business matters with a notary. Delays followed, and it was not until late on Wednesday morning that, burning with impatience, he got into a carriage at the railroad station at Nantes, and ordered the driver to take him to de Francheville.

As Gaston went up the avenue leading to the château, he noticed that the family carriage was waiting. He concluded that his mother was about to pay one of her visits of state.

"If so, I am just in time," he thought.

Just in time!

He found Madame de Francheville in the boudoir adjoining the salon. Her dress was unusually rich.

"Ma mère is probably about to visit the Archbishop or the Préfet, at least," muttered Gaston, standing in the doorway.

She saw his reflection in the mirror before which she stood.

"*You* here?" she cried, turning suddenly. "Have you broken our compact, Gaston?"

"No," he said. "I will return to Paris as soon as I have given you this packet, which Monsieur Blanque left in the cabriolet. It is addressed to you."

"To me? But go at once, Gaston. I have an important engagement, and there is no time for talking. Go at once," she repeated, eagerly. "You have only two days to wait."

She took the packet, looked at the address, and tore away the already mutilated wrapper.

"Au revoir, mon fils," she said, unfolding the paper.

"Au revoir, ma mère," returned Gaston, bowing ceremoniously, and then, turning on his heel, "until Friday."

"Martin! Adèle de Saluces!" gasped madame, hastily scanning the words. "Gaston! Gaston! Go! Follow them! I have been deceived! They have gone to the mairie for the civil ceremony—the religious marriage will take place at twelve. Go! Go, I say!"

Gaston had reached the middle of the salon, and was looking wistfully at the unoccupied piano-stool—Adèle's accustomed seat at this hour of the day. He turned toward his mother in surprise.

"Explain."

"Do you not hear me?" she exclaimed. "Monsieur Blanque and Adèle have gone to be married! Go after them," she screamed, "to the mairie, and prevent it before it is too late!"

Gaston rushed out upon the terrace, over the flower-beds recklessly, and sprang into the waiting carriage. Old Berthe's mouth and eyes opened wide in amazement.

"Don't spare the horses, Berthe. Use the whip! To the mairie!"

There was a tone in Gaston's voice that warned Berthe he had best do as he was told. Never before had the de Francheville vehicle rattled over sticks and stones at such a fearful rate of speed.

Reaching the mairie in about five minutes, Gaston ran madly through the hall into the principal apartment. Here Monsieur le Maire stood ready to perform the ceremony. Monsieur Blanque, in a capacious white vest, spotless tie and gloves, with a huge bunch of white lilacs in the button-hole of his glossy coat, was near the civil functionary. He held an open watch in his hand, from which his glances anxiously wandered to the corner of the room where a knot of festively attired ladies were gathered. They were surrounding Adèle, who had fainted on entering the room. Gaston, with long strides, neared the sofa.

"Adèle!"

Her eyes opened, and a faint tinge of color returned to her face.

"Gaston!"

Before anybody could interfere, half carrying, half leading her, he strode through the hall and deposited her in the carriage. Monsieur Blanque reached the steps of the mairie in time to see Gaston shut the carriage-door. The vehicle rolled away, leaving him standing in the midday sunshine, while the village children gathered around him and made remarks on his gorgeous appearance.

"I renounce you, perfidious girl, treacherous Adèle!" he cried, shaking both his fists in the direction of the departing carriage. Accidentally, his eye caught the blaze of Adèle's diamond on his finger. Nothing could force him to remove that. He smiled through his tears. The bargain was not so bad, after all! But, in spite of that, he felt that he had risked much and drawn a blank.

. . . .

Gaston and Adèle were married. They are perfectly satisfied with each other. Neither indulged in unreal, unnatural expectations regarding the other during the time preceding marriage, and there has been no disappointment. They are tranquilly happy—happy in each other's love, happy in the practice of our holy faith, without which human life is barren and human love entirely worthless as Dead Sea fruit.

Madame de Francheville shudders and refreshes herself from her *bonbonnière*, when she remembers how narrowly the heiress of a marquis escaped the plebeian appellation of "Madame Blanque"!

A MEASURELESS ILL.

"For years a measureless ill.
For years, forever to part."
—*Tennyson.*

OLD JOHN RUSSELL and I were standing on the bridge. The afternoon was lovely, though it was a January afternoon; the air had all the softness of early spring. Faintly, yet distinctly, over the silent hills and water came the strains of that saddest of sad airs, "*Ah che la morte.*" It is a hackneyed song, and brassy-throated singers have torn its passion in tatters, and the brassy-throated band at the fort had often practiced on it as they did now, and yet, sounding in this bright glimpse of spring in wintry weather, it seemed like a wail for all the sorrow in the world.

I listened until old John spoke: And so you never heard of the Berryls? I thought everybody knew the Berryls for miles around. They do say that the first Esau Berryl was an awful Tory in the Revolutionary time, and that he called young George Washington "a disloyal viper" one day; but then he was an Englishman, and I don't blame him for sticking to his country, right or wrong. You don't like that? Well, young folks have their ideas and old folks have theirs, but in *my* time young folks used to follow the ideas of their elders, and it seems to me they got along well enough.

Old Esau Berryl died, and left one son, the second

Esau. Young Jim Berryl, *his* son, was one of Mosehy's men in the war, and Esau, who liked blue coats better than gray, swore that he was no true Berryl, and so Jim never came home. But it's of Arthur, the elder, that I want to talk.

Arthur was a fine fellow—one of your tall, broadshouldered, deep-chested chaps—a real Southerner; you Yanks have nothing like it—with sharp gray eyes that could see through a bale of cotton, and a forest of brown hair on his face; yes, a regular forest, more fit for a savage than a Christian—not that Arthur Berryl was much of a Christian; but never mind that just now.

He went into the No'the'n army in '61, and came out three years later a colonel, with no right hand. A cannonball had shattered it. This one of the Berryls hadn't much use for his right hand in the way of work. He had a house over there in Virginia, and some money that his mother had left him; and, besides, everybody knows that old Esau is a mighty rich man. And the old fellow was swelled up with pride about his son, "the Colonel." I didn't blame him, though I always was a "Reb"—every man for his own way of thinking, *I* say—though it made me mad when I thought of my own poor boy, who fought might and main with Moseby, and then came home to his poor old dad with not so much as a stripe on his sleeve, but *we* had neither money nor rank to throw away.

Ah, you don't see that up No'th this time of year. Yellow jessamine, I swear!

[My old friend rested both hands on his hickory stick, and paused to gaze at a negro who was passing. The negro's arms were full of bright yellow blossoms, though the sun was not yet warm enough to break the ice on the Potomac.]

Yes, the jessamine reminds me of that day, for there was some of it growing near the grave. I don't boast much of education, *but* I have feelings, and education can't give a man feelings, can it? and that jessamine makes me feel downhearted.

And as Arthur Berryl had nothing to do, for a man with no right hand can do precious little, he went the way of all young men, and fell in love.

She *was* pretty, I tell you. Our nig, Julius—at least, he was ours before you Yanks took him—was courting her mother's Sue, and so we found out all the particulars.

Her name was Annie Desmond. Her mother was a widow with some little property. They lived over there, not far from the canal.

It was just after we were converted, my wife and I. Poor Rob, my son, would have died in prison up No'th, if the Sisters of Charity, Heaven bless 'em! had not taken his mother's place, and so when he came home, he made his mother and me believe there must be something in a religion that could turn out such women. We weren't much on religion; she was a hard-shell Baptist when she was young; I was a sort of Episcopalian, and when Rob grew up he just believed in Moseby.

Well, one fine day we three knelt at the altar-rails in Trinity Church, and we've thanked God ever since.

And so that was the way we first saw Annie Desmond. She was at Mass every Sunday. Pretty was no word for her. She wasn't tall, and she wasn't short; but when she walked up the aisle, you felt that there was a lady coming, her step was so light and firm. I'm no hand at describing looks. I only know that her face was bright and sweet, and it was gay sometimes, and reverent sometimes; but I never saw it sad until I saw it in despair.

Her cheeks were prettier than the color of my pink oleanders, and her eyes were dark, and blue, and clear. One day, when her hat blew off on the church-steps, her hair seemed a regular shower of brown and gold threads. I never spoke to her, neither did my wife; but if she had been our own daughter we couldn't have taken more interest in her.

Colonel Berryl was passing along the street that day when her hat blew away. He caught it in his one hand, and gave it to her with a low bow. I saw their eyes meet. Ah, I know the signs; I've been young; and I told mother that I wished it was Rob, instead of Arthur Berryl. And I doubly wish it had been now!

Colonel Berryl was in love, and Annie Desmond was the girl. The Berryls brag of their family, you know. We think a great deal of family down here. I know some people around here who wouldn't be anything if it wasn't for their families, but these Desmonds, though, they hadn't any family in particular. Mrs. Desmond, it is true, did say something about being descended from the kings of Ireland; but then that doesn't count for much down here; it's not like being descended from a Washington, a Carroll, or a Lee, and when I mention those names, I think of Russell, for we are an old family, I assure you, though we have worked hard in our time.

Mrs. Desmond was mighty glad to have Arthur Berryl come to her house, folks said. Annie liked him from the first; but I think her mother must have favored him, and made courtship easy for the young couple.

Esau objected to Annie. There were plenty of girls around the District and Virginia—girls of good family and all manner of creeds. He didn't see why a Berryl should marry a Catholic.

Arthur said: "Don't you mind her religion. She's been bred in it; but she's only a girl, and after a while she'll believe just as little as either of us. I love her, and I'll do anything to please her now; and, by and by, she'll do anything to please me."

Esau didn't keep up his opposition long; he believed that Arthur had the wisest head of the family.

Esau did not believe much. He was of the school of Jefferson and Tom Paine; his son swore by Huxley and Tyndall. The old man held that there was a Supreme Being; the young man was not certain whether he believed there was or not.

Old Esau disliked all forms of Christianity, but, quite naturally, he hated Catholicity more than all.

He said to Arthur: "If this girl becomes your wife you may let her go to her Popish practices if you choose; but if there are any children, and you let a priest come near them, or have any superstitious mummery over them, I'll leave every cent I own, and every acre of land, to Jim. So help me ——!" And he swore by a Name in which he did not believe.

Arthur laughed lightly. The Berryl acres were dear to his heart.

"Trust me," he said to his father.

One afternoon, just at sundown, I saw Arthur Berryl and Annie Desmond getting out of a boat after a row down the Potomac. How tenderly he helped her on shore, how proud and spirited he looked as he gave her his arm! And she looked up to him with such a light in her pretty eyes! My old heart was moved. It was a pretty sight. But the storm in the western sky made a very ugly background.

"It's all fixed," I told my wife when I went home

And, after a while, Julius came in, and told mother all that Sue said. Yes, it was all fixed.

Arthur promised Mrs. Desmond all she wanted. Bless you, he was ready to promise anything. He couldn't help it when he thought of Annie. He was too deep in love to mind what he said.

They would be married by a priest. The children should be baptized, and sent to school wherever Annie pleased, and, in time—who knows ?—he might become a Catholic.

At the last moment, it seems, Mrs. Desmond's heart misgave her. She consulted one of the Jesuits at the college, and then she cried all night; but she, like a woman, dried her tears when the marriage took place in her little parlor, and at the wedding-reception in the Berryl mansion she leant on old Esau's arm as smilingly as a darky in Christmas-time.

Time passed. Young Mrs. Berryl was 'iked by everybody. There wasn't a night that Arthur did not have her at some sor-ee or other among the bong-tong of Washington, as the papers say. He was very proud of her, and once or twice we saw him at eleven o'clock Mass with her.

"All went merry as a marriage-bell." That's out of Byron. You young folks don't read him or Moore nowadays. Perhaps it's for the best.

One day old Esau actually laughed. A little grandson had come into the world. He was a pretty baby, Sue said, like his mother, but he was quiet and still, and he never cried at all. All the life in him seemed to be in his pretty blue eyes.

Mrs. Desmond wanted to have him baptized at once. This made old Esau swear. He wouldn't hear of it.

Arthur sided with his father.

Mrs. Desmond looked at the child again. She entreated Arthur to send for a priest.

"Never shall a priest enter these doors, ma'am!" roared old Esau.

Mrs. Desmond appealed to Arthur. He said, "My father and you must settle this."

She reminded him of his promise. He only smiled. She was a hot-tempered woman, and she let her tongue have full swing. Then she left the house.

Days counted into three weeks. The child still lived, and moved a little, and cried a little. Sue said he wouldn't live; he was just like a snowflake.

Every day Mrs. Desmond visited her daughter. Every day the dispute about the child's baptism was renewed. Old Esau stood stiff; and, in this, Arthur was too much afraid of his father to yield to the pleadings of his poor wife.

Poor girl! Black Sue said it made her cry to see her young mistress' white, anxious face.

Mrs. Desmond made her usual visit, and looked at the baby. Sue said that Annie was lying back in an armchair, but she opened her eyes and watched her mother as if her life depended on it. Esau dropped his newspaper and watched her.

She saw something in her mother's face that frightened her.

Mrs. Desmond stood near the toilet-table with the child in her arms. Sue was in the doorway. She had left a pitcher of water on the table, and was going out, when Annie's voice, like the moan of the wind, made her turn

"*He is dying!*"

They called the baby by no name yet.

The young wife knelt at her husband's feet, and clasped his knees.

"Have mercy, Arthur!" she said.

Her face turned as white as a dead woman's at the look in his face. She fell back with a dull thud.

Esau, Arthur, and Sue went to her instantly.

Mrs. Desmond stood alone with the child near the toilet-table. The others had their backs to her. Whether she baptized the child or not, or whether it was already dead when she took it in her arms, she never told.

When Annie recovered her senses, the baby lay cold and still—dead.

The funeral was a grand one for such a little thing. It was a cold, damp day, but my wife and I went with the rest over to the Episcopal Cemetery, where the Berryls have a family vault.

Annie stood near the grave. I could not see her face for her thick black veil, but I could hear her sobs.

Mrs. Desmond stood next to her, stern and severe. On the other side was Arthur, as stern, but seemingly like a man in pain. Esau wasn't there.

They waited at the grave until nearly everybody had gone. My wife and I drew off a short distance and waited too. Women are so curious.

"*Come!*" said Mrs. Desmond, sternly, and she took her daughter's arm.

Annie raised her veil. Her face seemed frozen into despair. My wife almost screamed at sight of it. Annie gave her hand to Arthur. He took it in his.

"Good-bye!" she whispered.

"Good-bye!" he said, turning away.

And so they parted.

. . ..

John Russell looked thoughtfully down at the water, and a cold breath of east wind blew through his iron-gray whiskers, telling us that our glimpse of spring was past. The sky was gray with evening. A spray of jessamine, crushed and broken, lay at my feet. The band at Fort Whipple again began the music. This time it was a merry chanson from the "Grande Duchesse"; but the words it suggested chimed in with my mood and the sadness around me—

> "De n'avoir plus jamais sur terre,
> Un moment de felicité."

JOHN NELSON'S MARRIAGE.

"In general opinion, marriage in real life, as in a comedy, is the end. On the contrary, it is really the beginning."
—MADAME SWETCHINE.

JOHN NELSON was neither as vain as Lamartine nor as poetical as that sentimental Frenchman, but he met his Graziella in Italy, and her name was Tita Malatesta. If questioned about a certain tragedy which took place long ago, and in which two of her name were concerned, she would have smiled, for she had pretty teeth, saying, "I know not of it, Signor." And if you had taken your Dante, as John Nelson did, and read to her the story of Francesca and Paolo, she would have said, "It served them right," feeling that Francesca was a great fool not to be satisfied with Lanciotto, who gave her a palace and plenty to eat and drink. Tita was not sentimental. In most things she was very matter-of-fact; after she became John Nelson's wife it was odd to hear his American friends at Sorrento call her Mrs. Nelson, while Tita still wore her picturesque peasant dress, and her answer, with smiling lips, "Si, Signore; si, Signorita."

His marriage was very imprudent, Nelson's friends said; but his friends were few and far between, and their opinion was not expressed strongly, for John Nelson was a bachelor of thirty years' standing when he married;

and if he had not a right to do as he pleased, who had?
The relatives of his, at home in New York, were so distant that blood in his and their case was not much thicker than water; so he did not consult them. In Italy he was considered rich; at home he would have been marked in mammas' list of " eligibles " " well to do."

A note from his acquaintance, the Viscomte de Vaudrier, who, having spent four years in Washington, was justly regarded by his Parisian friends as a master of the English tongue, both in speaking and writing, will give you an idea of the light in which his friends regarded his launch into matrimony.

"DEAR FRIEND: You have no doubt great surprise for receive a letter of me, but i may make it only a billet, for my aunt, which is a priest, Monsieur l'Abbé de Vaudrier, have come to arrive in Paris. He have come last night, and it must that i give to him great attention, which is a plage, but right that it should be. You know how well I speak the English in Vashington, but I have much improve now, for i speak her all the day to my brother, the Marquis, which I teach, and even to my horses, of which i say, 'Go lon'—skedaddell!' And they go lon'.

"I have heard to speak of your marriage. She is a little Italian *paysanne*, is it not? As you go not great deal among the society, it is not great deal importance that she may be *paysanne au bout de ses ongles;* and as you Americans have no families aristocratics, it is not bad for you, if that she may be jolie and also good wife. I put my good wishes at the feet of Madame; i kiss her hands. My broter also have surprise of your marriage. He say you are not like the spirituel Lamartine, but you have *les défauts de vos qualités.* My aunt, M. l'Abbé, you send his blessing, and have great pleasure you have marry one of our Faith.

"Yours, ALPHONSE DE VAUDRIER."

Like De Vaudrier, all his friends were resigned. He received one indignant letter. It was from his cousin's widow, and it was stormily indignant. His cousin had been a Methodist minister,—a herald of wrath and hellfire among his brethren,—a man who lovingly read the inspired words of Eugene Laurence in *Harper's Weekly,*—who tried to believe that convent schools were ways to "the pit," who sternly forbade his daughter to wear *cardinal* ribbon ("that symbol of antichrist!") In a phrase, he was a collection of fossilized prejudices, preserved in malice and uncharitableness. During his life his wife had been a mild little woman, who might, had somebody proposed to convert the Pope, have answered, like the woman in Thackeray's novel, "Poor Pope, what has he done?" After her husband's death his spirit seemed to have taken possession of her. She was a living proof of the doctrine of metempsychosis. In her letter to John Nelson she implored him "to break the vile nets of the scarlet woman, to be another Samson, and pull down the temple of the idolaters"—

"She means St. Peter's," thought John.

"To put the Bible in the hands of his wife (she inclosed one for the poor deluded woman); to let her drink of the pure stream"—

John laughed, as he imagined Tita struggling with the pure stream of King James' English.

"To part from the Jesuit in disguise (Mrs. Greenough firmly believed that Tita was a Jesuit in disguise) if she refused to hear the truth."

"Are you a Jesuit, Tita?" asked John.

"What do you mean, G'ovanni? The good Jesuits are priests."

Tita looked at him in the most matter-of-fact way, and then a smile, a reflection of his, curved her lips, and she shook her head, suspecting that G'ovanni was enjoying one of those things which she never tried to understand —a joke.

The days were very pleasant at Sorrento. Sicilian muses, who since the days of Theocritus, live only as nightingales among the orange-groves of Sorrento, kept night and day awake with shakes and roulades sweeter than were ever heard at La Scala. The days passed in dreamy *dolce far niente*. Tita divided her time between her mother's farm and her husband's villa. Sunshine, bluest of blue skies and waters, even when set to the music of a nightingale, do not make life; and John Nelson longed for the less tender breezes of his own country.

Tita was good, loving, simple as a child; but there were many things that she could not understand in her husband's sayings and doings; and to John Nelson the worst of this was that she would not try to understand. She was willing to take too much on faith.

"Dear G'ovanni," she said to herself, "he knows no better; he means well; he has lived so long among the heretics."

Tita's ideas of geography were vague. She knew the world was round, and her knowledge was founded on as good ground as the knowledge of most of us—she had been told so. China and our glorious country were to her the same, and, though her state of mind may seem incomprehensible, she would have, with the same degree of distaste, gone to one as the other. Tita could read, but she never did. John had read to her *I promessi Sposi*. The novel interested her.

"Is it true?" she asked, when he had half finished it.

"No," he answered; "Manzoni made it out of his head."

"I do not like lies," said Tita, and would hear no more.

In matters of religion Tita was an authority. She could confound John's elaborate arguments in the fewest words. She knew all the Bible stories by heart, and as she had received them orally, they were, coming from her lips, like pale-tinted marble under ruby-colored glass. The legends of the saints were her history. In Italy she was playful, petulant sometimes, matter-of-fact, having a childish love for John—a love which he, after he had been married a few months, compared to a shallow stream. "It may run on forever, but it will never grow deeper. Tita will never be a woman." There was bitterness in the thought.

John Nelson had become a Catholic more from love of Tita than love of truth; but he believed in a lazy kind of a way. He went to Mass with Tita, yet heaven could scarcely expect from him, a refined American who had lived in Boston, the sort of cultus it got from Italian peasants. He did not own this thought, but nevertheless it was in his mind. He patronized Providence, and felt that he had made a sacrifice when the *contadini* pointed him out as one of the *forestieri* among Padre Lenceno's parishioners.

Tita did not want to leave lovely Sorrento. It was her home. Her mother did not urge her to stay. "Women must obey their husbands," said that matron; and married daughters did not fill much space in a mother's heart which already held nine other living Malatestas. "Wives must obey their husbands," said Padre Lenceno, too, so Tita dried her tears, and hid her face on John's shoulder as the beauty of Sorrento faded away.

Hotel life in New York, John thought, would not suit either him or his wife; and, to set Tita up as a housekeeper, inexperienced as she was in the ways of American life, was an idea that he could not entertain. It was not that John felt the want of near relations, sensible uncles and anxious aunts. There were the Greenoughs. He thought about them. Mrs. Greenough was zealously intemperate only in words, and, happily, Tita could not understand them; and his cousins, Vashti and Esther, as he remembered them, were mere girls. Besides, the Greenoughs were not rich, and two boarders who could pay well would doubtless help them.

Tita shivered in the May breezes that swept into New York from the sea. John left her near the register in the warmest room of the hotel, and started to interview the Greenoughs.

"John Nelson!—*c'est moi, mon ami!*"

"De Vaudrier!"

Nelson grasped the hand of a young man who had just dropped out of a car. It was his friend De Vaudrier, a stripling of about twenty-two, tall, slim, dark-eyed, with a flush on his cheeks and a slight moustache on his lip. De Vaudrier dropped his travelling-bag, and turned about to embrace John in the Continental fashion, when he remembered that he was not at home.

"I have overjoyed to view you," he said, his face lit up with a cordial smile; "I am come to arrive. I 'ave no 'otel yet. Where are you resting?"

"Stay with me," said John; "I will arrange everything for you."

De Vaudrier left his portmanteau at the hotel, and accompanied his friend.

"I am travel for instruction; but, *mon ami*, let us speak French. It is singular, I love best the English at home, and the French here. Hast thou brought thy wife?"

He was on his native heath, and he began to "tutoyer" John with much volubility.

The Greenoughs were at home. They lived in a cottage in the suburbs. The cottage had two gothic towers, a miniature carriage-house, an ornate balcony, and bay-windows in several unexpected places. It was built of brick, but coated with an imposing cement. Some people thought it was of stone. The house was too large for her family, Mrs. Greenough said; but, though she would not think of entertaining ordinary boarders, John, his wife, and friend might come. She could not refuse to receive her own flesh and blood. She looked like a martyr as she said this, but inwardly she rejoiced that now the taxes would not seem such an important item, and the girls might have new dresses, in time for the next anniversary at the Bethel Church. The matter was settled.

Mrs. Greenough was small, delicate, and serious-looking. In her solemn suit of sable, she looked like one who was always ready to cry out in her thin, artificial voice, "Woe! woe!" to the world.

The girls, Vashti and Esther, were different. One could see that by the books on the parlor-table. There were Spencer's *Sociology*, Matthew Arnold, and other new lights for Vashti; Rossetti, William Morris, and even Swinburne for Esther. They were both "advanced";

but they went to services, and Mrs. Greenough was too intensely interested in the heathen without her gates to think of the heathens within.

The girls were twins; they were much alike in appearance; both blondes, and rather pretty. Vashti was the taller, and she adopted the Greek style. Esther being shorter and plumper, was mediæval. They had "views" of their own on everything in, above, and beneath the sun.

"Never did your papa dream," said Mrs. Greenough, solemnly and sadly, "that necessity would force me to take Papists under his roof! What sacrifices we must make for the cause!"

"What cause?" demanded Esther.

"Mamma intends to convert them."

"I do," responded Mrs. Greenough.

And she did, especially the young Vicomte. What a sweetly pious account of the dear young man's deliverance from error she could write in the *Evangelical Times!* How envious the present Bethel clergyman's wife would be, as she entered anniversary meetings on the arm of her converted member of the French aristocracy! It was a consoling thought.

"For that I can bear it all."

"Even a fish-dinner on Fridays?"

"And Jesuits hiding in all the closets, as they do in Catharine Sinclair's novels," laughed Vashti.

"Never," said Mrs. Greenough, gravely; "to that I will *never* submit. I defy them!" And she folded her arms, and looked serenely before her.

"We will have a real Vicomte here, anyhow, and give *musicales* every Thursday. How those snobbish Glover girls will feel it! They are always talking of an Italian baron they discovered at the Exposition. 'Permit me, Miss Glover, to present Monsieur le Vicomte de Vaudrier,' I will say, carelessly, and Julia Glover will attack him in French, which he will not understand, and which I will interpret for him!" cried Esther, turning rapidly on the piano-stool, and began Mendelssohn's Wedding March.

"No," said Vashti, contradicting her sister's music, "I will be Madame la Vicomtesse!"

To decide the matter the girls tossed an antique medal, and Esther won De Vaudrier.

De Vaudrier was not so easily won. He was shy of these young ladies when he came to dwell beneath their mother's roof. Their manners rather frightened him. There was not the slightest impropriety in their "style" according to our American canons, but De Vaudrier did not judge young ladies by our American canons. He had lived in Paris, and yet he was not spoiled. He was manly, yet good and ingenuous to an extent which we rarely find among American young men, but which, in France, is often found in those families whose sons are not corrupted by the detestable government lyceums.

Esther's French, like that of the dainty man in Chaucer, was not of Paris, and her first attempt at æsthetical conversation was a failure. He knew nothing of art or literature, but much about vine-growing in his department in Burgundy, and other useful things. Esther struck him with Ruskin's *Stones of Venice*, and thought she had made a hit; De Vaudrier was certainly stunned.

"I know not Rutskin," he said.

She asked him if he had read Baudelaire's *Fleurs du Mal*, which she had heard was extremely æsthetic.

De Vaudrier opened his eyes in horror. *Ces demoi-*

selles Americaines were too much for his understanding. He took refuge with Tita. That silent little woman was much more congenial company than this Miss who talked boldly of everything.

Tita was alone on a rustic seat in the porch. The pale blue of the sky was fading to evening's gray. Tita looked very uncomfortable in a black silk dress. She seemed afraid to move her arms, and her head was kept stationary by an uncomfortable ruffle around her neck. How she longed for the freedom of her peasant costume!

"She looks like the kitten when I tie her up in my handkerchief," thought Esther.

She certainly did not offer a pleasing contrast to Vashti, who, in a faultless costume of gray and blue, with a fillet of violets in her golden hair, walked up and down the garden-walk with John Nelson by her side. He, fresh from a land of brunettes, thought he had never seen a woman so beautiful.

Tita watched them, and felt like crying. She felt and looked lonely. De Vaudrier, with his pleasant smile, brought a checker-table out, and offered to teach her the game. Youth is elastic; and Tita was soon deep in a game of checkers. De Vaudrier laughed at her blunders in the game, and she laughed at his broken Italian. Mrs. Greenough, anxious to improve each shining hour, drew her chair near them. In one of the pauses of the game, she said something about Popish superstition and Jesuitical wickedness ("I was merely stating facts," she afterward said, "without the slightest intention of offending the young man.")

"Madame," answered De Vaudrier, with severe politeness, "I am great surprise that an old hag like you, with two feet in the tomb-stone, should speak thus of our holy faith."

Mrs. Greenough was speechless. "Old hag!" It is true De Vaudrier thought that hag was a synonym for woman; but Mrs. Greenough did not know that. She gave him up; she felt that he would be damned, though, as she said, she tried to conceal the horrible fact from herself.

Vashti Greenough had received John Nelson with great cordiality. He was an old flame of hers, she declared, adding, "and, as we are cousins, of course your wife can't be jealous." It pleased John to hear her talk in this way, which she did with charming archness and candor. She talked so well. She could tell him everything that had occurred in the dramatic, literary, and musical worlds, since he had buried himself in Italy. The very first night she played his favorite nocturne, gave a crisp criticism of *Daniel Deronda* for his benefit, and recited a little idyl, which he had written for one of the magazines. John Nelson turned the leaves of her music-book with a warm consciousness of being appreciated—a delicate kind of flattery liable to turn any man's head.

De Vaudrier went to his room early. Tita sat outside the circle of lamplight, with an open album in her lap, gazing at the group near the piano. Her face was troubled. She seemed to be trying to understand. This was new to her; Giovanni had never before neglected her. She only smiled when he praised his beautiful cousin.

After this the days were full of weariness for Tita. Vashti and Esther tried to be friendly, but, as they could not speak her language, their efforts amounted to very little. Mrs. Greenough avoided her. John was always engaged. Vashti had discovered some new ferns, would he not come down to the green-house and look at them? Vashti wanted to go to the picture-galleries; Vashti liked the opera; Vashti enjoyed an occasional drive, and John was always her cavalier; for pictures, music, and drives, Tita cared only when Giovanni was with her alone. She would not divide him with any one; and so she sat in a sunny corner of the parlor, and thought De Vaudrier saw this with pain, and he tried hard to amuse Tita. These two grew friendly, and Tita sometimes forgot her troubles for a moment when he spoke.

Prejudice is a upas-tree that poisons all the air around it. Mrs. Greenough was prejudiced against De Vaudrier. She believed good could come as naturally from him as figs from thistles.

John Nelson ceased even to go to Mass with Tita. The girls, anxious to show off their handsome cousin at the Bethel, persuaded him to go to morning service.

"Tita mia," he said, playfully, "you will do the praying for us both, while I watch the pretty girls!"

If he could only have known the pain in her heart! Every Sunday De Vaudrier, with honest indignation in his mind, escorted Tita to High Mass.

One evening, when sunset was burning the west with crimson, purple, and gold, Tita sat on the porch as usual, sad, silent, lonely. Grief had made her a woman. She was no longer a child. Up the path came John. He seemed about to come to her, when from the arbor stepped Vashti. She stopped him, and pinned a rosebud on his coat. Tita grasped her heart.

"Oh, because I am dumb, do they think I can not see?"

John Nelson's eyes met Vashti's. A regret entered his mind. Why had he tied himself to a little Italian child?

The tragedy of Francesca di Rimini, which John, in the pleasant days, had read to her out of Dante, floated across her mind. "If I could kill them! if I could kill them!" she thought, and the burning pain in her heart seemed to burn her breast. "*O Santa Maria, ora pro me! ora pro me!*" And she fled to her room to weep and pray passionately.

Neither De Vaudrier nor Tita were at breakfast the next morning. De Vaudrier was often absent, but Tita—

"Tita is gone," said Esther. "Mary saw her pass the kitchen door, with a small bundle, last night. She thought nothing of it; Tita was always giving things to the poor."

"Good works are vain," began her mother.

"One moment, mamma; but when she found that Tita had not slept in her room, she came to me. Here is a note she left for John."

John, about to leave the dining-room, had paused in the door, and Esther entered by the other. He turned back, and took the note. In large, tremblingly-traced letters, he read, "Addio, Giovanni."

"And De Vaudrier has gone, too," said Mrs. Greenough, significantly.

John put his hands to his head. His face took a purplish hue.

"Mr. De Vaudrier is in the garden," said Esther, softly. Mrs. Greenough blushed, and, it is hoped, profited by the rebuke.

Detectives, telegraph, all the modern means for detecting fugitives were set to work. No Tita. Three weeks passed, and still she was not found. About this time John Nelson fell sick. "A cold, an overtaxed mind, headache, pain in the back," the Greenoughs said at first

"Small-pox," the doctor said at last.

Exeunt the Greenoughs and De Vaudrier over to those snobbish Glovers. John Nelson, the small-pox, and Mary, who had had the disease, remained; but the small-pox and Nelson were often left alone, for Mary, being unwatched, and "having a free foot," except in the morning, when the doctor came, went into town, to pay a number of calls she owed to certain nursemaids and cooks.

On one of these afternoons out, John Nelson awoke from a delirious dream, thirsting and parched with fever.

"Giovanni!"

Was it an echo from his dream?

A cool cheek was pressed close to his hot one.

"Tita, Tita!" he cried in horror, "leave me. My disease will kill you; it is killing me."

"Then I will die with you, Giovanni."

She would not go. He raved and entreated. She remained. Late in August, he arose, pale, thin, scarred; but Tita was happy. He was hers again.

"My heart was breaking," Tita said; "I went into the city, and found some of my country people. They gave me bread, and I made clothes for the little ones; but I could not stay away from you, Giovanni. I came, and you are mine again. I was wrong to go; Padre Lenceno would have said: 'Wait and pray'—but you are mine again."

"Yes, God's and yours," he says, devoutly.

"Thank God, whom I forsook, and his Blessed Mother!"

The Greenoughs returned to their house. De Vaudrier went to Brazil, with a kind adieu from his *bel enfant*, as he called Tita. John Nelson and his wife, happier than they ever were, are now on their way to Rome.

AMONG THE "OLIVE BRANCHES."—THE STORY OF A NEW YORK BOY.

I.

CHRISTMAS EVE.

WASHINGTON Square is like a huge, white sheet spread among the houses that enclose it on every side. Its benches, frost-bitten grass, and wide paths are all lost in the whiteness which is becoming gray as the twilight falls. The snow ceased to come down so recently that there are no tracks on its smooth expanse, except the prints of the feet of a little Scotch terrier which is making haste slowly on three legs—four being difficult to manage in the soft, clinging substance.

After a while, when twilight deepens, the crowd of cheerful people—it is Christmas Eve—returning from work will obliterate the little dog's prints and make a hard, firm path. It is somewhat too early for that. A heavily-laden man or woman, with the legs of the fowl of the season sticking out from among the greens under a high-poised basket-lid, or with one of those delightfully mysterious bundles that everybody carries at Christmas, struggles along against a high wind which the snow seems to deaden and make noiseless.

Hugh Desmond, a small boy with a broom, stands at one of the entrances of the square. He is waiting for somebody. He shivers in the wind and wraps his ragged scarf more closely around his neck.

Waiting there, Hugh thinks he discovers the contents of packages with which several passers-by are sailing against the wind. Hugh *knows* that this bundle holds a boy's skates; that, a girl's doll; he feels that the tall, thin man carries almonds and raisins, because he sees celery-tips sticking out of brown paper; and that the little woman—he knows her: she keeps the "charcuterie" in South Fifth avenue—has many boxes of candy for her eight children in that square package under her shawl. She has plenty of sausages, blood puddings, and strange French dishes in her shop. She does not need to buy anything solid to eat. She *must* have sweetmeats. He begins to smack his lips, but finding that process unsatisfactory to an empty stomach, cuts a double-shuffle, and whistles three times by way of distracting his attention from the mysterious packages.

If Kitty only had a doll, and Mary a new frock! and mother—oh, so many things! As for himself, turkey and cranberry sauce and a shovel would content *him*. Just now Hugh wants a shovel more than anything in the world. With it, if the snow holds up, he could perhaps dig out a turkey before Christmas morning. He has a broom, but it is half-worn, almost a stump. During the last snow he had been in partnership with Jules Roussel, the French shoemaker's boy, at the end of the alley; but Hugh's broom became so stumpy that the thrifty Jules had cast him out of the firm and taken in his own little brother, Auguste, whose father had generously donated a new broom which swept very clean. Poor Hugh could do little with his stump. A broom, without spade or shovel, is a poor thing in a heavy snow. He could not earn a nickel a day with it.

Jules, a ruddy-cheeked lad, warmly clad in a woolen

jacket, and boots that seem to reach almost to his neck, comes running around the corner:

"Le voilà
Nicolas!"

He sings with an Alsatian twang. Auguste, a fat little boy, puffs after him, flourishing the new broom in one hand and jingling two quarters in the other. They stop and perform a war dance in front of Hugh. "Aggravating" him, Hugh thinks.

"Your broom's no good," says Jules. "Why don't you go and sell papers?"

Hugh has no capital, and will not beg. But he would not let Jules and the greedy little Auguste know his poverty for the world—or a shovel.

"Sell papers?" returns Hugh, contemptuously. "Not much. There's nothing in it!"

Jules is astonished at the lofty tone of his former partner.

"It's better than nothing," says Auguste, frankly.

"You just hold your tongue, young fellow," Hugh answers, with a grand air. "The trade is broken up. Too much competition. Girl-labor has ruined the business."

Not caring to consider the question, Jules and Auguste disappear.

The little Scotch terrier has at last succeeded in reaching the entrance. "Hello, Chip!" says Hugh; "you *would* take a short cut, would you?"

Chip wags his tail with an air of relief and sniffs at Hugh inquiringly.

"Home," says Hugh, with a sigh, and they start down South Fifth avenue. *Home!* Well may poor Hugh sigh as he trudges along, feeling the cold snow against his foot in the rift between the upper and sole of his shoe. Home! Hugh knows that he will find his poor mother, sick, weak, working hard at the washtub, and Mary and Kitty trying to keep warm behind the curtain which divides their sleeping-corner from the rest of the room. He reads the signs in the fading light as he goes, just to keep his mind off home. If "Madame Tricot," blanchisseuse, would only rush out of her cellar and put a brand-new shovel into his hand! If "Mademoiselle Triquette," maker of artificial flowers, would only come from behind the sprays of roses in the window and say, "Here, boy, I want my pavement cleaned by a boy with a stumpy broom; no new brooms for *me!*" But neither Madame Tricot nor Mademoiselle Triquette does either of these things, though it is Christmas Eve, when people may be expected to do almost anything. If that man in the ulster, who is entering the French circulating library, would say, "Here, sonny, just let me lend you fifty cents until you get a shovel"; if Mr. Byrne, the landlord, would suddenly turn a corner and tell Hugh that the rent is paid. If—Hugh pauses, waiting for the landlord to appear. But Mr. Byrne does not come.

"I'm a fool!" says Hugh, looking up and down the street, with still a gleam of hope in his bright blue eyes, which are just visible above his woolen scarf. But the man in the ulster goes into the library and leaves no hope behind. Hugh thrusts his red hands into his empty pockets. He can not go home.

A German band in the cross-street strikes up. It is the "Adeste Fideles" they play—

"Let's hasten to adore Him, our God and our King."

Hugh's heart leaps. Yes, it is really Christmas Eve!

Last year his father was alive, and he sang that, with the other children, at the Christmas Mass. And the happy day that followed!—gifts for everybody—and mother, as she helped them all to the turkey, looking so fresh and rosy! But now! Tears, very unusual in brave little Hugh's eyes, blinded him. He can not go home empty-handed. Kitty and Mary will expect something. He can not meet their eager looks. Kitty has already spread the supper of milk and porridge, he knows. They are all waiting for him. He can not go home.

Nobody seems to want a boy to do anything. Everybody is carrying his own packages to-night. There is the ever-open church where mother, Hugh, and his sisters hear Mass every Sunday, and, sometimes, when mother's work is slack, other mornings. Hugh expects to make his First Communion there soon.

Weary, heart-sick, the boy crouches for a while in the doorway before he enters. He wants to get the tears out of his eyes first.

"Here, little boy," a voice says; and a coin drops into Hugh's hand. It feels like a fifty-cent piece. "I'm not a beggar!" he begins to say; but the woman has descended the steps. Besides, he reflects instantaneously, "She might take back the money, if I told her that."

Hugh is very thankful. He is only a ragged, alert-looking boy, such as you may meet on almost every corner of down-town New York streets, but a psalm of thanksgiving goes up from his heart as he bows his head before the Presence in the dark church. There are other boys there, kneeling near the confessionals, some of them as ragged as himself; and in their hearts, as in his, the wonderful, the incomprehensible, gift of Divine faith and love is raising their thoughts high above earth.

AMONG THE "OLIVE BRANCHES." 221

Hugh leaves the dim church, which, to-morrow, for him, for all the poor, will blaze with light and resound with the "Gloria in Excelsis."

Christmas-trees and many gifts may come from human love to some happy children; the Church's celebration and gift are for all! Something like this passes through Hugh's mind. Out of the church, he darts into a side-street.

In the fourth story of a tenement-house in that street, Hugh's mother has a small room and a large closet. The tenement is lit up when Hugh reaches it. There is a lamp behind every curtain in the lower stories; in the upper ones, where there are no curtains, the lamps are visible. There is no light in Mrs. Desmond's room. Hugh thinks that the light may have been put into the closet, which is his sleeping-place. He will give them all a hot supper. Sausage?—He runs back to the "charcuterie," and, after some bargaining with madame, who is generous, but not too generous at Christmas, secures a wonderfully cheap blood-pudding. The greedy Auguste is there, investing lavishly in pig's feet. Having the serene consciousness of better days, Hugh only calls the French boy a "galoot" once when Auguste makes a face at him. At ordinary times Auguste might not have escaped so easily.

Back again to the tenement-house goes Hugh. That blood-pudding under his arm has given an air of festivity to the scene which was late so gloomy. He snatches a tin horn out of a passing boy's hand and blows a blast in a friendly and jubilant manner, and then discreetly dodges the boy's fist.

On the stoop of the tenement-house several women and a man are standing gazing at some dark objects on the sidewalk. Another woman in the hall is shading a kerosene lamp with her hand.

"It's a shame and a disgrace on such a night!"

"An' sure the devil, when he has his own, will have Paddy Byrne."

"There wasn't a more decent woman in the house than this same woman."

"Ach!" Hugh hears the man say—it is Schimmel, the tailor up-stairs, who is generally "on a spree"—"if money vos not so scarce I would have paid the rent myself."

Hugh observes that a very usual thing has happened. Somebody has been "turned out." This is a monthly occurrence. A bed, a table, a stove, some chairs, and a small bundle in a quilt, lie in the snow.

"And faith here is little Hughey himself, poor boy! Come up-stairs till I give you a drop of hot tea."

Hugh's heart stands still. He has seen this often; but he has never imagined that—

"Where's mother?" he asks, as the light flashes upon his frightened eyes.

"It's the landlord's doings—more shame to him this night; and your mother and the children have gone down to Mrs. Donovan's, the lady she used to work for."

"Where?"

They are not sure. Bleecker street, somewhere. Mrs. Desmond had been almost carried to the car. She bade them tell Hughey, but everything had gotten mixed up.

"Come up-stairs and have something warm."

"Ja," says Schimmel; "unt something to eat."

Hugh can scarcely answer them. He treads by chance on a book in the snow. He picks it up. It has fallen from the bundle in the quilt. He knows that it is his mother's little prayer-book.

"Take care of these things, Schimmel," he says, "until I find mother. They are all we have, you know."

"Ach, Himmel!" says the worthy tailor; "I wish I could do more."

Hugh goes down the street. He has dropped the blood-pudding; and when Charlie Schimmel picks it up and gives it to him, he tells him to keep it, which is a lucky thing for Charlie Schimmel, who, otherwise, would have had no supper.

"My heart aches for the boy," says one of the women on the stoop; "he seems to have lost heart entirely."

"As for Paddy Byrne," returns her neighbor, a wrinkled old woman, with a clean, wide cap-frill, "I LEAVE HIM TO GOD."

It was the worst thing this old woman could say: so she said it. But the man so blessed, or cursed, is a respectable person, having a front pew in church—indeed, he sometimes takes up collections for the poor—and he never loses an opportunity of protesting against the evils of foreign landlordism. He is very patriotic, as he intends to run for the office of alderman in his ward. Mrs. Desmond's rent was much overdue, and Hugh can not vote. Mr. Byrne never "turns out" a voter.

Hugh knows the city well. In earlier days he sold his papers in nearly every locality. He does not find Mrs. Donovan's house. Toward midnight he has become very cold, very hungry, and desperate. He is afraid of being arrested as a vagrant; so he creeps into a packing-box when he sees a "cop" coming. But the "cop," to use his own phraseology, "nabs" him. All that night—all that night, the happiest night of the whole year for so many boys and girls—poor Hugh sobs, prays, and moans. If he only knew where mother and the children are!

The cell is warm, and the policeman, though rough, is not unkind. The Christmas morning, with its clamor of bells and horns, seems like a horrible dream. No Mass, no gifts, no happiness this year. The day is dreary, and after a ceremony in a magistrate's office, Hugh finds himself a vagrant, adjudged to the possession of the Little Bethel, an evangelical establishment, the managers of which, like the awful old giant in the fairy tale, smell the blood of little Roman Catholic Irish boys afar off, and take good care of them.

II.

THE LITTLE BETHEL.

The Little Bethel is managed in a way that is said to be "truly evangelical and characterized by a thoroughly Christian spirit of economy and industry. Verily," said the directors, in their ninth annual report, "the institution may be termed a little Heaven on earth, where the fortunate young orphans snatched as brands from the burning form a sweet cluster of celestial olive branches. Here the children of Romish parents have their eyes opened to the light, and learn from the shining example of the Rev. Virgil C. Gregg and his estimable lady— who, however, make no violent attempts at proselytizing —that the Popish superstition in which they were bred is a snare and a delusion of the evil one. 'Give me a Bible,' these poor, blinded children often say, thirsting for the water of life. Owing to the demand for Bibles and the expense of opening the eyes of Chin-Chin, a young Chinese half-orphan, and his father, the Commit tee recommend that an extra appropriation be made, that the Rev. Virgil C. Gregg and his estimable lady may be encouraged in their commendable work."

Hugh does not ask for a Bible when he is admitted into the little Bethel. He tells the Rev. Virgil C. Gregg that his mother is with Mrs. Donovan, in Bleecker street; but that estimable gentleman pays little heed to him. He does not even offer him a Bible. He sets Hugh to scrubbing the floor of the Little Bethel dining-room, and tells the boy to pray that his eyes may be made clear. Hugh notices that all the other "olive branches" have sore eyes, and he innocently prays that *his* eyes may not be made sore.

Accustomed to life in the streets—in the streets, but, happily, through the influence of a good mother, not of them—Hugh is inclined to laugh at the discipline of the Little Bethel. He feels sure that he can easily escape. There must be a back gate somewhere; or a fence. It is unfortunately true that he imitates the nocturnal raging of cats during the singing of "I want to be an Angel," after the evening repast of mush; and that when a bench tips over during Mrs. Virgil C. Gregg's warbling of "Almost Persuaded," Hugh is not unjustly accused of being the motor.

"You are a Romish child," says Mrs. Virgil C. Gregg, after she has rapped Hugh once on the head with a Moody and Sankey hymn-book; "I fear that the spirit of Anti-Christ is strong within you."

"No, ma'am," answers Hugh, with real simplicity; "I was born in New York, and my father came from Cork."

Mrs. Virgil C. Gregg evidently looks on this plain, unvarnished statement as a piece of ribaldry, and she remarks to the Rev. Virgil C. Gregg that this wicked boy had better be deprived of his allowance of molasses every day for a month. It is such a delightful novelty for Hugh to have an assured expectation of regular meals, that he can not help looking on his sojourn in the Little Bethel as an amusing but brief episode. Being a boy, he soon regains his good spirits, though he worries occasionally about Chip, who, like most New York dogs, knew a policeman when he saw him, and decamped. His mother will find him out, Hugh is sure; but how will Chip find him out?

At first Hugh has more freedom than the other little "olive branches." He is given plenty of hard work to do, but none that takes him even within sight of the back gate. The Rev. Virgil, a Connecticut man of great penetration, is aware that the Romish child who does not at once ask for a Bible is not to be trusted. In a week or so Hugh feels the "screws."

He has been told several times not to bless himself when the Rev. Virgil says grace, as Mrs. Virgil pours the blue milk over the saucer of porridge, of which the "olive branches" partake voraciously. But Hugh's mother has told him never to be ashamed of the sign of the cross. By this time Hugh has learned certain controversial terms much in use among the "olive branches." He was well drilled in his Catechism, but up to this time he has not made much application of its phraseology in every-day life. When Barney Ruark, one of the converted little Papists, remarks, in the hearing of the Rev. Virgil, that Hugh is a child of Belial, he can not retort in his usual language. "Galoot" seems utterly inadequate; so, when Barney is obediently carrying Mrs. Virgil's breakfast up-stairs and trying to drink her cream, and Hugh is engaged in sweeping the steps, he trips the pious convert in a style much practiced in South Fifth avenue, and Barney drops the tray. Hence there are tears. Barney has a black eye and Hugh many blue marks from the Rev. Virgil's thong.

Hugh, however, continues to make the sign of the cross.

"I must make an example of you, Desmond," cries the Rev. Virgil, taking off his spectacles and shortening Hugh's supply of porridge. "You must quit that Popish superstition."

Hugh does not dare to answer. Wishing to improve the occasion, the Rev. Virgil continues:

"What is Popish superstition, my children?"

Several hands go up.

"Ruark!"

Little Barney scratches his red head for an instant and then answers:

"An idolatrous abomination practiced by the followers of the Pope."

"That will do. Oh," says the Rev. Virgil, wiping his spectacles, as if they had been moved to tears, "what wisdom out of the mouths of babes and sucklings! Miranda, how blest are we to be humble instruments!"

Miranda is counting the spoonfuls of molasses she is putting in a sick boy's coffee; she merely groans in a general way.

"So no more Popish signs, Desmond."

Hugh raises his hand:

"Is the Pope Anti-Christ, sir?"

"Most certainly," with emphasis.

"Then the cross must be Anti-Christ, if it's Popish."

The Rev. Virgil looks at Hugh's face and becomes as

red as a turkey-gobbler. He says nothing; and the other "olive branches" fear there is something in the wind that may lead to a confiscation of the remains of their porridge, which is an evil ever present in their minds. Only one little boy, half-converted, who has been induced to ask for a Bible after some days of starvation, murmurs irrelevantly, "That's so!"

Hugh gets a "dressing," as the "olive branches" call the Rev. Virgil's hardest and longest application of the thong, and is kept on bread and water for a week. The little half-convert is similarly treated until he asks for his Bible.

Frequent "dressings" and sieges of starvation break Hugh's spirit somewhat. He no longer makes the sign of the cross; he assists at the services in the chapel without a murmur. But he hugs the little prayer-book close every night and keeps it safe in various hiding-places about himself, which even very small street-boys learn to contrive. Once Mrs. Virgil sees him kneeling, crying and praying at the side of his cot in the cold dormitory. She takes it for a sign of "a new heart," and tells the Rev. Virgil. If Hugh could imitate the hypocrisy of the miserable little Ruark, his name would soon have led all the rest among the "olive branches." There are fifty of them—twenty girls, who work hard and well earn their porridge, with beef on Wednesdays and pork on Fridays and Sundays. But Hugh, partly through faith and partly through love of his mother, is neither a hypocrite nor a liar; yet sometimes he forgets to say his "Our Father" and "Hail Mary." The teachings of the Rev. Virgil are beginning to have their effect. He wonders why his mother never told him about the Inquisition, and from much hearing of Scriptural texts imbibes the opinion that the Jews committed their great crime because they were Catholics!*

Mrs. Virgil's new tack of kinder treatment has something to do with this softening of the boy's firmness. He might perhaps have figured in the new report of the directors of the Little Bethel along with Barney Ruark and the expensive Chin-Chin, the converted Chinese, but the vigilant Rev. Virgil discovers the little prayer-book in his shoe one day, and seizes it.

Hugh's blue eyes flash and he clenches his small fist.

"Give me that!" he cries. "It's mine. It was my mother's; you sha'n't take it from me."

"Idolatry!—foul idolatry! A mark of the Beast, Miranda!" the Rev. Mr. Virgil says, solemnly.

"Be calm, Virgil," returns the aimable lady. "One of the directors is in the hall."

Hugh springs from the dormitory into the hall. Mr. Haskins, a pursy old gentleman, who does not believe much in religion, except as mingled with economy, as in the case of the Rev. Virgil O. Gregg, is about to hear the happy children, hungry and hating the place, sing a hymn in which the Little Bethel is entitled their Heaven on earth. Hugh, paler and thinner than when we first met him, bursts forth with his story.

"I am a Catholic little boy," he cries; "I don't want to stay here. That is my book, and I want it back. It was my mother's."

Barney Ruark breaks out, in his high, piping voice:

"He is a bad, Papistical boy, sir. *I* am a brand. *I* love my Bible. The Rev. Virgil O. Gregg, our dear teacher, has taught me the error of my benighted parents—"

---

* A fact.

Mr. Haskins, who thinks that Barney is unusually fat for an "olive branch," and fears that the Rev. Virgil has favored him, says, "Silence!" and examines the book.

"So it's your mother's, hey? Let him keep it, Mr. Gregg. It can't do him much harm in this atmosphere."

The Rev. Virgil smiles gently. "I feared that he might proselytize the other children with it or cause some to backslide."

"I didn't!" cries Hugh, anxiously and eagerly; "I didn't do anything to anybody since I tripped Barney Ruark on the stairs."

Mr. Haskins smiles, and Hugh is marched off to more bread and water.

"Likely to be a troublesome boy. Better send him West. If he has Catholic friends in the city they'll be inquiring after him. These Irish are safest away from their friends."

"Enormous appetite. Mrs. Gregg has, on several occasions, been forced to help him twice to meat, but we are compelled to keep him on bread and water on Friday. He will not touch pork, in spite of all persuasions."

Mr. Haskins winks: "*Persuasions?* Well, we'll send him West with the next batch. Luther McKillian wants a boy, doesn't he? The last one committed suicide. He's a strict disciplinarian—a righteous man. A good place for this obstinate little Irisher. He'll take the starch out of any boy."

Rev. Virgil assents. Inquiries have been made recently in behalf of Mrs. Desmond. Luther McKillian, a Protestant Irishman from Canada, having a farm in Oregon, is well known to the directors of the Little Bethel as an earnest Orangeman and a hater of the Scarlet Woman. He has a particular gift for the further conversion of young Catholic children. A few weeks afterward, Hugh, with a sigh of relief from the Rev. Virgil, is sent forth as one of the "olive branches" bound for Oregon.

Hugh is not sorry. He is going farther from his mother and Kitty and Mary and Chip, but he will see them all again. He prays for that nearly every day. Besides, he has the prayer-book, and reads the "Memorare," which his mother always loved.

Dreary and sleepless nights are those spent in the crowded immigrant-cars, often three boys crowded into a seat, half-stifled by the smoke from gross pipes and the odors of the steerage. Hugh is used to hardships, and yet he suffers and longs for his corner in the old tenement-house, which to him represented all comfort and a mother's love.

Luther McKillian's farm is well kept. Frugal, industrious, stony-hearted, and bigoted, this North-of-Ireland man has made the soil, both in grazing and farming, yield its utmost. Most of his farm-work is done by "bound boys" from various institutions. Labor costs him little. He will never permit any of his hands to work on the "Sabbath," but on other days he grinds them to dust, as it were; he is a brute, with a conscience moulded in the Orange way.

Hugh feels small and helpless as he enters the kitchen on the night of his arrival and has his share of the hands' supper. Perhaps better days are in store for him. He has heard his mother speak of an uncle, Tom Desmond, who went West. Hugh looks around the table, in the hope of finding this uncle. Who knows? He may be there. Anything is probable in a boy's imagination. But the young faces are weary, gloomy. The elder men are stolid and silent.

Luther McKillian says grace, and Hugh, in his new sense of freedom, blesses himself. He hears a gruff laugh near him. Then Luther McKillian roars, "Come here, you young Papist! Much good the Little Bethel has done you!"

Hugh trembles, and follows the sturdy, malevolent Luther to the cellar. Poor boy! Later he creeps into his straw in the loft, heart-sick, panting, with huge welts across his back, but with his dear prayer-book clasped tight in his hand. At daybreak he is driven forth, more dead than alive, to do "chores"; and heavy "chores" they are.

The winter goes. It is a season of torture for the poor boys who work for Luther McKillian. There is not much good-fellowship among them. They are afraid of the master's suspicious eye. Hugh is always alone. He sees no friendly face; even the dogs snarl. How he longs for Chip!

The spring comes. The stream, set with rocks, which skirts McKillian's farm, swells into a torrent and threatens to rise as high as its steep banks. This puts the master in a bad humor and the workmen feel it.

There is a clump of thick bushes just bursting into bud on this bank, and here, about noon, Hugh has gone in search of a strayed calf. The air is sweet with the scents of spring. The whole new world seems to say, "Raise up your hearts." Hugh, tired by the ceaseless morning's work, sits down among the bushes and takes out his little book. "Mary Desmond, from her husband, 1866," he reads over and over again. He turns to the familiar prayers for Mass. He thinks of the old church in South Fifth avenue. He recalls that Christmas Eve when he knelt— A blow on the head sends him several feet forward.

"At your Romish books again, you idle vagabond!" It is McKillian's voice. "Take that!—and that!"

Blood runs down Hugh's face, but he holds on to his prayer-book. He is blinded by the blood. He runs forward wildly. A step too far, and he disappears. He has gone over the bank.

. . . .

"And so," said Mr. Haskins, reading a letter from the West, "another of Luther McKillian's boys has killed himself. This thing must stop or it will get into the papers."

"I always said the Desmond boy would come to no good," said Mrs. Virgil C. Gregg, as she watered the supply of milk, that it might not be too rich for the stomachs of the little "olive branches."

. . . .

III.

FATHER RAPHAEL.

Some priests in the West have hard times all the year round. They are grateful for very little. A house, such food as comes to hand, and a borrowed horse, are worth much thanksgiving, if their scattered flocks prosper.

One afternoon, Father Raphael, a priest who served several scattered missions and many more scattered families, was riding toward his home. His road lay through lonely prairies. He knew the way well, and his horse knew it better; younger inhabitants would have been lost in the trackless expanse. No houses were in sight, and Father Raphael expected to see no human figure.

He saw, however, something move some feet ahead of

him. Was it a boy crouching in the grass? He called out; there was no answer. The figure seemed to draw itself together, as if to hide. He dismounted. A boy lay in the grass, crouching and trembling. The boy was ragged; the remains of a straw hat lay near him; his feet were torn and scratched. He raised the arm which had hidden his face. He looked at Father Raphael with bright, blue eyes, and, at bay, coolly drew a blade of grass through his lips. He would not speak. The priest tried every expedient in vain. The boy clung to the tall grass, and would not move. At last, the priest, by a happy inspiration, made the sign of the cross. The boy started up.

"I know that you are a good man now," he said. "I have been alone for four days. I have eaten only wild strawberries. May I go with you?"

This sudden change from distrust to implicit confidence surprised and amused the priest.

"Are you a Catholic, my child?"

The boy, with a flush of pride on his thin cheek, drew a worn little prayer-book from his jacket. This was his credential. The priest opened the prayer-book and read, "To Mary Desmond, from her husband, 1866."

Father Raphael started.

"The ways of God are inscrutable," he murmured.

"That was my mother's prayer-book," said the boy, very frankly, as he gave the priest his hand and trotted by his side to the spot where the horse had been left. "She is in New York. I want to work my way home. I can work; I used to be an 'olive branch,' and we had to work. It was harder than selling papers or shovelling snow. You bet."

Father Raphael made the little fellow get on the horse

behind him. Hugh laughed as he clung to the priest.
"I am glad I did not run away," he said; "I felt like
running away when I saw you. But you came too fast.
I was lonely, Father, in these big fields. It is not like
New York, here. We have many houses in New York.
The city is more like Heaven than the country, I think."

Father Raphael laughed this time. "Why?" he
asked. "Isn't the country more beautiful?"

"Oh, no," said Hugh; "no place is finer than New
York. New York is more like Heaven, because the
Bible says so—the Rev. Mr. Gregg used to read it for us
out of the Bible."

"Indeed!" said Father Raphael. "Well, go on."

"'In my father's house there are many mansions,'"
returned Hugh in the canting tone which the "olive
branches" were taught to adopt when quoting Scripture.
"There are many mansions in New York—big ones—
and none at all in the country. The city is more like
Heaven."

Hugh ran on. His lonely days on the prairie had
caused him to accumulate much to talk about.

"I don't remember much of my Catechism; but I can
say the whole Book of Proverbs and four hundred and
eighty verses of the New Testament!"

Father Raphael was soon in possession of Hugh's story.
He had fallen into the stream at the foot of McKillian's
farm; his practice in swimming at the New York docks
served him well. He regained solid ground, with the
prayer-book held between his teeth, in a few seconds after
he touched water. He hid in the bushes until McKillian
had grown tired of searching for him. Wild strawberries
abounded at this season of the year, and he had managed
to keep himself alive.

Hugh's artlessness pleased Father Raphael; his confidence touched him, though he was shocked by the street-boy's slang phrases and premature knowledge of the world.

When they neared the town, Hugh dismounted and trotted beside the horse as his own Chip would have done.

Hugh made himself at home in the kind priest's house at once. He attached himself to Father Raphael. He worked like a beaver. He did the "chores" with great fidelity, rang the chapel-bell for "Angelus," and served Mass every morning. He even helped to prepare Father Raphael's frugal meal when old Mike, his rheumatic sexton and factotum in general, fell sick. He seemed happy. Father Raphael began to prepare him for his First Communion. But the priest noticed that whenever he took a writing-lesson, in rare intervals of Father Raphael's leisure, he tried to write "Mother" and "New York." He had made a Novena for a mysterious purpose.

One day Father Raphael, after Mass, called Hugh into his private room.

"I have good news for you. This letter is from your mother. Your prayers are answered, my boy." And the priest read, from an open letter in his hand:

"REVEREND SIR:—I take my pen in hand to thank you for the blessed news that my child is safe. And also for the other news. Tom, my husband's brother, could not write, so we seldom heard of him after he left New York. We knew that he had gone to Oregon. I am happy to think that he was a good Catholic when he died, for he had been careless—"

"I find," said Father Raphael, "that your mother is the sister of a man who fell sick while here in one of the mines. His name was Thomas Desmond. He left some money—two thousand dollars—with me for your mother."

Hugh could not speak. He trembled all over.

"How have I suffered since I lost Hugh on that dreadful Christmas Eve two years ago! Tell him that the children and I are safe. Mrs. Donovan cared for us. We are all working hard, but doing well. Oh, I thank God for your kindness and for the kindness of the priests at the church here, through whom you found me out. I almost fear to meet Hughey. It would break my heart if he lost his Faith. Let him come to me as soon as you can send him."

Hugh covered the letter with kisses. Usually so garrulous, he could say nothing. When he had recovered the use of his tongue, he said:

"And Chip, Father?"

"Your mother does not speak of Chip," said the priest, smiling.

. . . .

After he is gone, Father Raphael misses very much the bright, docile boy. Letters go and come; and one day Father Raphael receives the following:

"NEW YORK, Christmas Eve, 1881.

"DEAR FATHER RAPHAEL:—Mother, Mary, and Kitty are well. Mother opened her little store just opposite Jules Roussel's father's last week. Mary and I sold a great deal of milk and cheese; but she took in a bad dollar, which I did not pass on any one, but burned. I have not found Chip. Perhaps he is dead. They make sausage-meat of dogs. I have another, named Chin-chins, because he *chins* a great deal. We send you a box; and a cover which mother made for the altar of the Blessed Virgin. I tend store when I am not at school. MERRY CHRISTMAS AND MANY HAPPY RETURNS OF THE DAY!

"Yours affectionately,

"HUGH DESMOND."

AT THE GATE OF DEATH.

I.

"Threads in the web of life."

SUNDOWN is situated on the Delaware. Its citizens delight in calling it a town, but impartial visitors, who have no fear of the inhabitants before their eyes, talk of it as a village. Its public buildings—of which the Sundowners are immensely proud—consist of two churches, a hall, a jail, and the long wooden pier, at which the steamboats stop daily on their way down. This pier is the first object that catches your eye from the river; behind it are thin fringes of houses, and beyond that orchards and well-kept farms.

On days when the wind blows up from the ocean, the air is full of Atlantic freshness, and the miniature waves that wash the narrow beach up to the roots of the bordering trees are capped with sea foam.

No sounds of busy trade mar the quietness, though occasionally a deputation of noisy sailors are sent from some brig or oyster boat to secure a relay of pork and biscuits from the grocery store, at which anything you don't want can always be obtained.

John Maitland lives in Sundown. His uncle, Andrew McVeigh, is decidedly the greatest man in the place, for he has been in the legislature of his native State; he has the loudest voice, the most money, and the finest house and garden in Sundown—gifts which inspire the Sundowners with respect and awe. Not finding in his natal place an opening worthy of his ambition, John Maitland secured a position as book-keeper to a prosperous and influential firm in the opposite city of Swedeston. He crosses the river twice every day in a superannuated steamer, which would go to pieces if it were not too old even for that exertion.

John Maitland is tall and handsome, and the outdoor life of his boyhood—Sundown boys are amphibious animals—has given him that athletic development that Americans too often lack. Looking at his face as he sits this bright spring day in the office of Seth Willis & Co., you can not help thinking that it is the face of an honest man. In his eyes, even now when he tilts back his chair in earnest thought, there slumbers a spark of laughter; his mouth is too mobile, perhaps too ready to express either anger, scorn, or good nature, as circumstances demand. His face tells you that he is sincere, frank, impetuous, and it may be, a little satirical; but it also tells you that it needs some rough discipline to teach him self-control.

John Maitland is past twenty-five; this year the firm has raised his salary to $2,000, and intimated that he will be offered a partnership in time. On the strength of this, he has asked Grace Lynch, the prettiest and best girl in Sundown, *the* question. In consequence of her answer he has built a gem of a cottage down by the Delaware; the wedding-day is only two weeks off, and he is now thinking about the bill for furniture. Mr. Kenzie, the upholsterer, has just left him.

"My dear Maitland," Kenzie said, "I know I am asking an unwarrantable favor, and doing an unwarrantable thing in presenting a bill before I have entirely finished a job, but I am awfully 'hard up.' A batch of unexpected payments have to be made, and if you would let me have a hundred on account—"

"If I could, I would; but I can't, you see," and John Maitland tossed his pocket-book in the air. "Empty. There is a tight little sum due me here, but I can't draw it till Monday. Will Monday do?"

"I'm afraid not," said Kenzie, his countenance falling. "I must have it to-morrow at the latest. Good-day."

"I wish I *could* help him," thinks John Maitland, falling into a reverie of ways and means. He is so deeply immersed in thought that he does not see a sun-burnt stranger who enters. The stranger drops his portmanteau and throws back his ulster overcoat; then takes a survey of the office and smiles.

"Have the cares of matrimony already begun to oppress my brother in future?"

"Why, Will Lynch!—Will, old boy!" exclaims John, starting up, and shaking the stranger by both hands. "How—when—where on earth did you come from? I thought you were in Rome."

"So I was until lately; but the *Echo* wants a correspondent to go to some festival in Iceland, or Greenland, or somewhere, and so I have been recalled, with orders to report at the editorial rooms in New York, to-day. And I go, like Cicero—isn't it?—but to return—some time."

"You have been over to Sundown?"

"Oh, yes, all the morning. Dear old Aunt Bridget, who used to scold me so awfully when I brought home stray dogs, and came into the parlor with unwiped shoes, went into an ecstasy of joy, and as for Grace—dear little Grace! She'll make you a good wife, John, and I think you can be trusted with her."

"You *think!*" echoes John, in a perfectly indescribable tone.

"Well, I *know*, then. At any rate, pray accept my blessing, as the little old woman says in 'Bleak House.' By the way, did you know that Father Augustin, that dear old director of studies at Notre Dame—how indignant our false quantities used to make him!—is stationed at the church in Sundown? I met him in the street."

"No. I haven't been at the church there lately. When I do go to Mass—which is only now and then—I go to one of the churches of Swedeston."

Will Lynch gives him a scrutinizing look.

"*When* you do go to Mass. Two years must have greatly changed you, John."

"Well," says John Maitland, with a slightly embarrassed laugh, "between business and other things, one finds such little time and so many things to think of. In fact, I'm afraid I'm growing rather careless."

Lynch made no reply at once. He is thinking and mentally weighing Grace's influence against the possibility of this carelessness becoming indifferentism and utter unbelief.

"Grace would make a saint of anybody," he says aloud, with a half sigh. "I had a conversation with your uncle to-day. He was very kind, very kind. I always was a favorite of his, you know; indeed, I don't know how I ever could have gone to college, after father's death, if it had not been for his assistance. Andrew McVeigh is certainly one of the worst tempered of men, and yet one of the most generous. We had a long talk, but he did not allude to your marriage. Are you on quite good terms?"

"No," answers Maitland, frowning, and digging his

pen nervously into the lid of the desk. "No. He is acting very meanly, I think, and since I told him so, we have scarcely spoken. I am his only living relative, and he tells everybody I am to be his heir, and yet—would you believe it?—he actually refuses to advance a dollar toward—toward our housekeeping."

Will Lynch can not suppress a smile as he observed the mixture of dignity and awkwardness with which his friend enunciates " our housekeeping."

"And," continued Maitland, "though he admires and respects Grace, he would prefer that I should marry a Protestant, or, at least, he has a prejudice against her religion."

"His sister, your mother, was a convert, a very fervent Catholic, and he has always been indifferent to all forms of religion. It is singular, but such extremes—faith and lack of faith—often occur in modern families. There are Cardinal Newman and his brother, for instance."

"Yes," returns Maitland, who had not heard a word of this. "My uncle says that we must begin life economically. 'If you can't afford to get married,' he said, 'don't. Two young people starting out into life ought to be satisfied with necessities.' He has no heart, except for money."

"He appears to have a great deal of sense."

"Only a moment ago I had to refuse Kenzie—you know Kenzie; he was in our class—I had to refuse Kenzie a hundred dollars on a furniture bill I will owe him in a short time, just because I hadn't the money."

"A very sufficient reason. But good-bye, old fellow. I must be off, or I'll lose the train. I regret that I can not be on hand for the wedding; but duty, you know. Good-bye. Oh, I forgot." And Will threw an envelope on the desk. "That's for you in honor of the great occasion. Take good care of Grace. God bless you!"

Lynch shakes his friend's hand violently, grasped his portmanteau, and leaves the office like a flash.

Maitland watches him, and then goes to work at his books; but times are dull, and before the clock has struck three he has nothing to do.

Suddenly he remembers Will Lynch's envelope. It has already been torn open, he notices, and he has merely to take out the three one-hundred-dollar greenbacks which it encloses.

"Generous-hearted Will," murmurs John Maitland, a haze coming between him and the notes. "I must manage to repay him somehow. Just now, however, the money is remarkably convenient. I will pay Kenzie's bill, and buy that carpet for the sitting-room which Grace admired so much, and which her aunt thought we could not afford. I'll go and see Kenzie at once."

Having gone into the back office and made sure that the firm had no further need of his services, he starts for Kenzie's, but the sound of a bell informs him that the Sundown steamer is at the wharf. This being the case, he forgets all about Kenzie, and turns to go over to Sundown to have a talk with Grace.

As the rickety machine shakes and struggles through the water, somehow or other he thinks of the old story of Hero and Leander, and wonders if he would have the courage to swim across to the lady of his love if there were no superannuated steamer.

Light, pleasant, careless thoughts; flowers on the brink of a precipice. Dreams to be dispelled by the touch of a hideous reality. It was well for him that no hand, at that bright moment, lifted the curtain of the future. God mercifully conceals the coming sorrow.

II.

PRAYER.

The cottage in which Grace Lynch and her Aunt Bridget live is in the main street of Sundown—the street which runs down to that work of architectural beauty, the pier. The cottage is a small, frame, chocolate-colored house, with a veranda and a tiny lawn in front. The frame looks so fragile that one would not be surprised to hear of its being carried away some day by a pair of muscular burglars; but Aunt Bridget covers her slight door and windows with bolts and chains, for Will, being a permanent man on the staff of the enterprising *Echo*, is seldom at home, and Aunt Bridget, though as an old maid she pretends to hate the male sex, does not like the idea of having "no man about the house."

On this afternoon Aunt Bridget has gone to church, for Father Augustin is holding the Forty Hours' Devotion, and Grace, having given all her music lessons and made her visit, is sitting before the piano, which, small as it is, fills half the room.

Grace is not beautiful. It is true that she has the dark blue eyes and the luxuriant black-brown hair of her mother, who was the prettiest girl in all Galway, but she lacks color, while the cheeks of her aunt, who is sixty-three at last, yet bear the ruddy bloom given them by Irish air. Grace is gentle and sweet, but a trifle too thoughtful for a girl. She deserves her name, for every action is stamped with that nameless quality which proclaims the perfect gentlewoman.

She is singing, playing a low minor accompaniment.

Her voice glides from the *Stabat Mater* to the *Dies Iræ*.

"There is sorrow in the air," she murmurs dreamily. "To-day I can play nothing but songs of sadness." She changes her accompaniment and tries her favorite song:

> Pray, though the gift you ask for
>   May never comfort your fears—
> May never repay your pleadings—
>   Yet pray, and with hopeful tears,
> Answer, not that you long for,
>   But diviner will come one day;
> Your eyes are too dim to see it,
>   Yet strive, and wait, and pray.

"Good enough, Miss Grace," cries a piping, feeble voice from the garden. "Good enough. Give us something livelier."

Grace goes to the window and sees a small, freckle-faced boy, with bright, saucy eyes, partially concealed by the hanging rim of a dilapidated straw hat. The boy holds one hand tightly on the breast of his button-up jacket, under which some bulky object is hidden, and plants his feet into the very heart of a bed of young pansies.

"Oh, it's you, Chip." Grace smiles, and then says sternly, "Get off the grass."

Chip obeys.

"Have you studied the Catechism lessons I gave you?"

Apparently, Chip is not eager to answer that question.

"Oh, Miss Grace, you sing nearly as well as the lady I heard once at a circus. Did you ever go—"

"Have you studied that lesson?"

"Oh, Miss Grace, Jonas Brown caught sixty crabs this morning."

Grace can not help smiling. The Sundown boys, and men too, say cra-a-a-bs, with an accent on the "a" like the crackling of thorns.

"Do you know your lesson?"

"Well," answered Chip, reluctantly. "Well—oh, Miss Grace, I shot a hawk, and nearly brought down—"

"Shot a hawk!" exclaims Grace, alarmed. "I hope John hasn't trusted you with a gun."

"I hadn't a gun," says Chip, clutching the object under his jacket, and very anxious to evade this new subject of conversation. "The steamer's in—and here comes Mr. John."

Chip knows that this diversion will be most effective. Grace, with a happy light in her eyes, goes down to meet him—John Maitland.

"How do you do, Chip? Idle, as usual, I see. Really, Grace, I am afraid you are spoiling that imp of mischief. Look here, Chip, you were in my room yesterday. I know by the way I found everything in disorder. If I catch—"

Chip utters a howl; for Nemesis has reached him. A stiff, slight, white-haired man on horseback had just turned from the lane into the street. He has dismounted, and with three or four stealthy steps reaches the gate where the three are standing. His riding-whip whistles in the air and strikes Chip's back.

"Is this the way you waste my time, boy?" the old man cries, his cold blue eyes blazing with anger. "Hey? I sent you with an important message this morning at eight o'clock, and I haven't seen you since. I'll teach you!" And the whip descends again, but Chip jumps over the low fence and escapes.

"Really, uncle, I don't think Chip has done anything—"

"It is not your affair, John Maitland," exclaims Andrew McVeigh, turning fiercely, and shaking the whip at his nephew. "I tell you it is not your affair. You have spoiled that rascally urchin until he has become as ungrateful as yourself. Yes, I repeat it, ungrateful," continued the old man, glad to have an object, Chip failing, on which to vent the vials of his wrath. "I have fed, lodged, and educated you; I have treated you as my son, and now you insist on bringing a Papist into the family, as if your mother, though religion could not spoil her, wasn't enough."

"I can't stand this, even from *him*," muttered John Maitland between his set teeth, his face whitening with suppressed anger. "Grace, leave us."

"I have nothing to say against her personally, and I've told you that before," interrupts the old man, "but I don't see why our family—your grandfather, John Maitland, fought under William at the Boyne—should be so fond of Catholics. It's just your confounded pig-headed obstinate desire to offend me."

In justice to Andrew McVeigh, it must be said that he does not mean more than half he says. He has had a day of disappointments, and his temper is worse than usual.

"You have thwarted me whenever you could, John Maitland, and I may repay you by cutting you off with a dollar, even if I have to leave my money to a Papist." And the inconsistent old man gives his whip a vicious flip, which, either by accident or design, makes a red mark on his nephew's cheek. Then chuckling, he walks slowly from the garden, takes his horse's bridle and proceeds down the street.

John Maitland, gasping with rage, looks after him.

"I could kill him where he stands," he mutters, hoarsely. "I will! I will!"

"John!" Grace lays her hand on his arm and then shrinks back. Fury has changed her hero into a demon. She feels powerless. She sees the golden cross of St. Paul's glowing in the sunlight, and the sight inspires her. "John," she says, pointing with her hand, "go, if you love your soul; if you love me, go and kneel before Our Lord. He alone can save you from your passion!"

John Maitland stands irresolute, and then, as the echo of her pleading accents enters his brain, he starts off with hurried strides toward St. Paul's without looking to the right or to the left, and keeping his hands on his breast as if to strangle the murderous thoughts within him. If Andrew McVeigh could have seen him now, he would feel sure that, however much in other things his nephew may have departed from the principles of his ancestors, he at least possesses the family temper in perfection.

All is silent within the little wooden chapel. There is a worshipper here and there among the rough benches, and two acolytes, in black and white, kneel before the Most Blessed Sacrament. A faint breeze enters with John Maitland and stirs the laces on the altar and the candle flames. He walks into the "dim religious light" from the glaring sunshine without, and finds himself in a new world of Faith and Love and Adoration. The subtle scent of the early flowers on the altar mingles with the odor of incense whose soul has flown to heaven, and brings back to his mind the morning of his first Communion. He kneels and breathes a loving, contrite prayer, taking no note of the time.

His old friend, Father Augustin, whom he knew in

his college days, has seen him enter. Father Augustin stands just behind the altar and watches him. Four o'clock strikes.

"Father," whispers a small boy, who wears a black cassock, "Father, it's four o'clock, and the two O'Brien boys have been out in the sanctuary since three. It's our turn now."

"Let me see." The priest refers to a small note-book. "The O'Brien brothers from three to four; John Dever and Miles Jones from four to five. Yes, it is your turn, Miles. Go on."

As the acolytes are changing, the sleeve of little Miles Jones' surplice brushes the candle. In an instant the light muslin is in flames. John Maitland quietly bends over the railing, and before the boy is aware of it, crushes out the flame between his hands. This has not taken a minute, and John Maitland resumes his prayer. But the boy will never forget the incident.

Nearly an hour passes before John Maitland rises from his knees, and then, catching sight of Father Augustin, he goes into the sacristy to speak to him. The priest is very glad to meet his old friend and pupil, but he has little time to spend in talk.

"I am going down to Maryland," he says, as they shake hands at parting, a few minutes after the clock has struck five, "on a mission. I shall start this evening, but I hope to return in a month or two, and then we will finish our chat about the old days at Notre Dame."

John Maitland leaves the chapel, and the demon of wrath that possessed him has fled. He shudders now as the shadow of his thoughts of an hour ago crosses his mind. He wonders that such strange madness could have been evoked by the querulous words of a weak old man.

The evening breeze is beginning to blow from the river, and the whole west is a gorgeous crimson and gold picture of blended clouds and water. He strolls along the beach. In one spot he sees several men standing around a small pool in the sand. Is it the sun's light that makes it crimson?

He approaches, and they draw together, whispering.

"Here he is!" One of them comes out from the crowd and says:

"I arrest you for the murder of Andrew McVeigh."

John Maitland laughs incredulously. His eyes fall on the pool. It is blood.

III.

"*For right is right, since God is God,*
And Right the day must win."—*Faber*.

At about half-past four o'clock Andrew McVeigh had been found dead by three farm laborers on the beach near Sundown. These men were repairing fences on land near the river, but shut out from view of it by a thick fringe of bushes that ran along the beach. They had heard the report of a pistol, followed by a succession of loud groans. Almost simultaneously breaking through the hedge, they had seen Andrew McVeigh lying upon the sand, a stream of blood flowing from his shoulder. His groans grew more tremulous and fainter. He could not speak. Before they could raise him he was dead.

At the water's edge, wet by the ebbing tide, lay a revolver with all its barrels empty. On a tiny silver plate in the side of this empty weapon were the words, *John Maitland from W. Lynch*.

The sand was covered with foot-prints, but as the spot where the murdered man had been found was a favorite bathing and crabbing place of Sundown boys, this went for nothing. And at the inquest the jury rejected the idea of suicide with contempt, and brought in the verdict that Andrew McVeigh came to his death at the hands of his nephew, John Maitland.

The following facts came out at the inquest:

Andrew McVeigh had remained at a sale of real estate which had taken place at the Sundown hotel. The auctioneer testified that he left the hotel shortly after four o'clock. A bystander, Seth Sunden, Chip's father—by the way, an inveterate lounger who always attended auctions and other free entertainments—swore that he had seen the deceased proceed to the river, leading his horse. After that, Andrew McVeigh had never been seen alive, except by his murderer and the three laborers in those brief moments immediately preceding death.

On John Maitland's person was found an envelope containing three hundred dollars. The envelope was addressed, "Andrew McVeigh, present." This envelope had been torn open at the end. Eli Woodbury, a dry-goods merchant of Ironborough, a town some distance from Sundown, proved that he had paid the three hundred dollars to the deceased on the day of the murder, for six months' rent of his store. He produced the receipt. Having been called out on business, he had placed the money in an envelope, written Andrew McVeigh's name on it and given it to his clerk.

Mr. Kenzie testified that early in the afternoon of the 16th inst.—the day of the murder—John Maitland had refused to pay his bill, or rather accommodate him with one hundred dollars on account of want of funds.

Rebecca Plummer, who lives next door to the Lynch cottage, affirmed that she had heard John Maitland and his uncle quarrelling in Miss Bridget Lynch's garden. She could not hear the words they used, but had seen him (the uncle) strike his nephew with a whip. Charles Chippeway Sunden, *alias* "Chip," and Miss Grace Lynch, had been witnesses to the quarrel.

Chip was missing. He had not been visible in Sundown since the day of the murder. His straw hat had been washed up by the tide down at the cove. He had lived with John Maitland and his uncle as "general utility," indulged by one, tyrannized over by the other, and half civilized by the efforts of Grace Lynch. It had been intimated that he had been "made away with" by the murderer, in order to destroy evidence. Seth Sunden, however, took the loss of his boy very philosophically. Sympathizing Sundowners gave him more drinks than usual, and after a certain number of glasses he seemed to find vague comfort in the time-honored axiom to the effect that "boys will be boys—they always land on their feet."

Grace Lynch's evidence was not taken at the inquest. She was too ill to attend. The scene in the garden had agitated her, and followed by this terrible shock had thrown her into brain fever.

Days, weeks, months have passed. The trial comes on. It takes place at Ironborough. Letters and letters have been sent to Will Lynch. No answer has been received. Chip has not appeared. The only new witness of importance is Grace. The poor girl is assisted to the stand. She is pale and trembling—a ghost of her former self. The buzz of many suppressed voices, the sea of upturned faces makes her giddy. She dare not look toward John. Oh, surely this is her sorrow's crown of sorrow.

The prosecuting counsel draws from her the story of the quarrel, slowly, painfully. John Maitland leans half over the railing of the dock, his heart and soul in his eyes. The counsel asks his fifth question.

Grace's lips whiten, and she presses her teeth into them. She will not answer. There is a dead silence.

"Spare her!" cried John, fiercely. "Spare her! I will tell you what I said. 'I could kill him where he stands. I will! I will!' These were my words."

"Were those his words?" asks the lawyer, apparently pitiless.

Grace does not heed him. The look of tender love and pity in John Maitland's eyes goes to her heart. She utters a heart-broken sob, and falls senseless into Aunt Bridget's faithful arms.

. . . .

The prisoner's lawyer, a man whose reputation has years ago outgrown his abilities, makes a florid speech. He has been sacrificing everything to the preparation of this speech all through the trial. He shows them what fearful odds are against him, and how gallantly he struggles to overcome them. His speech grows more and more brilliant, but he forgets the prisoner. To-morrow the newspapers will call it a telling speech and a masterly effort, and John Maitland will know that he has selected for his advocate the one lawyer of a thousand who could fail to save him.

The verdict was given clear and loudly: "Guilty."

John Maitland smiles bitterly. "And this is man's justice."

. . . .

AT THE GATE OF DEATH.

"You have come North just in time, Father Augustin," says John Maitland, "for in another week you may write at the end of my record, *non est inventus.*"

"In another week?" Father Augustin wipes his spectacles and glances around the narrow cell in the Ironborough jail. "In another week—"

"I must die. But, believe me, Father, among the sins I will confess to you to-night, murder will not be."

"I believe you. There is some horrible mistake. I heard no word of this until I arrived in Sundown this morning."

"Those papers on the table contain a full account of the trial. While you look them over, I will finish this letter."

Half an hour passes. No sound breaks the stillness except the rustling of Father Augustin's papers and the scratching of the prisoner's pen.

"My dear boy," at last said Father Augustin, with a smouldering excitement in every movement, "you and your lawyer have acted like a pair of fools. It is unpleasant, but true. Had you no memory? Had he no— he ought to be ashamed of himself! Why did he not attempt to prove an *alibi?* Listen. From this report of the trial I gather the following. On the fatal 16th your uncle was seen alive at about ten minutes past four P.M. He was found dead at half-past four. Now please attend. *You were in St. Paul's Church, at Sundown, either kneeling before the altar or talking to me in the sacristy, from four o'clock P.M. until five.* I will swear to it! You shall have a new trial, my boy. Thank God! Thank God!"

"My prayer! my prayer! I had forgotten it, and it will save me." John Maitland buries his face in his hands to hide the tears in his eyes. Sorrow could not wring them from him, but joy has done it. He tears up the letter, for it is his farewell to Grace.

. . . .

Father Augustin never loses time, and now it is doubly valuable. He moves Heaven and earth to save John Maitland's life. Hope, suspense, despondency, alternate in the prisoner's mind, but the priest does not despond; he has too much to do. At last the demands of red tape are satisfied. A reprieve and a new trial are granted. Two witnesses, Father Augustin and little Miles Jones, of Swedeston, who knew nothing about the former trial, triumphantly prove an *alibi*, and John Maitland walks out of court a free man, saved by his prayer.

John Maitland finds that his uncle, eccentric to the last, left a will bearing date of the terrible 16th, bequeathing all his estate without reserve to his esteemed young friend, William Lynch. But he, the heir presumptive, is content; he is innocent, he is free, he has Grace, for Father Augustin married them three days after the second trial. The Swedeston firm still trusts him, although Will Lynch has not yet turned up to corroborate his statement about the three hundred dollars, and his great sorrow has left him a wiser and better man. Grace is sweeter and brighter than before, and the two are as happy as human beings can be in this valley of tears.

. . . .

Returning from High Mass at St. Paul's one Sunday, late in autumn, John and Grace hear strange voices in their little sitting-room. Aunt Bridget is crying and laughing by turns, accompanied by the running commentary of a ringing bass voice. Of course, Grace at

AT THE GATE OF DEATH. 257

once jumps at the conclusion that the house is being robbed. She is agreeably amazed, however, to find her brother Will and Chip amiably finishing one of Aunt Bridget's apple lunches. Will looks the same, but Chip has grown taller and thinner, more freckled, and exceedingly forlorn in appearance.

"Aunt Bid has told me everything," cries Will, when the greetings were over. "I had never received your letters. When I had completed the *Echo* business, I started as companion and secretary to an English traveller, on a rather straggling and uncertain tour; that probably accounts for the failure of your letters. And so they brought the money as evidence against you! I'll tell you how it came into your possession. Your uncle, as you know, entertained a strong liking for me. Well, I happened to meet him on the 16th, just before I saw you, John, and I told him that I was about to start on a long journey. At first he spoke in his usual hot and inconsistent way, and then he became very kind. He pressed that envelope into my hand, saying: 'Take this, it's only part of what is to come.' He forced me to keep it, and so I thought it would make a nice wedding present for you. Now, Chip, clear up your mystery." But Chip's mouth is very full at this particular moment, and Will considerately gives him time. "I picked up Chip in Philadelphia. I found him selling papers, and glad enough he was to come home. How do you like selling papers, Chip?"

"Too much competition," answered Chip, gravely.

Chip's story was not long. He had entertained for some time within his breast an ardent desire. It was to shoot certain prowling hawks and crows. In order to fulfil this desire, he waited for an opportunity to borrow

17

clandestinely John Maitland's revolver. On the morning of the 16th, John cleaned and loaded it, and carelessly left it on his bureau. This was Chip's chance. John usually left his door open, and Chip, when his master had gone, secured the revolver. With it he shot the unfortunate hawk, of which he spoke to Grace, and during his interview with her it was the object he concealed under his jacket. After he had escaped from Andrew McVeigh's castigation, he ran down to the beach, and in blissful ignorance he was levelling the one remaining charge at another crow, when McVeigh suddenly grasped his collar. The frightened boy turned, and the charge took effect in the poor old man's side. Chip dropped the pistol and ran down to the cove. There was a schooner lying there. Chip, half dead with terror, hid himself among the barrels on deck. The crew coming on board at nightfall were a little "confused" by their sojourn on shore, and when they discovered him, which happened to be many miles from Sundown, they made him work hard. Chip's vicissitudes have subdued him considerably, and he is, indeed, very glad to get home.

"I will send you to school, Chip," says Will Lynch, "when he have induced the authorities to hear your story. And now fill your glasses with Aunt Bridget's currant wine. I drink to the health, long life, and happiness of Mr. and Mrs. Maitland." And every day since that eventful 16th those two kneel at the Holy Sacrifice in thanksgiving for John Maitland's prayer.

THE FINANCIAL CRASH.

I.

TWO FRIENDS.

"AS firm as a rock, sir—as firm as a rock!" was the unanimous opinion of the people of Eagle's Falls when anybody mentioned the Belforest Bank; and the people of Eagle's Falls, being Pennsylvanians with streaks of cautious Dutch blood in their composition, are not far behind their brethren of New England in "cuteness." If a clear record and unvarying steadfastness for more than fourscore years deserve confidence, the Eagle's Falls people were neither rash nor imprudent in implicitly trusting their great institution. It had stood all the shocks of Jackson's administration, partly because its conductors, the Belforests, father and son, were sagacious, and partly because it was rather an elastic sapling bowing before the blast than a towering oak.

Like the wealth of the Rothschilds—this phrase, by the way, is from the Eagle's Falls *Argus*—it was founded on an act of honesty.

One October night, in 1777, James Belforest sat beside his spacious fire-place in the stone farm-house. He was too old and feeble to fight against the invader, but his mind was active, and just then it was following his son in the army.

The distant thunder of cannon came from the direction of Germantown. Each detonation froze the old man's blood. He shuddered, and cowered close to the hearth. War is horrible to those who fight, but even more so to those who wait. In the midst of his torturing suspense, he heard a faint sound at the door, and then a groan.

Might it not be his son returning, wounded, dying?

With trembling fingers he pushed back the bolt, and threw open the heavy door. On the threshold lay a man in the uniform of a British officer. The face, upturned in the pale starlight, was young and handsome, though pain had made the features rigid, and drawn dark shadows under the eyes.

James Belforest slowly and tenderly moved the almost helpless man to the fire. His eyes, growing misty with the coming of death, spoke their gratitude. With an effort he tore a ring from his finger, and drew by a thin chain a diamond cross from his breast. James Belforest tried to stanch the blood that oozed from a wound in his side, just beneath the shoulder.

"It is useless," gasped the officer; "I am dying. Promise that you—send this ring and cross—to my mother in Lancashire. I am Henry Somerville."

Before James Belforest could speak, the young man made a convulsive movement, raised the cross to his lips, and fell back on the hard oak floor dead.

After the war old James and young James were again united. Some of their neighbors advised them to keep the "British spoil," but both the Belforests were honorable men, and, after some delay, the cross and ring were sent across the ocean to Lady Somerville, of Todmorden, Lancashire.

Two years passed. Young James Belforest worked on

the small farm, and old James took his ease in the stone farm-house, building castles in the air.

One day a letter came from London. Lady Somerville was dead. To James Belforest she had bequeathed five thousand pounds and the cross set with diamonds.

"Father," said James the younger, "let us leave the old place. I was not made to be a farmer."

"I have known that for a long time. You have submitted to necessity; you have done your best. I have made a plan for us both. We will go to Eagle's Falls."

Young America of to-day would have questioned, and probably doubted, "the old man's" wisdom. Years ago things were different; fathers were kings in their own households; and their power seems to have fallen with other monarchies.

And so one of old James Belforest's castles became a reality, and the Belforest's Bank was started, with Lady Somerville's five thousand pounds, after young James had been sent to Philadelphia for advice from the sapient Benjamin Franklin.

People shook their heads at first, and prophesied a failure, but old James, who had been in a London banking firm, knew what he was about, and the venture prospered.

James Belforest, third of the name, and grandson of the original James, associated with him, on the death of his father, Albert Verner. The bank flourished still, and the Belforest name was a power in the land.

Little Alice Belforest had a bright future before her, it seemed, although her mother had been dead one year; for all that wealth could give would be hers. This was in 1855.

On a bright morning in that year James Belforest

kissed his little daughter for the last time, and went down to the bank. As he entered, a clerk handed him a note.

"It was left here a few minutes ago, sir."

James Belforest carelessly ran his eyes over the contents, and then all the ruddy color left his face. He staggered into his office, closed the door, and read the note again:

"You have trusted me too much. The entireness of your trust tempted me. I have speculated with the money of the bank, and my speculations have failed. There is no need to go into particulars. The bonds and mortgages I have left will not realize twenty-five cents on the dollar. Flight is my only resource. Do what you can for my wife and son. A. Verner."

James Belforest sat, white and rigid, as if petrified.

"Fool! fool! to trust him!" he groaned at last. "Oh, consummate villain! he has destroyed the work of three generations. I am ruined!—disgraced! In a few hours our name will be a by-word in the streets! I can not live to hear it."

He drew a revolver from one of the draws of the desk, and prepared to load it.

The office door was pushed open, and a tall man in black entered. He had about him that undefinable air which distinguishes a priest among men. His tall, thin form was slightly bent; his face was calm and sweet, but there were lines around the mouth and a latent fire shone in the eye that spoke of firmness and deep fervor.

He started slightly at the sight of James Belforest's livid face. His eye fell on the pistol. In an instant it had changed hands.

"And now, old friend, what does this mean?"

"It means that I will not live—ruined—disgraced!" And James Belforest covered his face with his hands, and uttered a groan that seemed to come from a broken heart.

"It seems that you are a coward," said the priest, in a clear, distinct voice. "It means that, for some transient trouble, you would cast yourself headlong into hell. It means that you would rather defy God than bear the scorn of men. I knew that you were not of the true faith, James Belforest, but I never thought for a moment that you would become so meanly selfish as to forget your duty."

"Read that."

"From my brother-in-law," said the priest, with a light tinge of bitterness in his tone. "I warned you against him."

"I was a fool not to listen to you. I trusted him entirely; and now the scoundrel, after ruining me, coolly asks me to take care of his wife and child!"

"There is hope. An establishment like yours can not be utterly ruined in a day."

"Not utterly ruined, perhaps, but think of what we were—we, the Belforests! Oh, I can not bear it! I must leave the place at once, before it gets into the papers."

"And Alice? You forget your daughter."

"Dear little Alice! No, I will not see her. She will bear soon enough that her father is a disgraced man."

"It strikes me that you are talking nonsense, James Belforest," said the priest, sternly. "Admitting that Albert Verner has lost or embezzled some money, does it necessarily follow that the bank is ruined?"

"In this case it does. Verner and I have been speculating and losing until—but you do not understand the terms of business—we were compelled to cease or break the bank. This dishonest individual speculation of Verner's has done it. I can not remain here. I can not face those whose trust I have helped to betray. Let them take all—everything."

"Stay. Be brave. You may retrieve —"

"I will hear no more. Oh, John Lewis, if you have not forgotten our former friendship, watch over Alice! Call her Lewis—any name—but make her forget that name which has been disgraced."

He pushed Father Lewis aside, and, crushing his hat over his eyes as he went, walked into the street.

"God have mercy on him!" murmured the priest, as he gazed after his friend through the plate-glass window of the office. "If the blow fell on these two men only, it were bad enough; but the poor, whose hard-earned savings are invested here! May God and His Mother pity them, and keep them from cursing the causes of *their* ruin!"

John Lewis and James Belforest had been chums at college. They had not lost their old sentiment of friendship even when the former became a Catholic convert and then a Catholic priest.

James Belforest, touched by the words and example of his friend, had often promised to "look into the matter" when business would allow him time for religion, but business thus far had not been accommodating, it seemed. Little Alice, however, had been baptized in the Catholic Church.

"Poor little Alice!" thought Father Lewis. "After all, it is for the best. The Sisters of the Sacred Heart will take better care of her than James Belforest could! I must also look after my nephew."

But Mrs. Verner did not trouble the good priest. She was a very proud woman, and the news of her husband's flight maddened her. Taking her son Albert, who was a year older than Alice Belforest, she hastened to New York to hide her shame in the midst of a crowded city. The letters that came from her to her brother were signed with her maiden name.

"If any of the Lewis family should happen to go wrong," said the priest, smiling, "I wonder what these people would do for a name."

Eagle's Falls was panic-stricken, and with reason. Its great institution, the bank "as firm as a rock," had crumbled away as other rocks sometimes crumble.

II.

"Unfaith in aught is want of faith in all."—*Tennyson.*

Eleven years have passed since the failure of the Belforest Bank. The Eagle's Falls people have not forgotten it, for nearly every farmer for miles around had some deposit in the bank, and they all suffered, more or less, by its collapse. The unhappy event gave an aggravating advantage to that class of people who never save any money. "We told you so!" they said. "A bank managed by two-men power! Ridiculous! *We* never deposited anything." And some of the unlucky ones were more angered by this cool assumption of sagacity than by the loss of their money.

After a time, however, the creditors were paid in part

out of the wreck of the bank, and frequent remittances came from James Belforest, in Brazil, for that purpose. In 1857, Albert Verner died at Baden-Baden. "It is the best thing he could do," said his proud wife, bitterly "A disgraced man is safest in the grave."

The woman who spoke those hard, cold words had been one of the most loving of wives, but her husband's dishonor seemed to have turned her heart to stone, and the stern Calvinism in which she believed was not likely to soften it. She was well educated, energetic, and work was the only thing that could make her forget. She toiled early and late, sewing, sewing, sewing, as if it were her one hope in life. Unvarying industry and economy at last enabled her to start in business as a dressmaker. Even in crowded New York she held her own, and succeeded in giving her son a profession. The day on which Albert Lewis earned the privilege of writing "M.D." after his name his mother wept for the first time in many years. The icy pride that had frozen her heart melted for a moment under the influence of a mother's tender pride in her son.

Father John Lewis—everybody calls him Father John—has a few more wrinkles in his face, his tall form is more stooped, and he has much more need for spectacles than he had eleven years ago.

He is growing old; but for him the time has not yet come, "when no man can work." He serves two churches, ten miles apart, and, if you consider that the road, or rather path, between them lies through Jersey sand, you will admit that his office is no sinecure.

His house, a rambling old structure—which was considerately bequeathed him by a grateful parishioner—stands on a hill not more than fifty yards from the beach

In the stillness of the night, the roar of the ocean seems to shake the timbers of the house.

It is Sunday evening. Vespers had been sung at St. Paul's and the red afterglow of a sunset still lingers on the cross at the top of the wooden spire. Father John is sitting on the porch of the pastoral house enjoying his only luxury—a cigar.

"Father John! Father John!" cries a cracked voice, in a tone that an ordinary person might use in calling "fire!" But Father John does not start; he is used to it. It is only his old housekeeper, Cynthia Ann Spence, who makes her appearance from the house, carrying two letters. As usual, Cynthia Ann looks scornful; as usual on Sundays, Cynthia Ann wears a dress with many flounces; as usual, on week-days and Sundays, indoors and out, Cynthia Ann wears a calico and cardboard sunbonnet.

"Beggin' letters," snaps Cynthia Ann. "Tim Tooney just brought 'em from the post-office. Throw 'em in the fire without readin' 'em. *I* would." And Cynthia Ann disappears abruptly.

It is not yet dusk. Father John puts on his glasses, and opens the letter with the New York postmark.

"DEAR BROTHER: Many times you have expressed a wish in your letters to see my son Albert. I have not sent him to you sooner, though I knew that you could help his education much, because I feared that in your hands he would become a Papist. I speak plainly. Now, however, he is old enough to take care of himself. He knows the Old and the New Testaments almost by heart, as it has always been my custom to make him study the Scriptures on the Sabbath, besides taking him to the Rev

Job Hardwrinkle's three services; but, in spite of all this, his religious impressions are, I regret, not very strong. I warn you, however, that if you attack him with Catholic arguments, he will doubtless confound you with his Scriptural knowledge. You have probably forgotten the text about 'Wisdom out of the mouths of babes and sucklings,' which you learned in your youth, for I have often heard the Rev. Mr. Hardwrinkle say that with you Romanists the Book is a dead letter. My son does not know of his father's disgrace. I do not wish him to know of it. Call him Lewis, and let it be forgotten that he ever bore another name. He has lately graduated, as you will see by the inclosed paragraphs from the *Herald*. A few weeks' rest with you will do him good, and better enable him to enter upon his duties here as assistant to a prominent physician.

"He will be with you early next week.

"Your sister, M. LEWIS."

Father John laid down the first letter with a sigh, and opened the second.

"PARA, *May* 1, 18—.

"DEAR OLD FRIEND: A steamer, touching here on its way to Rio, gives me this opportunity of writing to you. The mail is about closing, which accounts for this villainous scrawl. You know, for I have told you several times, that my ventures in coffee and rice have made me—yes, I may safely say it—rich. A large amount of my wealth is invested in valuable property in New York and Eagle's Falls; besides, I have paid many of the debts of the old bank. I am growing old, and intend to start North to little Alice as soon as I can wind up my affairs here. Dear little Alice! When I see her, I will tell her the story of the old bank, and call her by her own name, 'Alice Belforest.' We Belforests can once more hold up our heads and look the world in the eye. By the same mail, I write to the Superior of the Ladies of the Sacred Heart, requesting her to send Alice to you. I will, if all goes well, be with you myself in a month or two. Alice has the Somerville diamond cross. I sent it to her as soon as I acquired funds to redeem it. Alice is an heiress, and when I have feasted my eyes on her, I have thoughts of hunting up poor Verner's son, and sealing my forgiveness by making a match. Is your nephew a better man than his father or I? By the way, a Jesuit here, Padre Torquato, has almost persuaded me to be a Catholic, but I have no time to think of that at present. The mail closes. *Vale*, as we said at school.

"JAMES BELFOREST."

"'Too late, too late; ye can not enter here!'" quotes Father John, folding up the letter. "I am afraid it will be with James Belforest as it was with the foolish virgins. He will have no time, indeed, when time slips from his grasp, at the last moment; but who can tell what Alice may accomplish? Bless me! she must be quite a young lady. What on earth will I do with her? And my nephew here, too! I'd better write, and ask the Sisters to keep her a while. No; that would seem inhospitable, and" (looking at the post-office mark on the envelope), "this letter has been delayed; she may be on her way hither already. I'll consult Cynthia."

"Law sakes!" says that valuable personage, throwing back her sun-bonnet, and allowing it to dangle gracefully by the strings. "Sure as my name is Cynthy Ann Spence, you'll have trouble, Father John. A feller and a gal comin'! The first thing you know she'll be his admiration and he'll be her admiration, and off they'll go an' git married, and both as poor as Job's turkey when he hadn't a feather, I'll be bound! Pooty doin's for a priest's house!"

"I can not prevent them from coming, you see," says Father John, ruefully. "There's plenty of room in the house—"

"Oh, that's all well enough," interrupts Cynthia Ann, resignedly. "An' I kind a'guess I can manage by borrowin' a few things from Mrs. Martin 'cross the lots, even if I do have to work my fingers to the bone."

"If they were both Catholics," begins Father John, rather thinking aloud than speaking to Cynthia.

"An' if they ain't," snaps Cynthia Ann, "don't have 'em here. Leastways, if she's a Catholic, she may turn him before marriage, but if she's a Protestant, keep him out o' her way. There was my Hezekiah an' me. When your teachin' opened my eyes to the truth, he was a rantin' Methodist, but I turned. 'Hezekiah,' says I—"

"Yes, I know," returns Father John, "I think you have given me enough advice for one evening, Cynthia."

"Maybe I have, and maybe I haven't," retorts Cynthia, recovering her bonnet with a jerk. "Tea's ready."

Father John is more absent-minded than usual, and half a dozen times has Cynthia Ann to interfere in order to prevent him from inadvertently misusing her pet china.

"Some men," she mutters, rather irrelevantly, "ought to be in Heaven; they ain't fit for this airth. But," after a pause, "that kind's mighty scarce."

A sunlit sky, with floating white clouds; stretches of meadows, vividly, brightly green, with here and there a wooded spot of shade; beyond, a thin strip of still brighter green—the marsh grass near the sea; and yet beyond, old ocean itself seeming narrow and crescent-shaped.

Alice Lewis sees all this through the open window of the railroad car.

The fresh, salt-tinged breeze tries to roughen her smooth brown hair, and then makes a swoop at the worn face of the tired-looking woman at her side. The woman closes her weary eyes—she has been travelling all night—but her baby finds it out right away, and utters a thrilling yell of remonstrance.

"Will nobody kill that child?" demands an awakened old bachelor. "I've given it all my cough-lozenges, and it doesn't seem satisfied yet. Why isn't there a special car for babies? Give 'em the smoking-car. I never smoke."

Alice stretches out her hands, and takes the baby, which, being allowed to tear her fan to pieces, condescends to be silent. The look of rest on the mother's face as she sinks to sleep more than repays Alice.

That young man on the other side, with the dark moustache and the frank-looking brown eyes, is pretending to read an illustrated paper, but in reality he is watching Alice. At the last station, she got into the wrong car, and their baggage became mixed up, because his initials are the same as hers, "A. L.," and they were obliged to hold a short dialogue, she speaking in the soft sweet voice which is so rare among American women, but which convent-bred girls have in perfection.

Her few simple words linger yet in his mind. He looks at a damsel at the far end of the car—a damsel with garments wonderfully ruffled and puffed, with a short fringe of hair on her forehead, and a *soupçon* of rouge on her cheeks, and then his eyes involuntarily stray toward Alice, with her smooth hair, innocent face, and tasteful raiment. As she bends over that child, he thinks of a picture by Sassaferreto—not irreverently, though he is a Protestant.

The *enfant terrible* having demolished the fan, utters a few notes preliminary to a grand fantasia, and Alice hums a little hymn. That finished, she is not allowed to stop, and she glides into Herrick's *Daffodils*, intended only for the baby's ear, but which her neighbor does not fail to catch. He listens attentively, and he never forgets the song, which is almost a murmur—

> "Fair daffodils, we weep to see
> You haste away so soon;
> As yet the early-rising sun
> Has not attained his noon.
> Stay, stay,
> Until the hastening day
> Has run
> But to the even-song,
> And, having prayed together, we
> Will go with you along!"

"Seaview!" calls the conductor.

The baby is restored to its mother, and the two A. L.'s step upon the platform of the little station.

The sexton, Tim Rooney, has driven Father John's old gig to the station every day of the preceding five days in the week; but to-day, for some reason best known to himself, he has rested. Luckily, St. Paul's cross is plainly visible from the station, and Alice guides her steps toward it. The young man, however, asks a boy at the station, whose directions are somewhat complicated, and consequently he makes a long circuit. Alice is the slower walker, and the two meet on Father John's porch.

"Alice, this is my nephew, Albert Lewis," says Father John.

And they are very glad to know each other. They say so, and, in this case, they mean it.

Six weeks have passed. Albert Lewis will leave Seaview to-morrow. Father John is not opposed to innocent amusements, and the Seaview people have made it pleasant for Alice with musical parties, croquet, and the like. Albert Lewis has seen her often, among the poor, among the rich, sympathizing in joy or in grief.

"She is a true-hearted girl, and she will be a noble woman," he has said to himself many times.

This afternoon Alice stands near the railing of the porch, holding a book in her hand. Amidst the lace at her throat glistens, for the first time, Lady Somerville's diamond cross. The glory of the sunset falls on earth and sky, and the creamy white roses which cling to the porch turn rosy-hued in the light.

"Alice!" Alice starts; it is the first time *he* has called her thus. Her brow and cheeks vie with the roses.

"Alice!" speaks Albert Lewis plainly and directly, "will you be my wife?"

There is silence. Alice steals a glance at his face, so grave, sincere, tender in its expression.

"I can not," she answers, tremulously; "I am a Catholic—you are not."

"Is that all?" he says, with a relieved sigh. "I thought that Father John might have objected on account of my poverty, or something of that kind. I have fair prospects, Alice, and I will work for you night and day, as I will for my mother, to whom I owe everything.

A difference in religious opinions need not prevent us from being happy."

"*You* can not understand," she answers, "and *I* can not argue. I have just been reading in this book," she continues, grasping at the first words that seem to bear on the subject, "faith and unfaith can ne'er be equal powers."

"You would say 'yes,' if I were a Catholic? Well, Alice, I will be a Catholic for your sake."

"No, no!" she says, eagerly, "if you can not be a Catholic for God's sake—for the sake of sacred truth—remain what you are. But, Albert, I am only a girl, and I—I like you a little. Speak to Father John, and I will abide by his decision."

"I agree. I will go to Mass every Sunday—for your sweet sake, and maybe after awhile—but I see Father John in his room."

Father John is a priest, but also a man, and, like other men, he is tempted. His nephew is poor; Alice—though she does not yet know it—is an heiress—an heiress to a large wealth. Why not endow Albert with this wealth, make these two happy for the present, and leave the question of Faith to the future? He breathes a silent prayer, and firmly answers, "No."

The next morning Alice and Albert say farewell on the little porch.

"Poor Alice!" sighs Father John. "But, after all, human hearts are of little worth if not crushed and broken to the will of God."

As he looks after the departing form of Albert, Tim Rooney brings him a letter. It is written in Portuguese.

"PARA, *June* 3, 18—.

"REVEREND SIR: As the legal adviser of Mr. James Belforest, it is my sad duty to inform you that my client was suddenly stricken with apoplexy on the fifth day of last month. Everything possible was done for him. Padre Torquato was sent for, but he arrived too late. I have communicated with Mr. Belforest's New York lawyer, whose name and address you will find below.

"SANCHO GOMEZ."

"Too late! Too late!" And the unaccustomed tears dim Father John's eyes. James Belforest was his oldest friend.

After a week has passed, Alice goes back in tears and mourning, to enter the novitiate of the Sisters of the Sacred Heart.

III.

"We have short time to stay, as you;
We have as short a spring."
—"*To Daffodils*," HERRICK.

"Yes," says Cynthia Ann, wiping her eyes with her black apron, "I am kind o' resigned like, but I did think that when God has so many saints in Heaven, he might have spared us one on airth. But I s'pose he knows best."

Cynthia Ann is talking to Alice Belforest, who, since her father's death, has resumed her own name. Father John, who survived his old friend only three months, is the subject of their conversation.

Alice entered the novitiate of the Sacred Heart, but it did not take long to discover that she had no vocation for the life of a religieuse, and so she and Cynthia Ann went to housekeeping at Eagle's Falls. They are now seated in Alice's pretty sitting-room.

Four years have changed Alice greatly. She is the same, yet not the same. She is beautiful, womanly, graceful; but now she is a grave, sad queen among women; then she was a joyous princess among girls.

The last four years have been busy years for her. Her large fortune has dwindled to a comparatively small sum; but in all Eagle's Falls there is no one who suffered by the collapse of the Belforest Bank who has not been repaid in full. The stain has been wiped from the Belforest name.

She thinks of Albert sometimes; but she has never heard from or of him, though Cynthia Ann has told her of his mother's death.

Albert, or Dr. Verner, as I ought to call him now, has prospered. He too has resumed his father's name.

"I will not tell you the wrong your father did," Mrs. Verner said, passionately. "I command you *never* to inquire."

"If our name has been disgraced, mother, I will redeem it!" he answered proudly. And blessing him, she died.

"*Domine, non sum Dignus!* I am unworthy—unworthy!" murmurs Albert Verner, kneeling before the Holy of Holies, in the Eagle's Falls church.

Alice's prayers have availed. God's grace has opened Albert Verner's eyes to the Light "which shineth in darkness."

"I will see her in Heaven, if I can never see her here.' This feeling, human and earthly as it was, drew him toward the Truth, and now Albert Verner is one of the most fervent of Catholics.

As he is about to leave the church he notices a bright glitter just made under the door of the tabernacle. He looks again. He can not mistake the great diamond in the centre. It is the diamond cross that Alice wore on that summer afternoon.

He asks a question of the sexton, whom he meets in the vestibule.

"Is it the cross you mean? Sure, that was given to the church by Miss Belforest, the best-hearted lady in the place, sir."

Miss Belforest! It is not *her* cross, then, he thinks. If the man had said that it was given by a nun of the order of the Sacred Heart, his conclusion would have been different.

Albert Verner has come to Eagle's Falls to attend a convention of physicians. After that was over, there were several important consultations, and his stay is prolonged.

He has letters of introduction to various people, and as "good" society is rather limited at Eagle's Falls, he meets Alice Belforest very often. She talks to him as she does to others, and makes no sign.

"My Alice would be like this one, if she were in the world," he can not help thinking.

On the morning of the day on which he intends to leave Eagle's Falls, he calls on Miss Belforest to say good-bye.

Alice is at the piano in the sitting-room when Cynthia ushers him into the parlor. He hears a faint sound of music on which softly float the words he caught that day in the car,

> "Fair daffodils, we weep to see
> You haste away so soon."

He is at her side in an instant.

"Alice, my Alice, at last!"

"I knew you all the time."

"Yes," snaps that oracle, Cynthia Ann, addressing the bridesmaids, "even the best of men haven't got no memories; but just show me the woman that can forget!"

A STORY OF TO-DAY.

I.

AT SEA.

ALL the last part of the afternoon there had been a yellow light on the sea, not the rich glow of an ordinary sunset, but a sickly glare which shone from the edges of the cloud masses in the west.

A boy, who had slyly crept into the boat at the brig's side, looked up, singing in the quaint old rhyme:

> "Mackerel's scales and mare's tails,
> Make lofty ships to carry low sails."

The mate, too, glanced upward, and impatiently turning, drove the urchin from his "coign of vantage." This brig, the *Hawk*, was not young, and time does not toughen fowls of her species. Fifteen days had she been out from Liverpool; she bore a full cargo and a few passengers, mostly friends of the captain, who were working their passage, or who had been taken on board from holy charity. Among the latter, two or three in number, were Kathleen Bryant and her little girl. It was enough to make the hardest heart ache—if the hardest heart *could* know such things—to forecaste what such a creature should have to suffer in the bustling new world, where even sympathy would take a form which her warm Irish heart could never understand. She was a widow, young, timid, gentle, poor, with no one akin to her except the little child.

The yellow light faded from the sky, leaving the sea a dark, undefinable color, throbbing as if it were the heart of the universe. Then sea and sky deepened in gloom, and the *Hawk* was dark as a funeral scarf from stem to stern; a low moan came from all quarters of the sea, and the winds were let loose.

Kathleen, in a dark cabin, clasped her child tight, for a crash, the sound of rushing waters, and many shouts and cries struck her ears. She shrank closer to the wall of the cabin, pulling her shawl around the girl.

Little Kathleen only opened her large blue eyes, and looked intently into her mother's face.

"Lord, have mercy on us!"

And when the mother got as far as "Holy Mary," the child answered as she had been taught, "Pray for us!"

"Kathleen," whispered the mother, aroused from the stupor by the little girl's voice, "keep near to me, shut your eyes, and keep sayin' your prayers; and here, Kathleen, darlin'," she said, with a touch of that prophetical inspiration which only mothers have, "take these, and if anything should separate us!"—

The ship shivered in every plank. Crash of timber, boom of thunder, and the weak voices of men! The world seems to be near its end. Kathleen and her child are dragged on deck. She feels a sharp pain in her arm, which is bruised against the gangway; she faints, clutching the old plaid shawl that holds her darling.

The wild waves have not left much plumage on that poor old bird, the *Hawk*. Captain, mate, and crew have done their duty. The two boats, with all the brig's load of human beings, are tossing to and fro like thistle-down on a windy day,

A voice sounds even above the shrillness of the wind.

"Kathleen! my child, my child!"

The men in the captain's boat look at one another.

"Too bad, too bad," mutters the captain; "the girl is in the mate's boat!"

"Sure she is in God's keeping, wherever she is," says an old woman, frightened by the stony look that comes over the young mother's face.

"My child, my child!"

Is it the wind that answers, "Mother"? for the mate's boat is out of sight.

II.

IN "SOCIETY."

"I don't know much about religion," said Alice Wesley; "but I do know what 'good' style is."

She daintily held her tiny teacup of scarlet and gold, and glanced around the room. She was of the prevailing blonde type, with fuzzy light hair, pulled down under her hat; a nose "tip tilted," as the laureate has it, and large, blue eyes, which she held under fashionable control; a complexion which was perfect "pale roseate" in gaslight or semi-gloom, but which showed a few freckles in daylight. She was standing near a cabinet of *bric-à-brac* in a costume, soft and dark, which seemed, like the pictures of Ingres, to be a study of form rather than of color.

"For instance, my dear—I always speak confidentially to girls, for they find out everything, anyhow—I am Ritualistic, because it is fashionable to be Ritualistic. It is quite a good style here in Washington to be Catholic, you know; but then there is something too *real* about you Catholics. Now, uncle declares that I am Irish (I am, anyhow, you know), and haven't any ancestors, though I *do* put the Wesley crest on my note-paper; uncle picked me up somewhere; he never will tell me where—and that I ought to be a Catholic; but, my dear, some of you Catholics, particularly the Irish, are in such *fearful* style."

She paused, to bow to a young man who had just entered the room.

"Felix Woodward, I declare! As I was saying, it's bad form to be a Methodist here, although the Administration is Methodist, and yet at home uncle knows so many young ministers that one usually has to assume *soupçon* of Methodism."

"But when you were at Notre Dame you liked to go to chapel."

The speaker was the young lady into whose ears Alice Wesley had been pouring her "ideas." She was taller, more graceful, not as pretty as Alice. Her brown hair was plainly arranged in the simple Grecian mode; her costume, while faultless, was not ultra-fashionable. Her complexion was not pale, but colorless, which, with the irregularity of her features, and the calm, thoughtful look in her eyes, suggested a head of Juno on an old cameo.

"Excuse me; I was not listening. I was watching the French Minister. I don't understand what the President means by letting foreign Governments send so many married men to this country. An ambassador *must* be unmarried, in order to give American girls a chance. What were you saying, Helen?"

Helen Winter repeated her sentence.

"Of course. It was quite the proper thing to go to Mass there. It pleased the Sisters. Some more tea?

Have some, do. It's really a pleasure to use these delicious China cups. I like this kind of thing," she said, turning to the cabinet; "here is a vase carved by Cellini, and there, at your elbow, some lovely amber Bohemian glass, and beyond, a set of Sèvres. Just look at that Cupid on the plates, driving his flock of yellow butterflies; and this majolica cat!"

"A lot of useless *roba*," said Helen Winter, indifferently, "which cost money, and does nobody good. It is not like a painting. Everybody can understand a picture; but how many people here know whether the shape of that vase painted by Boucher is modern or antique?"

"Well, Boucher vases and Minton ware mean culture—"

"What is culture?"

Alice showed her white teeth in a quizzical little smile, and said, after a pause: "To know more odd things than somebody else; to believe yourself superior to the *canaille*; to quote Brahma and the Vedas; to admire Wagner, Swinburne, and Baudelaire; to find moral things immoral because they are *not* true art, and immoral things moral, because they *are* true art. I am a critic."

Both girls laughed, and Alice continued:

"Mrs. Houghton is asking Felix Woodward to sing. He has a fair tenor, and sings rather nicely. I like the singing at a kettledrum; it relieves restraint; under cover of it you can talk in your natural tone, and you are not obliged to whisper as if you were at a funeral. He begins. Old Feoli (who has been *attaché* ever since Washington's time) plays the accompaniment."

"Let us listen."

"Turn, Fortune, turn thy wheel with smile or frown;
With that wild wheel we go not up or down;
Our hoard is little, but our hearts are great.
'Smile and we smile, the lords of many lands,
Frown and we smile, the lords of our own hands;
For man is man, and master of his fate.'"

Felix Woodward's voice was strong and clear, and he gave the words with an energy that seemed to bid defiance to Fortune. Helen looked at him with interest. He was young, not particularly handsome; there was an expression of reserved power about him that attracted her.

Alice betrayed a little amusement.

"You seem interested. He's only a book-keeper, or something of that kind, out on a holiday. Mrs. Houghton invites him because he is a Southern relative—has seen better days, and that sort of thing. He'd be nice to flirt with, but of course no girl who respects herself will ever marry him."

"Why not?"

"*Why not!* For the very sufficient reason that he has no money."

"But she might love him sufficiently—"

"Pardon me, my dear," interrupted Alice, with an air of patronage, "you are either very hypocritical or very unsophisticated. Love is bad form; but *you* haven't the slightest occasion to bother about the 'coming man.' Mr. Vincy—"

A flush reddened Helen's brow. Alice, fortunately, was enabled to retrieve her mistake. "Let me present Mr. Woodward."

Felix Woodward bowed and said something about a pleasant afternoon. Alice chatted gaily, but with more reserve.

"We have been talking of religion," she said, with a determination to force her companion to talk; "Miss Winter is quite devout—*enfant de Marie*, and all that."

"An excellent thing in a woman. Men are religious nowadays because they are good, but no man is good because he is religious. Religion has lost its power."

"He is rude," thought Helen, "or too frank." Her eyes sparkled. She spoke. "If you were a Catholic, Mr. Woodward, you could daily see that religion has not lost its power."

"Ah! you are a Catholic, Miss Winter? I know some Catholics, poor and rich; the poor ones, I admit, are devout, because they are taught to be; with the rich and educated ones religion is a mere æsthetic sentiment. They go to Mass, and like the music and pomp; but that does not prevent them from doing what they please. They are too 'superior' to mingle with the herd of their co-religionists. I admire your religion, Miss Winter; but I think that educated Catholics are generally supercilious to their brethren and apologetic to dissenters, and that the mass is uneducated and ill-bred."

Helen was surprised, and somewhat indignant. "He is ill-bred," she thought, "but there is, from his point of view, some truth in what he says."

"No doubt the crowds that followed our Lord were uneducated, and I don't suppose they all knew the best-bred manner of eating their loaves and fishes," she said.

"Oh, Mr. Vincy!" Alice exclaimed. A gentleman, apparently about forty years of age, stood beside Helen's chair. He wore mutton-chop whiskers, and was attired in the most pronounced English fashion. His head was bald on the top; his face florid; there was no expression about him, except one of exalted satisfaction. He was

Mr. Vincy, the millionaire. He had made his money by means of a great capability of laying out railroads in Russia. He believed in himself; he wanted a foreign mission and a ladylike wife. You know all about him that is worth knowing, except that he was supposed to be the man for whom Helen was destined by her parents.

Felix Woodward was not handsome; in fact, not as handsome as Mr. Vincy; but he looked like a gentleman, and wore no jewelry, while Mr. Vincy's malachite sleeve-buttons, studded each with a ruby, and his gorgeous ring and chain, made Alice curl her lip, while she admired the jewels themselves.

"Nice little party; nice little party! You should have seen the reception the Czar gave in my honor, though, after I had finished that railroad to Loutchinova. It was a stunner; no cakes and weak tea. Champagne, worth more than you'd make in four years, sir."

"Pardon me, but do you collect the income tax, sir?"

Alice held up her handkerchief to prevent giggling. "Permit me to introduce Mr. Woodward, Mr. Vincy!"

"Not necessary, not necessary," said Mr. Vincy, in swelling tones; "we have met before, down-town."

"I have forgotten you." And bowing to the ladies, Felix Woodward went to another part of the room.

A frown appeared on Mr. Vincy's pink forehead. "Clerk down-town. How does he come here? Mrs. Houghton ought to be more careful."

"This is a republican country, Mr. Vincy," said Helen.

"Wrong principle—wrong principle entirely."

Alice's nonsense soon made Mr. Vincy regain his good humor. In a short time Mrs. Winter, who chaperoned Helen, came up, and the girls separated.

Helen rode home in a state of satisfaction. *Cui bono?*

Alice made her sad; Mr. Vincy was vulgar and "horrid" (for the first time); the world was hollow. "I will be a nun," she thought. Before they reached her father's house, on Capitol Hill, she forgot this thought in the attempt to discover what interested her in Felix Woodward, who was certainly brusque and ill-bred, and yet there was something about him—

III.

"IPHIGENIA!"

Mr. Winter's pampered London coachman was drunk on the day of Mrs. Houghton's kettledrum, consequently Helen and her chaperon had to wait some time in the hall at Mrs. Houghton's while Jehu clumsily manœuvred the carriage up to the sidewalk. The strength and chilliness of Washington wind is proverbial; and Mrs. Winter, who was delicate at all times, took cold. She was one of those delicate people who are always on the verge of death apparently, and when, in ten days' time, she died of pneumonia, everybody was surprised, although everybody had expected that sad event for the last ten years.

The dead woman and Helen had loved each other devotedly. They had been confidantes, friends, companions to an extent which is very rare nowadays between mothers and daughters.

Mrs. Winter had lived a gentle, harmless life, and she died in the Catholic faith.

Her husband was of the worldly order. There had been little sympathy between him and his wife, and none whatever between him and Helen. He paid her bills and admired her because other people congratulated him on having such a charming daughter. He was the owner of some very wealth-producing cotton-mills in Massachusetts, and just at present he was much preoccupied in lobbying an important bill through Congress, consequently his wife's death was a matter of secondary interest, as she herself had been for a long time. Helen was the only real mourner, and the care and sorrow drove all other thoughts from her mind. Her days were spent in religious reading and prayer. What is life? she asked herself, and answered, The vestibule of death! These days were bitter-sweet and solemn. It was a relief that her father never required her presence except at dinner, when she usually met Mr. Vincy, who talked of the value of his new cottage at Newport, his railroad to Loutchinova, and his contempt for all men who were not self-made, until his host nipped him with a touch of gentlemanly sarcasm, and reduced the conversation to a monologue on the prospects of his bill. After a time these quiet days grew long. Helen became restless. She was tired of Mr. Vincy. He laughed too loud and jeered openly at everything he did not understand—religion, art, music.

"He is not a gentleman," she thought; "he despises poor people, and respects only those who are wealthy; he thinks that money is everything. I wonder if Mr. Woodward—but why Mr. Woodward? He is no better than anybody else—"

A knock at the door. Alice Wesley entered, bright, pretty, and voluble as usual.

"How well you look in black, dear—like a lady out of Dante Rossetti's poems—mediæval, you know; and you are a girl who need not trouble yourself about your looks either; your '*beau mari*' is secured; at the german the other night, Mr. Vincy posed for 'a forsaken swain,' you not being there."

" Alice ! "

"What a queer girl you are! You don't seem at all delighted at the prospect of marrying a million. I would be wild with delight, although Mr. Vincy is the most detestably vulgar man I know; still a million—"

"*Alice!*"

" Oh, what's the use of girls being hypocritical to each other. By the way, I just ran in to borrow a pin for the lace at my neck. I'm in a dreadful hurry to promenade on the avenue in this lovely sunshine; and I've lost my pin—the lovely one, with the figure of Œnone. Can't you lend me one ? "

Helen produced a box of glittering trifles. Alice selected a large, carved cross of black bog-oak.

" This is old and pretty. Ta! ta! ma belle! I wish you would come with me."

" I am going to Vespers. It is a holy day."

" Saint Agnes ! "

It was just after luncheon. There were several hours to pass before dinner. Helen was in the mood for a long walk. She had it in her mind to ride to Georgetown, and cross the bridge to Arlington. She knew the road, and the sadness of the place harmonized with her melancholy. But she did not care to go through the Virginia woods alone. She finally took an aimless walk, and at vesper time found herself under the arches of St. Dominic's.

The majestic swell of the organ, the forms of the Fathers in their black and white robes amid the haze of incense, and the atmosphere of prayer, were better for her than the sadness of Arlington ; and her mind, heart, and soul were satisfied.

Coming out, her eyes were full of the glory of the stained window over the organ, irradiated by golden light, and she did not notice a gentleman at the gate until he spoke, half involuntarily:

"Miss Winter!"

"Mr. Woodward! I have not seen you since Mrs. Houghton's afternoon."

There was a pause. Pauses are full of meaning, and this pause meant that one had been thinking of the other. In their thoughts they had become friends; and now it was necessary to go from the ideal to the real. They were both trying to do this.

"You had a sad time since that afternoon."

"Very sad."

"You said a few chance words that afternoon which have been in my mind ever since. You said that Catholics were *governed* by their religion, and that they did not make it a thing of convenience."

"I meant to say that, whether I did or not," said Helen.

"Well, I thought I knew to the contrary, and I said so; but I have discovered that I judged from superficial premises."

"I *know* you did," she said, earnestly.

"I had heard of *your* charity and goodness—"

Helen's face reddened, partly from annoyance, partly from pleasure that he should praise her, even with second-hand praise.

"I do not like compliments."

"I did not mean to compliment you. I meant to show you what your example has led me to; but you jumped at a conclusion. Do I look like a man who would pay compliments?"

Helen thought: "What a strange man! His apparent rudeness is only earnestness!"

"I have come to the conclusion that your religion is the only one that governs men's passions and impulses. All men need to be restrained and governed. In a few days I will be a Catholic. Pray for me!"

He bowed and turned the corner.

"He *is* rude!" thought Helen. "I wanted to talk to him."

And Helen thought of him until she reached Capitol Hill.

He had come back to the corner, and watched her until she reached the avenue.

"A true woman," he said; "what a wife she would make for a good man! And yet I know so little of her!"

That evening, after dinner, Alice brought back the cross. There was a worried look on her face.

"I had an adventure," she said, in an agitated way. "I had not gone far to-day, when I noticed that I was followed by an old woman, with a basket on her arm; a withered, meanly-dressed old woman, Helen; she passed and repassed me, turned around, and looked sharply at me several times; at last she cried out, as if she were about to have a fit, 'Kathleen, Kathleen, is it you, my child?' Her voice frightened me. I ran into a store, and somebody sent her away. Oh, Helen, if that common woman should be my—my—MOTHER!"

Moisture came into Helen's eyes.

"It would be happiness—"

"*Happiness!*" cried Alice. "I am nearly wild with dread! That coarse, common thing *my* mother! I will go away and hide. I will deny her, even if she prove it. I will!"

"There is no fear," said Helen, trying to conquer a feeling of repulsion to this heartless Sybarite; "I heard your uncle telling papa that you are the daughter of his brother, who married a poor Irish girl—"

"I know! He says that; but I don't believe it. He will tell me nothing of my parents; and *she* may be my mother. I will *never* own her!"

Alice's culture and refinement had become weeds which had killed those flowers that spring from the heart and soul.

"Mr. Vincy will call to-morrow evening," said Mr. Winter, when Alice had gone. "He intends to propose. Of course you will say yes."

The blood flew to Helen's brow.

"Papa, I do not love him."

"What has that to do with the matter? Don't be foolish, girl. He is worth a million."

"I don't care."

"*I* do. My bill has been defeated. I was so sure of its success that I mortgaged everything to push it. I must have this millionaire for my son-in-law, or I shall be ruined. You *must* marry Mr. Vincy." He said all this slowly, calmly, as was his wont.

Helen burst into tears.

"Iphigenia!" sneered Mr. Winter, "a modern young woman weeps at the thought of sacrificing herself for a million. 'Tis passing strange!"

She prayed for strength, for light. Marry Mr. Vincy! The thought filled her with horror. Be the means of ruining her father. She could not, she could not!

The next morning, after a sleepless night, she sought relief in one of her long walks. Again, fatigued, she knelt in St. Dominic's. The church seemed cold and empty. She prayed desperately. God could save her, if He would.

"*Are there two of them?*"

These whispered words made her turn.

There was an old woman, with pinched features, poorly clad, at the end of the pew.

"If you please, Miss," said the old woman, timidly, "an' I hope you'll not think it strange for me to be askin'. Is that cross you wear at your throat yours?"

"Certainly," answered Helen, amazed.

"Have you a rosary, Miss; an old one, of small white beads, and big black ones, with no crucifix, but only a broken sixpence, the first thing my husband gave me, on the chain?"

The woman ran over the words with such trembling eagerness that Helen scarcely understood her at first.

Helen hesitated. In a drawer at home lay an old black and white rosary, from which the crucifix had been broken; and to which was attached a broken sixpence. This was the first plaything that Helen remembered.

"I have such a rosary," said Helen, "but let us leave the church. We can talk elsewhere."

The woman did not heed her. Her wrinkled face turned pale, revealing very plainly the blue circles around her eyes, set there by years of suspense and tears. She staggered and fell against the side of the pew. Helen caught her hands.

"Thank you, acushla," said the woman, with a wistful look. "Sure you have her eyes clear as the sky at home! Do you go by the name of Winter?"

"I am Helen Winter."

"Not Kathleen?"

"No." Helen's self-possession was taking leave of her.

This woman must be insane, and yet, as usual, Helen could feel, but not think.

"You are my girl! My Kathleen!"

Kathleen Bryant—aged by care and the hope that maketh the heart sick—prostrated herself in the aisle and said her *Nunc Dimittis*. After a silence which was eloquent, Kathleen arose, her face bathed in tears.

"If you're happier, my child, with your rich friends than you would be with me, stay; but oh, let me see you sometimes."

Helen was bewildered. She said, "Come home with me, and speak to Mr. Winter."

As they went along Kathleen Bryant told how she had lost her child the night the *Hawk* was wrecked nineteen years ago; that, after a long search, she found the mate of the brig in New York, and heard that he had given the child into the care of a rich lady, Mrs. Winter, who had promised to bring her up in the Catholic faith. Kathleen now ceased to seek her child. She worked hard and was thrifty. She wanted money, only that she might find her child; and she had amassed sufficient to allow her, with frugality, to search everywhere, from morning to night.

"Sure, I put that cross into the old shawl that was around you, and gave you the rosary the last thing, darlin'!"

Helen led her mother up to her luxuriously furnished room.

"I can't take you away from all this, darlin'," cried poor Kathleen, with a heavy weight at her heart. "I am poor."

"I will go where you go, mother." This broke the ice. Helen felt that she had found her mother. That withered old woman had suddenly become more precious than the whole world.

What scientist can explain the thing? It was not reasonable. Helen wanted no proof. This woman was her mother.

Mr. Winter did not come home to dinner. The mother and daughter dined together up-stairs, much to the amazement of the servants. Later, when Mr. Vincy came, Helen led Kathleen into the parlor.

"My mother, Mr. Vincy."

The millionaire opened his mouth until the gold plate of his false teeth showed. His face expressed surprise and disgust when he recovered himself. Then Helen explained.

Mr. Winter entered at this juncture.

"Look here, Winter, is this true?" And Mr. Vincy ran over the story.

"I suppose so," said Mr. Winter, indifferently; "Helen is not my daughter. Mrs. Winter found her somewhere. If she wants to go to her mother I have no objection; but I suppose you have, as you want to marry her."

"Winter, I say; you don't expect me to marry the daughter of that old hag!" the millionaire said, swelling with rage. "If Helen will give her up, and keep the thing quiet, I'll think about it."

"Never!" said Helen.

"You're a brute, Vincy!" said Mr. Winter, politely. "It's all for the best, Helen, for I intend to marry Mrs. Houghton in four months' time, and Mr. Vincy might not like a stepmother-in-law."

Mr. Winter could afford to be independent now. Mrs. Houghton had agreed to advance all the money he wanted.

"You can stay here, Helen," he said, "if you like;

you have always behaved well; but I can't have the old lady here."

. . . . . .

In a little house in Philadelphia, Kathleen Bryant and her daughter live happily and contentedly. Peace and love dwell there.

"Frown, and we smile, the lords of our own hands."

Helen remembers those words. And the singer, whom she remembers too, has obtained a position in Philadelphia; when the little home is made ready Kathleen Bryant will again lose her daughter.

"Well, well," says Kathleen, between a smile and a tear, "sure, what's the difference? She's in God's keeping."

Alice Wesley, now Mrs. Vincy, tries to forget a longing for higher and better things in the dash and glitter of society, and sometimes she succeeds.

THE LISLES.

I.

"My dearest foe."—"HAMLET."

A GREAT change had long been taking place in Arthur Lisle's mind. The influences surrounding him had not been favorable to such a change. He could not tell where or when the first swell of this great wave had arisen in the ocean of his life; he only knew that now it had burst through all impediments. He stood, as it were, happy, yet fearful, watching the gates of his soul open to the flood of Faith.

Although he had scarcely passed his twenty-sixth year, he was rector of a fashionable church, St. Bonaventura's. This church was "high," but not extremely high. In its decorations it admitted florid crosses of all styles, but, as yet, incense, vestments, and possessions had not entered within its walls. Among its congregation there were no poor people; silk did not jostle serge, and clumsy shoes never profaned the soft carpets of this literal "chapel of ease." In its cushioned pews one was sure to see the latest things from Paris every Sunday; therefore its services were attended largely by that class of vacant-headed youths who on the sidewalk "most do congregate."

Of this church Arthur Lisle was deemed worthy for various reasons. His father, Eric Lisle, was one of the "best" people in Central City. No man was considered more respectable, no man more wealthy, consequently no man was more "looked up to" than "old Lisle," as people called him, though he had barely reached the shady side of fifty. All his pride seemed to be in his only son; and now that Arthur had gained the position of rector of St. Bonaventura's, his father had hoped that he might one day enjoy the delight of uttering " Bishop " Lisle, not dreaming that his son was beginning to regard that title, in its Protestant Episcopal signification, as a delusion and an empty sham.

Arthur Lisle was a favorite among his parishioners. He was gentlemanly, eloquent, handsome, the very *beau phraseur* of a youthful reverend, but he was married. Of course this was a serious drawback in the eyes of the maidenly devotees at St. Bonaventura's; in consideration of his extraordinary good qualities, however, the amiable beings graciously permitted their papas and brothers to support him in vestry meetings and similar conclaves.

Thus far his path in life had been strewn with rose-leaves. And now it was his will—or rather, God's will—to thrust aside the roses, and to search for the sharp thorns beneath them—thorns that pierced his heart to its very core.

Once only had he seen his father in anger, and this was when he had hinted at the change his belief was undergoing. And then the old man gave way to no sudden or fierce burst of rage. His face became white, and his hands trembled.

"If," he said, slowly, "this delusion should ever lead you to embrace the Romish Belief, I would discard you—pitilessly. It is impossible—impossible! Yet, if it were not, I could never forgive you. Never speak to me of such a thing again. Forget it."

Eric Lisle was a man of few words, and these deeply impressed themselves on Arthur's memory. He had counted the cost. He knew his father too well to believe that he would relent; still, he hoped, in spite of better judgment.

One bright Sunday morning he ascended to the pulpit as usual. The blood-red spot which the sun threw from the stained-glass window upon the white velvet of the pulpit cushion, lay as it had lain there before for many Sundays. He had learned to watch it, and to notice that it always changed to purple when he came to the third head of his sermon. The same rustling of silks and preparatory coughs of other Sundays settled into silence. A vague, unreasonable thought passed through his mind: Could it be that, while nothing without was changed, he could have changed so utterly within?

To-day the sun had not time to turn the stain on the cushion from red to purple while he spoke.

In a few words he said farewell, and left St. Bonaventura's without a rector. He descended as the sound of his voice died away, and slowly walked from the scene of his labors, never to return.

"Gone over to Rome!—deplorable!—outrageous!—but I told you so!"

And for once Arthur Lisle's sermon was unfavorably criticised at the luncheon-tables of St. Bonaventura's select flock.

From the church, Arthur Lisle went to his father's house—for the pastoral residence had for some time been undergoing repairs. His earthly future was clouded; but all along the way his heart seemed full of sunshine. The light of peace had entered it. Feverish doubt and indecision had fled.

Agnes, his wife, sat in an arm-chair filled with pillows, near the window of a pleasant room. Agnes Lisle was one of those pale, *spirituelle* women who seem like greenhouse lilies, fit only for an atmosphere of warmth and care, ready to wither at the first chill breath. Her brown hair, gold-tinted by the noonday sun, had become dishevelled; as she turned her wan but beautiful face toward him, it seemed as if the halo of a higher life had already fallen around her. He paused, startled, and a cold thrill ran through him. Something in her expression reminded him of the look his dying mother had worn.

"Is it over?" she asked eagerly.

"Yes, Agnes," he answered, "it is over."

"Thank God!—thank God!" she murmured fervently.

Only a few days had passed since the waters of Baptism had purified her brow, and in her new strength she rejoiced in her husband's sacrifice.

"God has given me strength," he said; "may God give me strength!"

"The worst is over."

He felt that the worst was not over. He must meet his father; and, looking at Agnes, he saw the dim shadow of the angel of death.

The first trial did not come in the form he expected. He did not meet his father face to face.

An hour had scarcely passed when a note was brought to him. He opened it with a feeling as if it were a death-warrant. It contained a few terse sentences:

"Arthur Lisle:—After what you have done this day, I can not recognize you as my son. You have destroyed all my hope in you. Do not attempt to see me. It is useless. Go—I will not curse you, but I can not bless you.   Eric Lisle."

Arthur crushed the paper in his hand, and for an instant it seemed that *this* was too much to bear—even for God; but he dashed the temptation away from him; in his heart he said—

"Fiat voluntas tua."

"Agnes," he said, after a pause, "we must leave this house."

She looked startled, and then, with a glance of tender pity, arose from her chair.

"I am ready," she said, putting her thin hand on his arm. "Remember what Christ suffered for us; remember her who said: 'What sorrow is like to my sorrow?' and be strong."

"It is hard—hard," he groaned. "Forgive me, O Lord! *Fiat voluntas tua.*"

"Fiat voluntas tua," she repeated.

And together they left the house, the master of which they loved better than life, and who now was their "dearest foe."

II.

LITTLE AGNES.

Tall masts, taller warehouses, a glimpse of the river between huge piles of bags and barrels, a combination of odors in which salt-fish is prominent, yells, shrieks, bustle—imagine all these, and you have an idea of the neighborhood in which Arthur Lisle lives.

It is not a pleasant place. Few places near the waterside in a great city are pleasant; but these surroundings matter very little to Arthur Lisle now.

A month ago Agnes Lisle was carried to the grave. He had seen the shadow of death growing around her darker day after day. And yet, when the blow came, he could not realize that she was dying. Even now it seems like a dream—that slow, gradual parting from life and him. He can not realize that she is dead. Even while he utters prayers for her soul, he turns, half expecting to hear her join her low voice to his, as she was wont to do.

Another Agnes—a little Agnes—smiling like her mother, but with her father's eyes—has come to bear him company. Sometimes he holds the sleeping baby in his arms for hours, musing over the joy that "might have been," were she alive; and then he awakens, with a start, to the necessities of the present. This little Agnes— her legacy—must be provided for. Thus far, he has been unable to obtain employment. The talents which showed so brilliantly in the pulpit seem to be useless now. All his attempts at earning a livelihood have failed. The market is overstocked with clerks—trained clerks, too. Newspapers and magazines offer to open their pages to him if he will write "spicy" articles; but, to a man inured to sermon-writing, "spiciness" and flippancy of style are not easy acquisitions. He can teach nothing, though his mind is well stored, because he feels that he does not possess the faculty of imparting instruction, and because no one has offered him the opportunity. He can not work with his hands, because his hands have neither skill nor strength. To him it seems that the most stupid laborer on the wharves is his superior. The man may be stupid and ignorant, but he is not helpless. He is a producer. He can work; he does not cumber the earth. Following this train of thought, Arthur Lisle groans. And well he may, for in all the wide world there seems nothing that he can do to gain bread for the little child in his arms. His small stock of money has begun to find wings; his father has shown no sign of relenting; and he will soon be at the end of his resources.

Mrs. Mulligan interrupts his gloomy reverie with one of her double knocks. Mrs. Mulligan is the washer-woman, who lives on the second floor. She is a tall, masculine-looking woman, with a weather-beaten complexion, red hair, and high cheek-bones; but the good-natured expression on her face amply compensates for its lack of beauty. She supports, by the labor of her hands, five small Mulligans and a big Mulligan. The last is her "worse-half," who can not be persuaded to prefer work to whisky, and who gives this heroic woman more trouble than all the young brood. She works cheerfully as only an Irishwoman can work. She carries her cross loyally, though, it is true, not very humbly to outward-seeing eyes. Her faith is firm, and her deeds would shame many a professional philanthropist. Ten months ago, about the time that little Agnes Lisle was born, Mrs. Mulligan lost her youngest child—an Agnes, too; and so, when Arthur Lisle came to live in the third-story room of No. 9 River Place, she "took to" the new baby at once. A stranger would have thought that she had children enough of her own; yet her motherly heart seemed to be warm enough for all little strangers in distress.

Mrs. Mulligan's loud but cheery voice brings to Arthur Lisle's mind a new sense of life and light. Her bustling presence seems like a fresh breeze from the outer world.

and raises his spirits in spite of himself. Willingly he resigns his helpless burden to her care.

"Sure, sir," she says, rocking the baby gently to and fro with a movement which she could only have acquired through long experience in that soporific art, "sure she's just the best child I've ever known, barrin' me own Mickey. Och, it's me that has the trouble! Sure Mike's been at it again, sir." Arthur is following a passing ship with his eyes, and contemplating an idea that it has put into his mind.

"At what," he asks, absently.

"At what, sure?" replies Mrs. Mulligan; "at what would he be at, except the dhrink?"

"Oh," he answers, with a belief that he is saying the proper thing, "I thought it was something new."

Mrs. Mulligan, who reserves the right of finding fault with her husband solely to herself, fires up at once.

"Sure you're mistaken entirely, sir, if you think Mike Mulligan would be after demeanin' himself in any way barrin' his takin' a sup of the crathur now and then; and sure we all have our faults—"

"No doubt—no doubt," interrupts Arthur, feeling like a man who has unwittingly turned on a shower-bath, and who is unable to stop it.

"I'll make bould to say you have some faults yourself, sir; an' there wouldn't be a more harmless crathur on the face of the earth than the same Mike Mulligan, if he'd let the liquor alone. Bad luck to it! Faith, I'm disturbin' the baby!—bless her pretty face!"

"Mrs. Mulligan, would you like to keep my little girl?"

Mrs. Mulligan looks startled.

"Faith, sir, haven't I got enough of me own to keep?"

A very natural question!

"Not always—for a time," he answers, pursuing his own train of thought, "until I return. I am going away."

"And where, sir?"

"I don't know. I can not tell yet."

As he leaves the room, Mrs. Mulligan shakes her head, and the pitying expression of her face says as much as Ophelia's "sweet bells jangled."

Arthur Lisle walks rapidly through the streets that border on the river. Once or twice he pauses as if to turn back; but again he goes on. At last he stops before a dilapidated house, with "Boarding" painted on the dingy green door. He asks one of the seafaring men who are lounging around the steps whether Captain Halstead lives there. He is answered in the affirmative.

He has met Halstead, who commands the brig *Osprey*, several times during his weary search for employment.

When he comes out of the dingy boarding-house, he has bound himself to serve as a common sailor on board the *Osprey* during the term of her next voyage to Cuba.

He had made a desperate plunge—a rash, impetuous plunge, many would say; yet to himself it seemed his only refuge from starvation.

He thinks of little Agnes as he goes home, and for a few moments doubts the prudence of leaving her with Mrs. Mulligan. Mike, it is true, is a drunkard; but he is never violent. The children are good-hearted, but rough, and ready for any mischief. Still, as Agnes is scarcely a year old, their companionship can slightly influence the little maiden. Besides, Mrs. Mulligan likes the child, and Arthur knows that she will be taught the dear old prayers of the Church night and morning.

"I will only be away a few months," he thinks, "and the sum which I shall pay Mrs. Mulligan will be of great service to her—small as it will be."

Mrs. Mulligan, on being consulted, joyfully accepts the responsibility, and the little money that he can afford to deposit with her for the child's maintenance. Indeed, the honest woman is rather inclined to consider herself elevated in social status by the addition to her family, and the young Mulligans take infinite delight in alluding to little Agnes as "the boarder."

The *Osprey's* sailing-day comes. In spite of his resolution, Arthur feels that something *must* occur to prevent his going; but nothing does occur, and he sails for Cuba in the *Osprey*.

If he had caught, a year ago, one glimpse of the future, how it would have appalled him! Now he accepts his fate resignedly, and his great compensation is that, with a pure heart, he can say, *Fiat voluntas tua*. After all, he thinks, does it matter much whether his life is spent on land or sea—whether he toils with brain or hand—if God's grace is only with him? Each day is a step nearer the grave; what matter whether this day be bright or dark? And yet, when land is out of sight, he thinks of little Agnes; and, looking round the bleak, wind-swept deck, he discovers that he is neither a stoic nor a perfect Christian.

Days are lost in weeks, and months lengthen into half a year. No tidings come from Arthur Lisle. The Mulligans have changed their abode several times, for landlords are exacting, and Mrs. Mulligan does not find business as brisk as usual. Whenever Mike is sober—at rare intervals—he goes, by his wife's command, to inquire for the *Osprey*. The brig has come into port more than once. Captain Halstead can only say that Arthur Lisle left the vessel at Havana, and did not return. No message, no letter, comes. Mrs. Mulligan is not as cheerful as she has been. The money which Arthur Lisle left for little Agnes has long since gone the way of all lucre. Mrs. Mulligan grows more anxious every day. Six small mouths to fill and six small bodies to clothe, force her to strive unremittingly in her efforts to make "both ends meet." But in the winter a time comes when she feels as if she must sink under the burden; and in this time happens the great temptation of her life.

One blustery day, as she goes down the ice-coated street with a large bundle of new-washed clothes, her foot slips and she is about to fall, when an old gentleman, who has watched her, restores both her equilibrium and her bundle. She thanks him with effusion, and then stands looking after him.

"What is his name, sir?" she asks of the first passer-by.

"Who? Oh—Eric Lisle. I thought everybody knew old Lisle."

"Sure, it must be," she murmurs; "that must be his father, for one's the very moral of the other, barrin' he's older."

Mrs. Mulligan's curiosity is excited; when Mrs. Mulligan thirsts for knowledge, she generally finds means to quench her thirst. She has many acquaintances among the servants of the place, and two days have not passed before, by judicious inquiries, she has possessed herself of a full and true history of the Lisle family.

The winter grows colder, and somehow the Mulligans grow poorer. The new landlord—the Mulligans of late have not had an old landlord—threatens ejection. The children cry of cold in the night, and the mother looks at little Agnes, and thinks that one little one less would make a difference favorable to the others.

At first she drives the thought away. After a while

she asks why this child should add to her poverty, while Eric Lisle, one of her natural protectors, rolls in wealth? Why should not he take charge of her? He is not a Catholic, Mrs. Mulligan knows, and under his care Agnes will never be a Catholic; Mrs. Mulligan knows this also. And yet, she thinks, the son may return in a short time, and he will reclaim the child, and no harm be done. In spite of all her reasoning, the idea of transferring Agnes to her grandfather makes Mrs. Mulligan feel guilty. To her it is like selling a soul. She waits, holding temptation at bay, hoping that Arthur Lisle may return. She waits in vain.

The night is cold and windy. The streets are white with hard frost and chill moonlight. In the Mulligan household the fire faintly glimmers; there is no cheery glow, for coals are dear, and wherewithal to buy them is scarce. The children shiver and cry for more bread. There is not sufficient for all.

The mother, with set teeth and frowning brow, selects little Agnes from the group crouching around the fire. Saying nothing, she wraps the child in a shawl, and taking her in her arms disappears in the outside gloom.

III.

THE ANSWER TO MANY PRAYERS.

Eric Lisle sat in his study, an octagon-shaped room, small and cosy, with all the appliances for luxurious reading. He is a handsome man, much resembling his son. During the last year his hair has grown grayer and the lines around his mouth and on his forehead have deepened, so that now he almost deserves the epithet old.

He is bending over a pile of dusty books and papers which he has just dug from the depths of an old-fashioned cabinet. In his hand he holds a paper-covered book, with gorgeously-colored prints of impossible birds and beasts. Its pages are dog-eared and tattered. On the first blank leaf he sees the drawing of a small hand— a hand that had evidently been laid upon the paper, and then outlined with a dull pencil. Underneath are these words, in great sprawling letters, "Arthur Lisle, aged eight."

Eric Lisle's face loses its stern, fixed expression. He covers it with his hands, and a bright drop falls between his fingers.

"Oh, my boy—my boy!" he groans.

For the first time he pities Arthur instead of himself; for the first time a vague thought enters his mind that he has been too severe, and perhaps wrong.

Again he looks at the childish outline, and a vision of Arthur's mother arises before him. He sees her now, as he often saw her, bending over the pretty, blue-eyed babe, building realms in the air of which the tiny Arthur was always the happy prince. He remembers how full of happiness his heart was one bright day when the mother and child—

A ring at the door-bell, followed by an altercation, interrupts his train of thought for a moment. How sweet the mother looked, and Arthur, with his large, blue eyes, and golden ringlets!

A knock.

"Come in!"

Mrs. Bell, his old housekeeper, stands in the doorway.

She seems agitated and unusually confused. She approaches hesitatingly, with what seems to be a bundle in her arms.

The ragged shawl has fallen aside. Eric Lisle's cheeks and lips turn white.

"Arthur!" he exclaims.

The housekeeper does not notice his changed countenance, or even the emotion in his voice.

"Somebody left it on the doorstep. What shall we do with it, sir?"

Eric Lisle does not answer. The vision of his baby son seems to have become a reality. Mrs. Bell repeats the question.

"You are a woman, you ought to know; I suppose it wants something to eat."

"Do you mean to keep it, sir?"

Little Agnes opens her eyes. They are like Arthur's.

"Keep it? What else?"

Mrs. Bell retires, speechless with amazement. This incident materially strengthens her belief that wonders will never cease.

In this way Agnes Lisle enters her grandfather's house. On a handkerchief tied around her neck was the name "Agnes," and so they called her Agnes.

"She is my granddaughter, without doubt," Eric Lisle says. "My son is too proud to acknowledge the error of his ways, and so he has sent me this little waif as a peace-offering. He'll come to reason himself, by and by, I assure you."

Eric grows brighter and apparently younger from the night of the child's arrival. She furnishes him with a means of unceasing occupation. He worries her nurse to desperation.

The child wore a little medal, with the image of Our
Immaculate Lady on it, when she came. With trembling
fingers Mrs. Mulligan had placed it on her neck. Eric
Lisle frowned when he saw it, and ordered Mrs. Bell to
throw it away. The housekeeper put it in the old cabinet, along with Arthur's childish books.

. . . .

Agnes passes through her childhood, and all the ills to
which childish flesh is heir, bravely under the care of
Mrs. Bell and her satellites. Her school-days pass at a
fashionable seminary, and she returns to her grandfather
"finished," which means that a very thin veneer of book-knowledge has been added to her other qualities.

By this time everybody that knows Eric Lisle is aware
that this girl is his granddaughter. Of her father's story
she is utterly ignorant, through her grandfather's desire.
As far as education could make her, she is a Protestant.
She firmly believes all the horrors which have been
taught her about Catholics, and they have been measured
out to her with no stinting hand. She is full of prejudices, for false representations of her father's belief have
impregnated the atmosphere she has breathed since childhood. Yet she is not satisfied with her own creed. She
longs for something higher, less lifeless. The waters of
Baptism lie hidden in her heart; but the rod is needed
to make them burst forth.

Her life in her grandfather's house is quiet, uneventful.
She reads to him, for his sight is failing; and sometimes
she plays for him the old airs he loves. Her occupations
are unvaried. Often she wishes that her lot had been
cast among those who are compelled to work for bread.
She seems so useless.

The beautiful Miss Lisle is very much admired, though

in her secluded life there are very few to tell her so
Still, she knows it, for she can not walk in the street
without being followed by glances from all quarters.
She walks "in maiden meditation, fancy free," and, after
a time, cares little for the effect she produces.

One afternoon, during her usual walk in the quiet
street, an incident occurs. She is in the act of crossing
from one sidewalk to the other when a young man steps
hastily toward her. He is rather handsome, she notices,
and is dressed in plain gray clothes. He pauses near her.

"Allow me, Miss Lisle—"

He has passed. To her astonishment she finds that he
has left a little book in her hand.

Mechanically, without thought, she opens it and reads
the word "Catechism," and underneath, "Arthur Lisle,
November 18th."

What can it mean? This is her father's name!

She hurries homeward. She says nothing of the book,
but questions her grandfather. He evades her questions.
Full of perplexity and curiosity, she goes to the old cabinet. For the hundredth time she reads a commonplace
note written by Arthur Lisle, and looks over the tattered
primers with tender interest. Then she takes up the
medal, which—Mrs. Bell has told her so much and no
more—she wore when she came to her grandfather's
house. It puzzles her. She applies herself to the Catechism, and reads slowly for half an hour.

"My father was a Catholic!" she exclaims horrified.

Later she says:

"All this is beautiful!"

And, when darkness makes reading impossible, she
cries—

"*If* this is Catholicity, I would like to be a Catholic!"

She is a young girl, consequently she is enthusiastic, especially regarding novelties. The next day she repents and takes to one of her books of lies. That does not satisfy her. She throws it aside and reads her Bible. Somehow, that seems to chime in with the Catechism. She can not close her ears to the concord. She becomes weary, troubled. Who was that young man? What did it all mean? She has no one of whom to make a confidant. At last she resolves to try the effect of this curious book upon her grandfather. As usual, he asks her to read something to him at evening. She produces the Catechism as a "curious pamphlet."

Eric Lisle does not interrupt her. She goes on, watching his face at intervals. After a while she pauses.

"It is all very clear and simple," he says; "go on."

She resumes.

"Agnes," he says, after she has read for some time, "as I grow older, I grow more doubtful of what I have believed all my life; and this little book fills my mind with strange thoughts. It may be the devil tempting me. Leave the book with me, child. If this was Arthur's belief," she hears him murmur as she steals from the room, "I have been the most cruel and unjust of men. Lord, pardon me; I knew not what I did!"

Agnes goes to her room, terrified. What power has possessed her? Why should this worthless little pamphlet have wrought such a sudden effect?

A week passes, and when Agnes explains how the Catechism came into her possession, no further allusion is made to it.

A sudden change in the weather takes place, and old Eric is laid low with rheumatism.

"Child," he said to Agnes, after a day spent in thought

and silence, "I want to see one of these Catholic priests. It may be—I do not know yet—that I have followed false gods all my life; and now, though at the eleventh hour, it is not too late to turn away from them."

Early on the following day, Agnes, with feelings of trepidation, goes to the Catholic church in the next street. The priest's house is not far off.

Father De Young is out on a sick call.

"Wait," the servant says, noticing the expression of her face. "He has been gone some time; and from High street, where he is now, he will probably go over to the Orphan Asylum. If you will walk down toward High street, Miss, you may meet him."

Agnes thanks the girl and adopts the suggestion. It never occurs to her that, as she has not seen Father De Young, he may be difficult to recognize. She goes on, confident that she must know a Catholic priest when she sees him.

Several people are gathered around the door of a house on the north side. Among them is a policeman, looking as important as if he were keeping the world at bay.

Agnes pauses a moment to watch a group of curious-looking children, who seem to be stricken with awe by the majesty of this minion of the law. A man, tall, thin, and bent, comes from the house and crosses the street rapidly. The policeman takes off his hat. Agnes feels that this is the priest. There is an indefinable something about him that tells her so. She approaches him.

"Father De Young, I believe?"

"Yes, child," he answers, gravely scrutinizing her.

She tells her errand.

"I will see Mr. Lisle," he answers, "in a quarter of an hour. In the meantime you can do an act of charity.

In that house, which I have just left, there lies a man suffering much. A few minutes ago a scaffold in front of a new building fell. This man, passing at the time, was severely injured. There is nobody with him now but an old woman. I am on my way to get a Sister to nurse him. Until she comes, you can be of great use, if you will."

He leads the way into the house; Agnes follows him, feeling rather timid, but resolving to do her best.

The injured man lies on a hastily-improvised couch in the little parlor of the house. His head is wrapped in bandages. An old woman, seemingly very nervous and excited, makes room for the priest and Agnes.

"The doctor has gone, sir," she says in a grating undertone intended for a whisper, "and *he* must be kept quiet and nursed well."

"You can go," the priest answers; "this young lady will remain for a time."

The priest gives Agnes a reassuring glance and some words of advice as he hurries away, promising to send the Sister at once.

The old woman, glad of the opportunity, leaves the room. The wounded man turns his face from the wall and opens his eyes. Agnes almost drops the glass of water in her hand. This man, in spite of his disfiguring bandages and deathly pallor, has her grandfather's face!

She stands motionless, gazing at him. He looks into her eyes.

"Agnes!" he cries, hoarsely. "Agnes!—have you come back to life?"

"I am Agnes," she answers, a strange joy in her heart —"Agnes Lisle."

"Then," he murmurs, "I am either in Heaven with my wife, or on earth with my daughter!"

He sinks back unconscious.

As soon as the physician gives his consent, Arthur Lisle—for the wounded man was Arthur Lisle—was conveyed to his father's house. The old man can not believe in his happiness. To have his son again!—to feel that they are reunited in heart and soul, in love and faith,—this seems too much joy for earth.

When Arthur Lisle is well enough, he tells his short story. When the *Osprey* reached Havana, he had gone ashore, intending to remain only a short time. The weather was hot, and the malarious fever, so prone to attack foreigners in Cuba, seized upon him. Some good Samaritans carried him to the hospital. Recent shocks had impaired both his physical and mental strength; consequently his illness was long and dangerous.

The Jesuit priest who attended him soon knew his wants. When he recovered, the good Father obtained for him a position as teacher of English. He wrote to Mrs. Mulligan twice, and received no answer. The suspense was unendurable. He returned to the United States, to search in vain for Mrs. Mulligan. Her old neighbors knew nothing of her. They believed that one of the children had died. Was it the little stranger? They were not sure.

After a fruitless search, during which he suffered a century of agony, he went back to Havana. Careful work brought him all-teaching experience, and he rose, step by step, until he found himself possessed of a competence which a well-managed sugar plantation yielded him. But he longed for home, and home he came, to find his child—to find his dearest foe ready to receive the Faith, and be again his dearest friend.

When an opportunity occurs, Agnes speaks of the

Catechism which has made the wilderness of their hearts blossom as a rose. Arthur Lisle looks at the book attentively.

"Ah, yes, I remember," he says; "I gave this to Edward, Mrs. Mulligan's eldest boy. And you say a young man brought it to you?"

Agnes describes him.

Arthur Lisle smiles. "Considering that you saw him only once, mademoiselle, your description is very minute. Father Dé Young may know him. I will ask."

It happens that Father De Young does know a certain Edward Mulligan, a pillar of his parish; and when the priest comes, that young man comes with him. That young man colors when he is introduced to Agnes, and hastens to explain the affair of the Catechism.

From his story, it appears that if his mother had only waited a few days, she might have spared herself years of remorse and self-reproach. The tide of fortune turned. A brother of worthless Mike's died in Ireland, and his savings, bequeathed to the Mulligans, made them comparatively affluent. Mrs. Mulligan, however, never regained her old cheerfulness. She felt, she averred, as if she had given a soul to the devil. When dying, she implored Edward to give Agnes Lisle her father's Catechism. She could think of no other reparation, and all the prayers and penances of her later life were bound up in that reparation.

On the happy day which sees Eric Lisle and Agnes admitted into the Church, Arthur, with his heart too full for many words, can only utter the prayer of his adversity:

"*Fiat voluntas tua.* Thy ways are not our ways, O Lord!"

INEZ.

I.

IN SPAIN.

INEZ RAYMOND thrust aside the window-curtain, and turned her face toward the sombre old church. She stretched out her hands, and wrung them with a movement that expressed intense agony, and the forgotten tears on her cheeks seemed to dry in the ardor of her look of supplication.

Beneath, in the open patio, under the shade of orange trees, a procession wound through ranks of kneeling people, and entered the church-door. Clouds of incense, faintly tinged by the setting sun, entangled themselves in the tree-branches, and then arose like prayer escaping from the grasp of earthly thoughts.

In the room, on a low couch, lay a man past middle age, with streaks of white in his dark hair. His eyes were closed, and the many wrinkles on his cheeks and forehead seemed to be traced in the palest wax. Apparently, he was immobile. No breath parted the closed lips—only a slight dilation of the nostril showed that he still lived. He had received the viaticum. The priest, Père Zacharie, held the crucifix before him. All was silent. The Sister of Charity ceased for an instant to read the prayers for the dead.

On one side was the dying man, serene, peaceful; on the other, his daughter, living, yet suffering intolerable anguish, and almost fighting with Heaven for her father's soul. Death seemed easier than life.

"Inez!"

In an instant she was at his side. Could it be that God had answered her? was her thought. Could it be that he had restored this life?

He tried to smile—that old, sweet smile which Inez knew so well. His eyes spoke. Père Zacharie understood him at once, and taking a small packet from the table, he put it in Inez's hand. The dying man looked into his daughter's face again, and then turned his glance toward the crucifix.

De Profundis—

As he turned to stone—a statue of despair—Inez stood, silent, tearless. She was an orphan, alone in the wide, wide world.

From the patio came the adoring chant of priest and people before the Host. Slowly, softly it sank into silence with the departing soul.

> "Qui vitam sine termino
> Nobis donet in patria."

Those words, fragrant with the sweetness of a thousand benedictions, aroused the girl from her frozen dumbness.

"O God!" she cried, "only give him eternal life—eternal peace with Thee, and do with me as Thou wilt!"

II.

A LETTER.

In a quiet street, a kind of no thoroughfare, in which the houses, as much alike as a dozen pins in a row, are best described by that detestable word "genteel," live the Leighs.

On this dazzling bright September morning the little dining-room looks very pleasant and comfortable. Carved brackets, hanging baskets, and a hundred nameless tokens of good taste and woman's care, are everywhere visible. The place is bright and cheery, which qualities the sunbeams enhance by peering through the sparse and russet grape-vine leaves at the window, and, having gained courage, making gradual encroachments among the silver and delicate china of Martha Leigh's cherished heirloom— her grandmother's breakfast set.

Martha Leigh puts on her spectacles, and opens a letter she has just received. The postmark is foreign, and the paper thin and crackling. As she bends slightly forward, you notice that her refined and gentle face wears a careworn look that can only have been impressed there by years of patient sufferings. She is past forty, but she looks older. Her dress is precise and Quakerlike. Her gown, of her favorite stiff, gray material, falls in ungraceful folds around her, and her dark-brown hair, still untouched by time, is covered by a cap of black lace.

Opposite, lazily sipping his chocolate, and shading his face with a white hand, on which sparkle several rings, sits her brother, Archer. He is older than his sister, but he has taken more care to conceal the ravages of time, though he has not succeeded in covering the traces of early dissipation. His face is flabby and of an opaque whiteness, but well covered by a luxuriant and artistically dyed beard and moustache. His eyelids droop a little, and when he smiles—which he seldom does at home—his lips disclose a set of teeth too brilliant to be true. He puts down his cup, toys impatiently with the tassels of his gorgeous dressing-gown, and then says irritably:

"Well, Martha?"

Martha has averted her face, and her glasses have become so damp that she can not see writing.

"*He* is dead," she answers in a low, tremulous voice.

"I am not in the habit of trying to solve conundrums," returns her brother. "*Who* is dead?"

She does not answer. She does not hear. Her mind has gone in the past. She sees him—the dead—in the pride of youthful manhood. She hears his voice mingling with hers in the old-fashioned duets to the music of her grandmother's tinkling piano. She goes back to a certain afternoon, when, beneath the mulberry-tree in the prim old garden, she plucked apart the petals of a daisy, repeating the school-girl charm, *il m'aime, il ne m'aime pas, passionément, pas du tout*, and when she said, "he loves me," he, standing beside her unseen, had made her pause. And then!—tears fill her eyes, and she drops the letter. Her brother bends forward and seizes it.

"The spectacle of a woman of your age acting in this way is simply ridiculous," he says, with a sneer. "It is John Raymond who is dead. I thought if *I* were to die you would be less concerned, no doubt."

"Archer!" she says, in meek deprecation.

He applies himself to the letter, which is dated from Cadiz, and written in French by Père Zacharie, S. J.

"Died on the 15th day of August, in the hope of a blessed immortality, having devoutly received the last consolations of the Church," he mutters. "Umph! so John Raymond died a Papist. What is this about a daughter? I have forgotten all my French."

"When alone with me a short time before his death, he solemnly implored me to place Inez in the care of you, Mademoiselle Leigh, whom he termed his earliest and best friend. I have obeyed him as far as I could. She will sail for your city in the next steamer, in care of her father's old housekeeper."

Archer Leigh's face flushed with anger.

"Do you mean to let that man's daughter come here?" he demands.

His sister answers "Yes," without raising her eyes.

"She shall not come, I say. John Raymond left his own country to avoid imprisonment, and now he sends this young beggar here to live on our charity. I'll not stand it! You know very well that our income is insufficient for my—our wants."

"We must economize," Martha says, timidly.

"Haven't I economized until I can no longer associate with gentlemen? Look at the miserable claret we had at dinner yesterday, and I can hardly raise enough money for gloves and the hire of a horse! When the season really opens, I shall be ashamed to show myself anywhere! Economize, indeed!"

Martha was silent. Forbearance with her was a virtue daily practiced. She did not remind this specimen of masculine selfishness that for years he had been living on her slender income, and acting the *rôle* of a man of leisure and fashion wholly at her expense. Archer Leigh—handsome Archer Leigh *then*—had been spoiled by foolish parents. Martha, living with her grandmother, had escaped their influence. Before he was twenty-one he had made his *début* as an accomplished "society man," and before he was twenty-five he had rushed through the fortune bequeathed him by his father. After that he allowed himself to be supported by his sister, waiting to marry money. The spider watched; the flies were wary; and he still waited. His life had been a failure—a deeper, darker, more miserable failure than even his sister believed.

"Now, don't be absurd, Martha," he continues, in a calmly argumentative tone. "Show some respect for my opinion, on this occasion at least. Do something to prevent this girl's coming."

"I can not. If I were base enough to refuse asylum to John Raymond's child, it is too late now. This letter has been delayed. Inez Raymond, Father Zacharie says, was to start in the *Aspen*. The *Aspen* is due to-morrow."

"I will not have this girl here—to be a burden on us, and to make things uncomfortable for me! Dick is bad enough!"

"Archer," says Martha Leigh, slowly, and with a visible effort, for she has been accustomed to bow to her brother's will in all things, "Archer, you force me to do a hard thing, which is to remind you that this house is mine, and as long as I live John Raymond's daughter shall never lack a home!"

Her thin hands tremble, and she nervously casts down her eyes; but he sees that she is resolute.

He mutters something under his breath, and then says, brutally, as he leaves the room—

"I will make this house too hot to hold her!"

"On whose devoted head is my amiable uncle's vengeance to fall now?" demands a clear voice; and a young man enters the room. His eyes are blue, his face is ruddy, and his hair light and curling. His very step has a cheery sound. He takes Martha Leigh's face between his hands, and kisses her.

"Good-morning, Aunt Mar!"

"Behave yourself, Dick. Late, as usual, and you didn't get home until after twelve last night. When will you learn to keep good hours?"

"How can you expect it, Aunt Martha? You refuse to let me have a night-key," he says, in an injured tone, "and it takes at least three-quarters of an hour to climb the back fence and open the kitchen door. If I had a key that time would be saved; consequently I would be in bed three-quarters of an hour sooner. Logic is logic, that's all *I* say."

"Oh, Dick, Dick!" Aunt Martha says, between a smile and a tear.

"Uncle Archer is getting more disagreeable every day. I wouldn't stay here another hour if it wasn't for you. By the way, who came in for his ill-humor this morning?"

"There's a young lady coming here," returns Martha, evasively. "A young lady from Spain, Inez Raymond. Her father was American, her mother Spanish. She has lived in Spain all her life."

"A young lady coming here! That *is* news. When is she coming?"

"Probably to-morrow. You will take me down to the steamer to meet her. You can get off from the office?"

"The people down there *may* manage to spare my valuable services for a few hours. Uncle doesn't like this *senorita*, and intends to make the house 'too hot to hold her!' That's it, is it? Well, I hope she may turn the tables. Is she pretty, Auntie?"

"I don't know, yet she must be handsome if she resembles her father. Why?"

"Because," answers Dick, with preternatural gravity, "I don't want to fall in love; I'm in love already."

"Oh, Dick, Dick! with whom?" cries his startled aunt.

"With you, of course, Aunt Mar!" And having finished a huge breakfast, Dick Leigh makes his exit, laughing.

"Poor, dear Dick," sighs his aunt, "I am afraid he is drifting into bad company. Oh, dear, I wish I knew how to keep him at home more—but Archer never gives the poor boy any peace."

And, full of doubts and perplexities as usual, Martha Leigh takes up her burden of household cares.

III.

"FROM TAWNY SPAIN."

Inez Raymond has come, and a week has passed since her arrival in the quiet, shady street. Her companion, Margaret Daly, an old Irish woman who lived for many years in the Raymond household, and who loves Inez as if she were her daughter, is trying, under Miss Martha's teaching, to learn American "ways." Inez, however, has not seen much of New World customs, for since her arrival she has kept within her room. This is her father's country, and the sight of it brings him back to her. All day long, with the warm fervor of her nature, she weeps and prays for him. Thus far her uncle has contented himself with a cold bow to her whenever they happened to meet, which was only twice. Dick Leigh thinks that "she is a regular stunner," and, having boldly proclaimed his admiration, receives a five minutes' lecture on slang from his aunt.

Inez Raymond is, without doubt, beautiful. Her hair and eyes are black, like her mother's. Her complexion is rather dark, with, at times, a rose-tint, which she derives from her Northern blood. She is somewhat below the middle height. Her voice is very low and sweet, "an excellent thing in a woman." In her moods, she is as changeable as the wind. One moment grave, dignified, ladylike; another, laughing, mischievous, girlish. In two things she is always the same—in her love for her Faith, and her love for her dead father. Her mother she can not remember.

On Sunday she comes down to breakfast, but speaks little. Although she has spent many a weary hour over Ollendorf, and her mind is stored with many thrilling sentences relative to the "golden candlestick of the tailor," etc., she is still doubtful about her English. Talkative Dick is reduced to silence in her presence. After breakfast he betakes himself to a sofa, where, under cover of a newspaper, he can watch Inez.

"I have forgotten to give you something," she says, turning to Martha Leigh. "Here is a letter for you from my father, and also this packet, which Père Zacharie desired me to tell you must be kept in a safe place."

The letter was addressed to Miss Martha Leigh. The packet bore Inez's name, "to be opened on her twenty-first birthday." Archer Leigh takes it in his hand, and scans it curiously.

"And now," says Inez, and her sweet tone robs her words of the *brusquerie* they might seem to have, "I am going to Mass. Are you going, Senorita?"

"No," whispers Margaret Daly, who happens to be passing behind Inez's chair; "no," she says, "they are heretics."

Inez looks regretful, and turns to Dick. "And you, Señor, are you—I beg pardon if it be not the right word—are you, too, a heretic?"

Dick, not quite understanding, shakes his head negatively.

"Then, Señor," she continues, gravely, "you should go to Mass. It is not good for a young man like you to be— what you call it—lazy, idle on the Sunday. Margaret and I are going. We will wait for you. Is it not the custom here, Margaret?"

Margaret Daly is divided between laughter and frowns. Dick hurries away to brush his hair, without having the least idea whither he is expected to go.

When the three start, it is discovered that Inez deludedly believes every ecclesiastical-looking edifice to be a Catholic church, and, consequently, they wander into several Baptist and Methodist chapels before reaching the object of their search.

"It seems, Señor," says Inez, severely, "that you have not been at Mass for a long time, since you do not even know where the church is."

Dick, not wishing to commit himself, smiles vaguely. They are in time for High Mass. Inez, who has arrayed herself in black, and who would have done so for church-going, even were she not in mourning, is astonished by the gay dresses of the ladies. She thinks their attire in bad taste, and longs to lecture them. Accustomed to the churches at home, she is struck by the long lines of straight pews. When the *Kyrie* begins, however, she forgets these minor differences. Dick has never been in a Catholic church before in his life. From his heart he admires the rapt devotion of the people, and at the Elevation he feels a sudden thrill himself, and almost involuntarily bends low with the rest.

Margaret lingers behind them as they enter the street. "Oh, you here yet?" exclaims Inez, as if she had forgotten him. "I hope your unusual devotion has not fatigued you, Señor."

"By no means, Miss Raymond; the ceremonies were new and interesting. That was my first visit to a church of your religion."

"And you are a her—not a Catholic? Oh! I beg your pardon. Margaret did not tell me, or perhaps I did not understand. I am very stupid in English, though my father often spoke it."

"Nor did I understand; but, all the same, I have spent a most profitable morning."

"And why are you not a Catholic?" asks Inez, after a pause.

"I'm sure I don't know; probably because my parents were not Catholics."

"Yes? But then," earnestly, "I do not think that you are a fool—"

"Thank you."

"And you have eyes and ears and reason. You are not like a mule—"

"No—that is, I hope not."

"Then why are you not a Catholic? Why do you not believe?"

Dick searches his mind for an answer to this rather *naïve* question.

"Well, I don't believe in some things your Church teaches. There's the infallibility of the Pope."

"The in-fal-li-bil-ité," repeats Inez, trying to catch his pronunciation. "Well, continue, Señor."

"Now," returns Dick, determined to do his level best, "you believe that your Pope is infallible because St. Peter was infallible. If St. Peter was infallible, how came he to deny his master? I have her there," thinks Dick, triumphantly.

"Oh," says Inez in a desparing tone, "you will never

understand! My father knew a heretic at Cadiz, and he did always say what you have said, over and over. The Apostle Peter was a man, he could sin like other men, yet he was infallible. To be infallible is not to be impeccable. The Pope can sin, but when he decides on matters of Faith and morals, he is infallible. *Do* you understand?"

"Yes," Dick replies, "I never saw it in that light before. A prophet, the Scripture proves, may fall, and yet be truly inspired."

"You are not as stupid as I thought, Señor," Inez consolingly remarks.

Martha Leigh has read John Raymond's last letter, in which he solemnly intrusted Inez to her care. "There is no other to whom she could go," he said; "no other from whom she would receive a mother's care."

"He did well to trust me," she thinks. "I thank him for it. He knew that my heart was his daughter's rightful place."

"Inez is not penniless," she says to her brother, as she locks the sealed packet in her old-fashioned sideboard, where the remnant of the Leigh plate is kept. "She has about three hundred dollars a year. Père Zacharie has made arrangements to have it paid regularly."

"Umph! An immense sum!" responds Archer, sneering. "John Raymond did not thrive in Spain, it seems. Disgraced men seldom thrive anywhere."

Martha starts and shivers at the word "disgraced," as if, Margaret Daly would say, somebody were walking over her grave.

"How old is this girl?" he asks.

"Eighteen."

He walks over to the sideboard, and carefully examines the lock.

Inez's life flows smoothly enough. She is an enigma to everybody, including herself. She is as variable as an April day, yet through all her moods there runs such an undercurrent of good intention that Aunt Martha can not scold her.

"She will be a noble woman, I hope."

"An' sure she will!" responds Margaret Daly, up to her elbows in dough. "The changeable spring comes before the constant summer."

"Yes," sighs Martha Leigh, thinking of *her* spring, "these girlish vagaries are only the spray cast up when the streams of girlhood and womanhood meet."

In another room Inez is heard playing the piano, and singing an Andalusian peasant song:

"Si me pierdo, que me busquen."

Dick tries to follow the joyous measure with his flute; he is her devoted slave now. Inez's presence has accomplished what his aunt's mild expostulations never could. He stayed home o' nights, and Archer—the season had not yet opened, and he is at home too—remonstrates in vain against being disturbed by their music.

In a short time, Inez learns silently to manage everybody. Even Archer reluctantly allows himself to be influenced by her. Once he asked Inez, in his insufferable way, to bring his slippers. Martha would have obeyed as a matter of course, but Inez, with a sudden impulse, threw them across the room with a force that made Dick stare and sent the cat in a fright from the room. She apologized to Dick and the cat. He fears and respects her, for he has an uneasy idea she has fathomed his arrantly selfish character.

Aunt Martha no longer sacrifices all her little comforts

for him. Inez, with wonderful tact, gently but effectively interferes whenever Archer makes an unreasonable demand.

Inez, having found the church, goes to Mass every morning, and Martha Leigh has acquired the habit of accompanying her. Dick generally sees them as far as the corner on his way to the office.

Martha Leigh seems to have grown five years younger since Inez has come. Gentle to a fault, yielding and somewhat undecided, willing at any time to sacrifice her dearest wishes for those she loves, it has been her lot to meet with ingratitude and lack of sympathy. Her orphan nephew Dick never voluntarily gave her pain, but he could not understand her. In Inez Raymond she has found a soul that appreciates and strengthens her own.

She is finding peace—the something for which she longed during her unrestful life—the peace of God.

IV

A STRANGE SCENE.

Inez, like many of her mother's countrywowen, has a remarkable talent for improvising melodies. This morning she feels sad and cheerless, for the winter has come, and it seems as if summer will never again fill the world with light and perfume. She finds it difficult to sew, and going to the piano she tries to make music for the sad, sweet words in Hamlet—

> "Why let the stricken deer go weep,
> The hart ungalled play,
> While some must watch, while some must sleep;
> So runs the world away."

But Margaret Daly's tones, high and loud in the kitchen, break discordantly into her music. Inez hastens to throw oil on the troubled waters, if possible. She pauses at the door of the kitchen.

Margaret seems greatly excited; but she is generally excited while composing her culinary specialty, which is a cross between an olla podrida and an Irish stew.

Near the table, his gloves and hat in his hand, his coat buttoned up, and a tuberose in his buttonhole, stands Archer Leigh. He is arrayed for conquest and morning calls.

"Be calm, be calm, my good woman," Archer is saying, as he waves his hand gracefully. "I don't care whether John Raymond was wealthy or not. I asked only out of curiosity."

"You have your answer. It's neither your business nor mine."

"But," returns Archer, determined to exasperate the old woman, "I can't help feeling amused when I see Inez Raymond queening it here, and I remember that she bears a tarnished name—that she is a felon's daughter."

"Say that again if you dare, Señor."

The words are low and clear. Archer Leigh steps back. Inez stands before him. Fire seems to glow in her dark eyes, and she holds her hand on her breast, as if to keep her passion from bursting out.

"You had better not say it again," cries Margaret, seizing Archer Leigh by the arm. "*I* know all, Mr. Leigh. Whisper. I nursed my master through the fever, and, in his ravings, I heard it *all*. Tell my young mistress you have lied!"

"You are a perfect fury, woman!" responds Leigh, not altogether at ease. "I am sorry that you listened,

Miss Inez. Your father may have been a very good man—in his way." He bows mockingly, and leaves the room.

"What did he mean, Margaret?"

"How should I know, child?"

"You do know!—you do know!"

Neither tears, caresses, nor entreaties move Margaret from her firm silence.

Inez waits until Martha returns from some housewifely expedition on which she is bent. She wonders how she can find what she wants to know without alarming Martha, and she hits on a leading question.

"And so some people think that my father did a great wrong, Aunt Martha?"

"Yes, child, but I never believed it," answers Martha, unguardedly. "But who told you?"

"Never mind. *You* do not believe it. Tell me it, Auntie, quick!"

"Well," sighs Aunt Martha, "it is a sad, sad story, but a short one. Your father and I were to be married, Inez. Did he ever tell you that? I thought not. Well, John Raymond and Archer were both clerks in my father's counting-house. John used to come to my grandmother's often. Ah, those were happy days!—so happy that I would give all my life to see them again, Inez. I, poor, thoughtless girl, expected that they would stay forever; but they flew away very fast. Somebody in my father's employ committed a forgery, which involved great loss. John was accused; the evidence was against him; he could not prove his innocence. The thing was kept quiet, but my father and Archer made me release John from his engagement. After that he went to Spain, and I—I have suffered cruelly ever since. If I had only been firm and true!"

Inez says nothing. Her mind is a chaos. Oh, if her father had spoken only once of all this! If he had said, "I was not guilty," she would be content now. He had spoken no word. It could not be possible that he—her father—whom she had loved and reverenced as a being almost perfect, could have done this thing!

"Oh, my God!" her heart cried, "save me from believing him guilty. Let me know that he was innocent, and then do with me as Thou wilt! I give myself to Thee!"

For days there was no more music. Dick's flute sounded once or twice in a melancholy way, but Inez seemed not to hear it.

Several times lately Martha Leigh has missed the key of her precious carved sideboard. She has always found it again, however, in unexpected places.

"I am becoming old and forgetful," she thinks.

Archer Leigh has grown kinder, and exceedingly courteous toward Inez lately. Dick is surprised and somewhat jealous; Martha can not understand, and Margaret Daly is suspicious.

Inez is quiet and thoughtful. She seldom speaks. She is trying to solve a problem. Was her father guilty? The state of her mind could be comprehended by few among us, because among Americans of the North there are not many natures like hers. Her whole life just now is one meditation on this question.

Archer Leigh wears his new disguise well. An inexperienced observer would probably take him for a gentleman. His manner toward Inez is half-paternal, half-loverlike. She avoids him.

One evening, Inez is alone in the little parlor. Warmth and light are within; darkness and fast-falling snow without. Her thoughts are more in sympathy with the cold and the darkness.

Archer Leigh enters, and draws a chair near hers. She does not notice him, and yet in a few short words he asks her to be his wife.

She arises, and looks at him. That look is sufficient to make him lower his eyes.

"You must have a very poor opinion of me, Señor."

Her cutting tone exasperates him. He can not keep his temper.

"I have a poor opinion of you—but not of your wealth," he retorts. "And I tell you that Dick Leigh shall never be your husband. I hate him—the impudent, young puppy! I would kill him sooner than see him a rich man and me a—beggar."

Inez thinks that he has taken too much wine. She scrutinizes him closely. It is not so.

"And so you think that I am rich?"

"I know it. I will tell you something, and I defy you to use it against me in any way. I have opened that packet in the sideboard."

Inez starts, and then says coolly, "Indeed? You are a villain, Señor. Père Zacharie told me that the packet contained a copy of my Spanish grandfather's will—"

"So it did, but it contains it no more. Here is the will, and also my con—"

Archer Leigh does not finish the sentence. A strong hand arrests his arm in mid-air. Before he can move, or even speak, the two papers change hands, and Dick Leigh towers above his uncle like a wrathful giant.

For a moment or two the three stand motionless. Then Dick gives the papers to Inez, while he holds back his uncle with his right hand.

Inez moves as if to interfere, but she involuntarily obeys Dick's words. "Go!" he says, "leave us. I wish to speak some words to this man."

"Stop!" says Archer Leigh, averting his face. "That paper which you hold in your hand is my confession. I forged the check, and threw the guilt on your father. In a fit of remorse—I was young and foolish then—I wrote that confession. In fact, he forced me to write it, but he never used it, because he loved my sister."

Inez devours it with her eyes. Again and again she reads it. A joyous light illumines her face.

"I thank Thee, O God!" she cries, in an ecstasy of gratitude. "I thank Thee! My father was innocent!"

It is as if she said *Nunc Dimittis*.

"Now that you have read this paper," Archer Leigh says, "I may as well tell you that I was glad to find it in your packet, among other documents not so important. Your father loved me once, and for the sake of that early friendship, as well as for the love he bore my sister, he was merciful. Will you be less so? I do not plead for myself; I have no right to your mercy; but for the sake of my sister and the good name of our family, I ask you to grant my prayer. Say you will do this, and I will leave this place forever."

Inez does not answer in words, but taking the paper in her hand, she walks to the gas-light, and holds it beyond Dick's reach until it drifts to the floor—light ashes.

"What have you done, Inez? What have you done?" cries Dick, in a tone of angry surprise.

"What have I done!" replies Inez, calmly, and with tears falling on her cheek, "I have left a sinner in the hands of God."

Martha Leigh's eyes are red from weeping. Margaret and she are bending over a huge trunk. Inez, dressed as if for travelling, stands near the window, looking dreamily into the street. Dick, pale and worried, is tugging at a pair of shawl-straps.

"The carriage is here," Margaret says, and in the next minute the four enter.

Inez is putting into action her secret resolution. For three years she will remain in the Convent of the Sacred Heart. After that she will go to Spain, and take the veil if her vocation is proven.

"Good-bye, Dick," she says at the railroad station, holding out her hand.

"Inez," he falters.

She puts her hand up. "I know, Dick. Learn to love God, and we will meet in heaven! *A dios.*"

The train flashed past. She is gone. Martha Leigh bursts into tears. Dick feels as if the sun had set forever.

Inez, Sister Maria of the Cross, is happy in her convent. The wayward humors of her childhood are past. A great, sweet peace has covered her soul. Margaret Daly lives among the Little Sisters of the Poor, working with them, and aiding them in many ways. Aunt Martha and Dick live together in the quiet street. Dick is older and graver. He can never forget Inez. He, too, is a Catholic.

Archer Leigh kept his promise, and is now in another land. Now and then a letter from "over the sea" reaches his faithful sister, which tells a tale which makes her heart throb with gratitude, for out of the wreck of her brother's blasted life God is rescuing a human soul.

"A SORROW'S CROWN OF SORROW."

I.

RELIGION can touch even the deepest sorrow, for God sees and comprehends all; but it is rare for human sympathy to reach below the surface griefs of life. Who is there that has not had a sorrow—dumb to his fellow-men—crying out in agony to God? Love, friendship, may solace; but he alone can understand the hearts he has made. You may hear the story of others' sorrow, and call it an idle tale, because, forsooth, there are no mock heroics, no passions torn in tatters; as if the silence of a Stylites were not immeasurably more expressive than all the words a great poet has put into his mouth.

I do not imply that these two people, between whose life-paths a great gulf opened, are silent saints. No; I only mean to say that the real depths of their sorrow could be fathomed only by themselves and God.

Charles Wernly was the great man of Glenborough. Indeed, a proposition to make the name of the town Wernly City had been rejected only by the steadfast opposition of the man whom the Glenboroughites delighted to honor. He has spent the prime of his life in building the prosperity of the place, and now, in his declining years, it was just that he should be rewarded. He had changed the little village, with its slow and sure population of Pennsylvania Dutch, into a thriving, smoky town, with thousands of hurrying workmen. The voice of the energetic little stream was drowned amid the ceaseless clang of machinery, and the silver and gold of the field-daisies had long ago been crushed under piles of rubbish. Well, it was all for the best; the little country village had had its day, and the toilers of Glenborough would have soon been conscious of an aching void, if the Wernly iron works were replaced by wild flowers and stream murmurs.

Charles Wernly was rich—so rich, people said, that he knew but half his riches. That was nonsense, however, for Charles Wernly was not a man to be content with half knowledge of anything that interested him. His pride and his perseverance were unlimited. He was proud of himself first, of his wealth, of his daughter. His pride was not meant to be vulgar and ostentatious, but he showed it, in a gentlemanly kind of way—not like self-made pride generally—in every inflection of his voice, every movement of his body. His wife had died in giving birth to his only child, Mary, who had just passed her seventeenth year when she completed her education at the Convent of the Sacred Heart, Riverside.

He was not a Catholic. He did not trouble himself much about religion, he admitted. He had no prejudices; his father had been a Quaker, his mother a Presbyterian, and he was nothing. Somehow or other, he had always got along well enough without religion. He thought, though, that convent-educated girls were better than girls taught in secular boarding-schools. And if Mary wanted to be a Catholic, he didn't care; a woman without religion seemed to want ballast. He guessed Catholics were as good as other people.

And though he "guessed"—as even the best of us poor, unenlightened Pennsylvanians will do sometimes—he was not an uneducated man. He read most of the popular works of the day. He liked Herbert Spencer, and Mill, and Tyndal; detested Swinburne and Joaquin Miller; admired Longfellow and William Morris; and had "skimmed" the Gladstone-Manning pamphlets, not because he felt much interest in the subject, but because people talked about it.

When Mary wrote to him for permission to embrace the faith, he readily gave it, and, at the same time, a munificent donation to the little Catholic church in Glenborough. And the men and women toilers who frequented the little church, breathed many a prayer for the girl whose influence had brought them this good.

If you are one of those—too numerous now—who reverence physical beauty as if it were a virtue, you would not find your ideal of womanhood in Mary Wernly. She was not beautiful, not even pretty. She was rather small and slight. Her features were not regular, and her cheeks were rarely flushed with color; but the expression of her face would have redeemed worse faults. The brow, which shone beneath the plainly parted brown hair, was serene and unruffled; her gray, clear eyes seemed to show a soul pure and true, and a sweet gentleness, that was almost humility, tempered all. Her quiet movements were singularly graceful, and even the motion of her small hands expressed something of the firm gentleness that characterized her.

When she came home from school "for good," all Glenborough, from the "best" people, who lived in stucco villas and boasted of "grounds," to the others who existed in hovels near the railroad bridge, and had nothing of which to boast, were on tiptoe to see the heiress of old Wernly's wealth.

Charles Wernly was a prouder man than ever, when his daughter laid her school-trophies of flower-crowns and gilded books at his feet; and prouder still when he drove her in her new phaeton through admiring Glenborough; through the long street, past the massive workshops, glittering stores, and rows of dwellings which he called his own, out into the open country, through the sunny air, and under the fleece-flecked sky, past the fields where clover and daisies still grew unmolested, singing all these, of hope and pleasure to him; but the words set to this summer melody, if he could have heard them, spoke of other things.

Mary was full of the girlish gossip of her convent-home. Her father's brow relaxed, and a smile played around his lips while she told him of Sister Paul's stately manner and common sense, of her "pet" sister's wonderful perfections, and her own attempts at teaching. Matters simple enough in themselves, but inexpressibly refreshing to this world-worn old man.

The phaeton stopped near the edge of a deep ravine crossed by one of the railroad bridges. Wernly dropped the reins, and enjoyed the influence of the time. A wood, thick with damp undergrowth and sweet-smelling fern, cast its cool shade over them. They could see the glitter of the stream as it curved through a meadow, and settled into a lakelet where the grave cows loved to stand knee-deep. The water-lilies, having drawn into their golden hearts all the scent of the new-mown hay, languidly opened their eyes to the noonday sun, and Mary watched them rising and falling with the faint pulsation of the tide. The rest of the landscape was level and green; but the blue sky and the sun-painted air gave it that charm, which in a different way, youth seldom fails to give to the plainest of human beings.

In the wood, hidden from view by a tangled hedge of wild grape-vines and blackberry-bushes, sat, or rather lounged, a young man. A fishing-rod lay by his side; a book, face downward, upon his breast. He was too idle to read, too idle even to think or to dream. It was the perfection of *dolce far niente.* Verily, Gerald O'Conor was thoroughly enjoying his time of rest, after long months of monotonous work in Charles Wernly's counting-house.

A spider ran down its airy stairway, to investigate the cover of his book; a bee buzzed within an inch of his nose, yet he never moved, but only murmured sleepily,

" 'I know a bank where the wild thyme blows;
Where ox-lips and the nodding violet grows.'

" ' Grows,' drowsily, 'faith, I believe, that's bad grammar for Shakespeare! But, never mind,'

" 'Quite over-canopied with luscious woodbine,
With sweet musk-roses, and with eglantine.' "

Here he paused from sheer laziness, and half-closed his eyes, as if he expected the fairy queen, Titania, to appear from the waving fern.

The face of Gerald O'Conor, even in its repose, expressed more strength and power than are usually seen in one so young—he has just entered his twenty-third year. The strength was latent, the power undeveloped; but both were there. When he spoke, there was a richness in his tones and a music in his accent very different from the thin, discordant American enunciation. He had been born and educated in Ireland; but the characteristics of some remote Italian or Spanish ancestor seemed to have reappeared in him. His skin was as dark as that of Wernly's book-keeper, Firandola, who was a Cuban. His hair was black and curling, and his eyes were so dark in hue that they seemed black. The short, thin upper lip had a somewhat supercilious curl at times, and his expression was often scornful and defiant; and yet he should not be judged harshly, for the world seemed against him; he was young, and scorn and defiance seemed his best defences.

He had been left an orphan in care of his father's brother, who was only too glad to take charge of the boy's wealth. No expense was spared in Gerald's education, but before it was quite completed the uncle died, and it was found that Gerald's inheritance had taken itself off on the wings of speculation.

Preferring to work for himself rather than to apply for aid to his relatives, he started for the United States, on whose sacred soil we have found him.

Suddenly he started from his reclining posture. A clear, sweet sound rippled through the air. What bird's note was it? Again he heard it, and pushing aside the shrubby screen he saw the phaeton standing under an arch made by two oaks.

"Old Wernly! and that's his daughter, I suppose."

Gerald softly swept away the undergrowth, and crept nearer. He had often heard of Mary Wernly, and had caught occasional glimpses of her during her vacations. According to Glenborough belief, she was a paragon of goodness, and a protectress-regnant of the poor.

"Sure, it's many a poor man's wages she's had raised! Heaven be her bed!"

Exclamations like this Gerald had heard many times, and was naturally curious about their object. Again Mary laughed, and the pony pricking up his ears seemed to enjoy it.

"I wonder if angels do not laugh in that way—if angels ever laugh," thought Gerald, and then his lip curled in scorn not so genuine as the thought.

"Yes, Mary, we will go to Europe, you and I," Charles Wernly was saying, though Gerald could not hear him. "We will see all the wonders of the Old World together, and when we are tired of each other," Mary laughed incredulously, "you shall marry some foreign grandee with a hundred orders. I am ready to go at once. I can trust Firandola with everything."

"Firandola?"

"Narcisso Firandola, my book-keeper and confidential clerk; you remember him?"

"Oh, yes!"

"That man is worth his weight in gold. He possesses more versatility, greater capabilities than anybody I ever saw. You never know what he can do until he does it."

Mary turned her face away, and made no reply.

She could not praise Firandola, for she involuntarily distrusted him, so she was silent.

"Yes," said Wernly, with a sigh of satisfaction, "the world is very pleasant just now, the future very bright."

"The train is coming," said Mary, as the whistle sounded. "Will not the pony take fright?"

"Oh, I can trust Bob," returned her father.

The whistle again shrieked piercingly, rudely shattering the noonday stillness.

Bob raised his ears, trembled, and then snorting and struggling, backed obstinately. Before the old man could grasp the reins, the hind wheels of the carriage were over the edge of the ravine. Neither voice nor hand could control the frightened animal. Behind the occupants of the phaeton was an almost perpendicular descent of two hundred feet—jagged rocks and matted roots. Mary knew this; she did not scream. While her father endeavored to make use of the tangled reins she spoke soothingly to the pony, and her voice, controlled by a great effort, was very plaintive and pitiful.

From his place in the wood Gerald O'Conor saw the dilemma. He saw, too, that three lives depended, under God, on his coolness, nerve, and courage. The train passed swiftly. The pony's struggles grew wilder. Wernly, who had arisen, lost his balance and fell sideways. The pony still backed. In another instant—

Gerald crossed the road like a flash, and caught the head of the furious little beast.

Events sometimes annihilate time. When Mary stepped from the phaeton, and Gerald stood in the middle of the road holding the panting pony, an age or an instant, neither could have told which, seemed to have passed.

"Oh, father—father! He is dead!"

Charles Wernly lay pale and motionless at the foot of an oak. The only sign of life about him was the movement of the mocking breeze in his steel-gray hair.

"He has only fainted," Gerald answered.

"No, no! here is—blood! Oh, father, father!"

His head had struck against a projecting root of the tree. Gerald brought water and soaked moss from the stream. He did not revive.

"Wait, I will go for a doctor—"

"And a priest! Do you know where?"

"I know him well."

Without another word he sprang into the phaeton, and forced Bob to dash at a break-neck pace toward Glenborough.

The priest and the doctor soon reached the scene of the accident. Wernly breathed easily, but he was still unconscious.

The doctor shook his head, and aided in lifting him into the comfortable carriage which Gerald had thoughtfully secured.

"These shocks often prove fatal to men of his age," whispered the doctor to Father Moran.

"Hush!" returned the priest, for Mary was watching the doctor's face intently.

A week of tearless agony and torturing suspense fell to Mary Wernly's lot—the first thorn of the crown of sorrow which she was to wear for many days. And during this week Charles Wernly's mansion was like the vestibule of a tomb. Silent footfalls, hushed voices, and foreboding thoughts filled it.

At last he spoke; at last he opened his eyes. Mary's petition, uttered from hour to hour, before the Blessed Sacrament, was answered. Her father had regained his senses.

"He will never be himself again," said the doctor; "I doubt that he will ever leave that room."

He asked for Gerald O'Conor when Mary had told him how she had been saved. Gerald came in the evening, and saw Mary in the twilight, by her father's bedside. Wernly would have offered him money, but Mary, with womanly tact divining his intention, checked it by a look. Gerald saw it, and thanked her in his heart.

"I am very grateful to you, O'Conor. You are one of the junior clerks in my office, aren't you?"

"Yes; I have been there a year."

"I don't remember you; but Firandola always arranges the office business. By the way, I appoint you Firandola's assistant, with an increase of salary, and you can bring any letters and papers that may require my attention here every afternoon until I get better."

He paused and sighed. Gerald thanked him, and arose.

"As proud as Lucifer," said the invalid under his breath; "I must keep my eye on him. I actually believe that he would have the presumption to fall in love with *you*, Mary." And he laughed at the absurdity of the idea.

Gerald, who had barely crossed the threshold, heard the words, and his face flushed. Presumption! Would it be presumption? and then he called himself a fool.

Firandola looked at O'Conor with his penetrating black eyes, showed his perfect teeth, gave him some letters to write, and said, "It is well," when he received notice that he was to have a new aid.

Firandola was a Cuban about thirty years of age. He had left his own country for political reasons, it was said. He was tall, slender, with a drooping moustache that hid his mouth. His face, to an observer, would have been of no use as an index to his thoughts. It was always calm and smooth.

A month passed. Charles Wernly had not risen from his bed, and Gerald visited him every evening with the important letters of the day. Wernly began to like him; his frankness, fearlessness, and fancied knowledge of the world amused him.

Mary enjoyed his talks with her father, and sometimes joined in them. "If all men were like him how different the world would be," she thought. Unconsciously she thought of him while reading of her favorite heroes of history and romance.

"Mr. O'Conor," she said, meeting him one afternoon, with an unusual flush on her cheeks. "See! Is not my father the kindest man in the world?"

She held toward him a casket. The lid sprang up, and revealed a nest of dazzling gems—an elaborate necklace of diamonds and emeralds. "And this?" she showed him a rosary of pearls, with a heavy gold cross. "Is it not kind—and yet papa is not a Catholic, you know."

He expressed his admiration; his hand trembled as he returned the casket, and looked into her smiling face.

"O'Conor," said her father, when he had finished the letters, "take those fol-de-rols of Mary's to Firandola, and tell him to lock them in the safe. Nice things for a poor man like me to buy."

Gerald smiled, as he was expected to do, and sighed. "What is the matter with him?" thought Mary. "I wonder what can be the matter with him."

Late in the afternoon of the next day Narcisso Firandola was ushered into his employer's room. His suit of spotless white linen fitted him perfectly. He managed to pass the mirror as he entered, and twirled his moustache with his left hand, for all his rings were on that hand.

"I have brought the letters myself," he began. "O'Conor has not been near the office to-day."

"What?—did he not give you the jewels?"

Firandola looked at the invalid in surprise, and then turned to Mary, who sat in the vine-curtained bay-window. Wernly explained. Firandola showed his teeth, and shrugged his shoulders.

"Car-r-r-amba! He has gone off with the spoil."

"It is a lie! It is untrue!" cried Mary, rising from

her chair; "Gerald O'Conor is a gentleman and a Catholic! I will not hear—" Remembering herself, she burst into tears and left the room.

"I wish I could hang the rascal!" savagely exclaimed her father, when he had recovered from his amazement.

II.

"They were worth five thousand dollars—not a cent less!" This was the burden of Charles Wernly's complaint, for neither Gerald O'Conor nor Mary's jewels returned.

"Father," Mary said, "he saved my life. Write the value of my life against that of the jewels, and try to forget the loss if the account does not balance."

This suggestion made her father irritable, and then struck him as supremely ridiculous. The idea was too good to be lost. He sent for Firandola.

"I am glad that you have repented of your unladylike outburst," he said. "You have come to the conclusion that your favorite is guilty, then?"

"No," she said, slowly; "I believe that those jewels brought him death. He has been murdered."

Firandola entered, jauntily.

"Do you think that O'Conor can have met with foul play?"

"I wish I could think so," answered the Cuban, with a strange light in his eyes; "that is, I mean, for the sake of his reputation, and," with a glance at Mary, "his soul; but, unfortunately, he was seen to enter the 12 M. train last night, for New York, the ticket agent says."

"Are you sure?" asked Mary, hastily turning away, to hide her face.

"Rogers and Arkright, two of our clerks, saw and hailed him."

A cry of anguish went up from Mary's heart.

"He were better dead—dead!" she thought.

"He is a base, ungrateful scoundrel!" cried Wernly. "You have set the detectives on his track, Firandola?"

The Cuban nodded, and then said, in a low tone, intended more for Mary's ear than her father's:

"Do not think too hardly of the poor boy. It may be, as one of your poets says, that heaven has permitted him to fall that he may rise, and take a firmer stand,—

> "'Or, trusting less to earthly things,
> May henceforth learn to use his wings.'"

Wernly, in amazement, raised himself on his elbow. Mary abruptly left the room.

"Saul among the prophets! You are a hypocrite, Firandola. I thought you did not believe in heaven or hell."

Firandola showed his teeth. "I am liberal," he said, "except where the Jesuits are concerned, and women have prejudices that must be conciliated."

Wernly knit his brows, and fixed his eyes on Firandola.

"You will gain nothing by conciliating my daughter's prejudices. Do you understand?"

"What should I gain?"

"Nothing. Unearth O'Conor, if possible, Firandola."

Outside the door, Firandola ground his teeth, and muttered, "Fool!"

* * * * * * * *

The most poignant thorns of sorrow generally press more cruelly into the heart of the one who waits. The woman, watching with straining eyes the last flutter of the sail that bears her fisher-husband away, suffers more than he who breasts the waves. The reason is plain.

Mary Wernly, pure-hearted maiden that she was, felt her face flame and blush when she thought of the defence she had made of Gerald O'Conor before her father and Firandola. But for worlds she would not have unsaid her words. Suddenly she had become aware that she regarded Gerald with a deeper feeling than gratitude. And now he was gone! gone! leaving a trail of guilt and infamy.

She had felt that her affection for him would always remain in her heart a closed blossom. She never thought that it could become a perfect flower. In her eyes he was a true knight—a Sir Galahad. She would love him as a sister, and help him, and he should never know it. This had been her brief dream.

But where was her Sir Galahad now? A thief? a felon? She *would* not believe it, and yet—

Perfect love casteth out fear. But what human love is perfect? And Mary Wernly was perplexed and tortured with doubts and fears. It was grievously sad to feel that she would never see her hero again,—most bitter to know that he had left her with a stain on his escutcheon. It was the crown of her sorrow. When she remembered him, candid, sincere, true, sitting in the twilight by her father's bedside, and read and heard what people said of him now, her heart seemed as if it would burst. In her grief and perplexity, her only resource was to kneel before her whose sorrow was like to no other. She, the Mother of Sorrows, could understand all.

Of course the Wernly jewel robbery made a sensation in Glenborough. The two rival newspapers metaphorically smacked their lips over it, and waxed rich by capturing Gerald O'Conor in one edition, and setting him free in the next. Reporters tried hard to interview Mr. Wernly and Mary. Narcisso Firandola was an easy victim; he liked it. Even the "hands" in the foundries were pounced upon by the enterprising agents of the press. Cuts, which had done duty as authentic portraits of Lincoln, Marshal MacMahon, and the last murderer, were re-presented as counterfeit presentments of the defaulting clerk. Glenborough, you perceive, was not unprogressive.

Time flew. Six months passed. The man so often a prisoner on paper was still at large. The detectives had found no trace of the jewels.

This question often occurred to Mary, Was he dead, that he did not appear to clear himself? And then followed another question, Was he guilty, hiding his shame? The girl could not answer either. It tore her heart to think of him; she could only pray that he might be proven innocent in the end.

"If he should prove himself stainless," she thought, "I would resign myself to his absence without a sigh."

As years went by, Mary came "out" under the chaperonage of one of her aunts. Many were the eligible and ineligible young men that old Wernly's daughter refused. And old Wernly, still bedridden, congratulated himself on having such a devoted daughter. If Gerald O'Conor could only have presented himself among the eligibles!

But Mary would never have deserted her father, that is certain. As it was, everybody agreed that she had a right to be fastidious. An heiress! and such a modest, amiable heiress. Some people thought her pretty, for time had improved her, though her smile was slow and infrequent, and there was a sad look in her eyes; when inspired by beautiful thoughts or words, she was lovely.

Scarcely anybody in Glenborough chanced to think of Gerald O'Conor now, except Mary Wernly. In her memory, his image grew fresher every year, and his name was never unmentioned in her prayers.

The Glenboroughites were grumbling at the dearth of news. There hadn't been a murder or anything for over eighteen months. The oldest inhabitants shook their heads. Glenborough was getting behind the times. The rival newspapers were dying for lack of a new sensation; and it came.

One morning all Glenborough heard that Charles Wernly had failed. This announcement was a shock that shook the place to its centre. Workmen and their wives talked over the rumor with anxious minds. Failed! Wernly—the strong—the impregnable—the man of iron! It seemed impossible. It was true, however. In a few days the foundries were closed, and laborers stood idle.

Narcisso Firandola came to the surface, as usual; the newspapers declared that he was free from all blame, and depicted his manful struggle against ruin in glowing terms. The failure had come of old Wernly's careless indifference. Wernly himself knew that it had come of his implicit trust in his book-keeper.

Firandola listened to all his employer's furious reproaches with a martyr-like smile, and taking a respectful leave of Mary, withdrew from Glenborough.

"I will not stay here!" cried Wernly. "I will leave this place in spite of all the doctors in creation. 'There is Wernly,' they will say, 'who was once a millionaire, and now is a beggar.'"

His indomitable pride and will enabled him to do what no other stimulants could. He went to New York with Mary. There, in three small rooms, they took up their abode. Wernly would accept no help from any one; he determined to live within the small income allowed him by his creditors, at the same time laying by something for Mary's future. Poor Mary, unused to economy, found it hard to make both ends meet; but her convent training had not been wasted, her talents as a cook and nurse shone brilliantly in the morning; in the afternoon she went out to give French and music lessons to three little girls.

"Don't talk to me about religion," her father had often said; "if I wanted to be a Catholic, your example would do more toward converting me than all your arguments; so don't argue, Mary."

Now, in his affliction—for loss of wealth and power were the greatest afflictions that could befall a man like Charles Wernly—he began to feel the emptiness of earthly things. In the evenings he and Mary held long and earnest conversations; and one afternoon she went rejoicing for a priest. Mary was almost happy; one of the thorns had been plucked from the crown of sorrow.

Mary had not forgotten Gerald O'Conor. Often, in the crowded thoroughfares, she saw a face that resembled his, and her heart gave a great bound. She believed that he was innocent. If Narcisso Firandola had been wicked enough to rob her father, he certainly would not have hesitated to murder and rob Gerald. Like most girls, she jumped at conclusions.

. . . .

On a certain evening Mary was detained much later than usual at the house of her small pupils. One of them being sick would not condescend to go to sleep unless her gentle teacher remained with her, and Mary stayed with the little tyrant until dusk. Then she started homeward. It was not a long distance, but dusk became gloom before she had accomplished it.

Was it the quiet repose of the hour that made Mary's thoughts travel into the past, with all its hopes and fears? Never before had the face and form of Gerald O'Conor arisen so vividly before her. A footstep behind her made her turn. In the half light, not three yards from her, was the same face and form. Was it Gerald O'Conor? If it was he did not see her, for his attention was fixed on a group on the opposite side of the street.

In front of a saloon, made painfully glittering by rows of colored gaslights, two men were standing, engaged in a low, though passionate conversation. Mary, from the other side of the street, observed them. One of them seemed familiar to her. His white vest and bosom glittered with jewelled pins and chains.

There was a loud oath, the report of a pistol, a low groan. The man in the white vest staggered, and fell at the foot of the lamp-post. The other fled rapidly.

Instantly Mary was at the side of the wounded man. Timid and gentle though she was, the suffering of another always aroused the courage of her nature. The man so like Gerald followed her.

"You—and *you!*" murmured the wounded man, Narcisso Firandola.

"He wants air—keep back," said a rich, full voice, which made Mary raise her head suddenly. The rapidly increasing crowd obeyed. "And now half a dozen of you run for as many doctors."

"Car-r-r-amba!" muttered the wounded man; "you shall not move me. I will die where I am. Ask me no questions. I will not tell his name. It was an old grudge."

He paused, panting. Mary wiped his forehead with her handkerchief. Gerald O'Conor raised him in his arms while she held a glass of cold water to his lips.

"O'Conor," he gasped, "keep everybody away! I am dying; I will not be troubled with a doctor. O'Conor, the casket you gave me one night five years ago—water!—water!—you will find all the jewels in a belt around my body. Miss Wernly, tell your father that his money has gone to help the cause of Cuban lib—"

The pallor of death showed on his face; he sunk into Gerald's arms.

"Pray for him! pray for him!" cried Mary, turning to Gerald. "Oh, Blessed Mother, save him!"

Gerald murmured the Our Father. Loud and sweet, Mary's voice rose above the chattering of the crowd.

"Oh, my God, I am heartily sorry for all my sins—"

Firandola's livid lips moved slowly, as if repeating the words. Mary went on. His lips ceased to move.

"He is dead," said Gerald, for the weight grew heavier.

The crowd fell back in reverence.

Five days later. *Scene:* The little sitting-room of a cottage near the sea. *Personages:* Charles Wernly, sarcastically benignant; Mary, radiant with happiness; Gerald O'Conor, calmly content, and without a trace of superciliousness about him.

"I suppose Firandola did not dispose of the stones, because they would have easily been traced to him,"

Charles Wernly is saying, "but what an awful fool you were to go off so suddenly without a word. Didn't you hear about the loss of the jewels?"

"I started at once for Ireland, where it was not likely that I would hear Glenborough news. Do you know, Mary, that I have been in Glenborough twice within this year; but nobody knew whither you had gone. God directed my steps through that street the other night."

"God is very good," murmurs Mary.

"I say, O'Conor," exclaims Wernly, with a gleam of fun in his eyes, "why did you leave us so suddenly? Had you really the presumption—"

Gerald interrupted him, "I have concluded to adopt your suggestion, sir. With the money I recovered from my father's farm in Ireland, I will lease the foundries in Glenborough, if you will come."

"I have no alternative," responds Wernly, smiling. "If Mary goes with you, I will have to go with Mary. Tell me, why did you leave us so suddenly?"

"Because," he answered, "I was afraid of loving Mary too much."

"And now—"

"I can love her as much as I please, can't I, Mr. Wernley?"

There are no happier people in Glenborough than Gerald O'Conor and his wife—his wife, who no longer wears her "sorrow's crown of sorrow."

ROSE.

I.

A ROSE IN JUNE.

> "A face that's best
> By its own beauty drest."—*Crashaw.*

THE breeze from the Schuylkill scatters far and wide the scent of June roses and honeysuckle, and Mrs. Earle Vincent's favorite heliotrope extract becomes decidedly sickly in the presence of this exquisite bouquet of the golden month.

The sun is low, and the clouds that show behind the green tracery of trees on the opposite bank are lit with carmine fire. No sound breaks that stillness which always seems to be the precursor of twilight, except an occasional shout from some boatman on the river, or the monotonous click of croquet-balls on the shore.

Mrs. Earle Vincent's garden-party is in full blast, which means that three dozen people, more or less, are grouped on her well-kept lawn laboriously doing nothing; for croquet-playing can not be called doing anything. Mrs. Earle Vincent is a widow, fair, forty, and with a talent for generalship; moreover, she can afford to be exclusive, for, though wealthy, she is not a *parvenu*. Has not Watson, in his *Annals*, written the name of her great-grandmother among the fair guests at the tournament given by General Howe's officers nearly one hundred years ago? A doubtful honor; some outside barbarians—mostly New Yorkers—sneer at this claim to distinction, but all true Philadelphians revere it in their hearts; consequently, Mrs. Vincent's garden-parties are "the rage." Her tact in securing "good" people is remarkable. There are few officers of any note in the army who have not, at some time or other, attended her parties; literary men and artists from all parts of the world, "caught on the wing," are plentiful; Senators common; and Congressmen, unless exceptionally eminent, are never invited.

"We *must* draw the line somewhere, you know," says Mrs. Vincent, sinking into a rustic seat beside her intimate friend, Mrs. Bolton, and fanning herself violently.

Mrs. Bolton is a tall, slim woman, with short, gray curls, who looks as if she ought to be an old maid, but has missed her vocation.

"Well, my dear," returns Mrs. Bolton, in an acidulated tone, "in drawing your line, you should be careful to exclude clerks and people like that young Burns, you know—very good in *their* way, no doubt, but not *quite*, you know."

"My love," Mrs. Vincent answers, with dangerous sweetness, "we can not establish an American aristocracy based on birth or occupation. It would, as Saxe says, be always 'a thing for laughter, sneers, and jeers.' Everybody knows who our fathers were."

Mrs. Bolton's father was a butcher before he secured a "war" contract, and she reddens—not, alas! on account of the contract.

"I like noted people and people of talent, and these will always come to the top, no matter who their fathers were," continues Mrs. Vincent. "There are very few Americans who can boast of their ancestors.

> "'Their family thread they can't ascend,
> Without good reasons to apprehend
> They may find it waxed at the farther end
> By some plebeian vocation;
> Or, worse than that, their boasted line
> May end in a loop of stronger twine,
> That plagued some worthy relation.'"

Mrs. Vincent delicately omits the poet's second person, in order that her friend may not consider the application of the lines personal. Mrs. Bolton looks angry; but, protected by the halo thrown around her by *Watson's Annals*, Mrs. Vincent smiles complacently.

"But this young Burns has nothing to recommend him that I can see."

"He has good morals, a clear head, and a true heart, I believe—qualities sometimes not discovered at the first glance; besides, he is engaged to Rose."

"Engaged to your niece!" exclaims Mrs. Bolton, casting an alarmed glance toward her son Paul, who is absorbed in conversation with the said Rose. "How *could* you?"

"*I* couldn't—that is, I had nothing to do with it. Her father arranged it before he died, and left her to me. I can't break off the affair by force, for Rose Vincent, *comme moi qui vous parle*, has a will of her own; therefore, like Micawber, I wait for something to turn up."

"Paul ought to be informed of this."

"Oh, let Paul alone. He may waste some of his sweetness on the desert air, but he can take care of himself."

He certainly looked as if he could. He was tall and stalwart, and his manner of wielding even the delicate mallet told of well-trained muscles. His face was handsome, though flushed—not with health or the heat, a keen observer would say, but with too much wine. Though not yet twenty-seven, Paul Bolton had " seen life"—which means the life of dead souls—in all the principal cities of Europe, and had come to increase the remnant of his fortune by taking a wife.

"Rather fast," mammas whispered.

"But oh, *so distingué!*" cried the daughters.

Paul Bolton was a favorite in society. His manners were perfect, his dress was faultless. But some, with whom manners and dress carried little weight, felt intuitively that there was a dark, deep current beneath this surface-flow of glitter and brilliance.

Just now he is twirling his moustache and talking nonsense to Rose Vincent during a pause in the game. Rose Vincent, in his estimation, is merely an unusually pretty girl, with no mind to speak of—a girl who will swallow an inordinate amount of sugared nonsense, and take it for truth ; a girl who may be married for her money.

"Ah, Miss Vincent," he says, with a confidential air, "can life hold in store for us anything sweeter than a day like this ?"

"Life would be very dreary if it could not," answers Rose, throwing a significant smile over at her " enemy " in croquet, Miss O'Neil. "An idle day is a lost day."

"And can you call this idleness, when all the best feelings of our nature are awakened by the supreme loveliness of earth, of sky, of air ?" He speaks with an affectation of intense enthusiasm. "When every sense is engaged in absorbing the sweetness with which each moment is crowded to repletion ? Oh, Miss Vincent!—without *you* this scene"—he pauses abruptly and turns away, as if his feelings were incapable of expression.

Rose shades her face with her fan, and the dimples in her cheeks come and go. She is silent, with the amiable intention of letting the man make a fool of himself, if he will; but she is too womanly to be an utter coquette, and her conscience reproaches her.

"It is your turn, Mr. Bolton."

Paul Bolton takes his turn, and then rejoins her.

"There's poetry in the air, Miss Vincent," he resumes, in a respectfully sentimental manner.

"My aunt appears to be quoting something very emphatically to your mother."

> "'For she and the clouds and the breezes are one,
> And the hills and the sea have conspired with the sun
> To charm and bewilder all men with the grace
> They combine and confer on her wonderful face.'"

Can any woman be deaf to such a delicately flavored compliment? he thinks.

"Ah, yes, that is rather pretty," responds Rose, contemplatively. "And it suits Miss O'Neil exactly. Do you know," with that artlessness which is the perfection of art, "I like to hear a gentleman compliment one lady in the presence of another. Direct compliments are often worthless, and always in bad taste."

Paul Bolton feels that he is checkmated—and by a mere girl. He is piqued; consequently, he makes a hasty move.

"I scarcely know your friend, Miss O'Neil. I mean you, and you know it. Rose Vincent, I love you!"

He leaves her, and quickly walks across the ground to the farther end.

Rose's face flushes and her blue eyes flash. She watches him for an instant, and then dropping her mallet she rushes into the house.

"Oh, what have I done to deserve this?" she cries, safely locked in her own room. "Have I been forward or unmaidenly? Have I given that hateful man any reason? Oh! what will Alban say? I have been insulted! Oh, dear! *dear!*" Here comes a fresh burst of tears. "After all, I believe I'm a flirt—a silly, frivolous flirt, whom I despise."

Having exhausted her breath in incoherence, Rose subsides into what is technically called "a good cry," and feels refreshed. Perhaps the sight of Alban Burns coming quickly up the walk helps to produce this effect. He pauses near Mrs. Vincent, bows to Mrs. Bolton, and, after a few words, offers the former his arm.

Alban Burns seems unusually silent, and thoughtful. The accustomed look of earnestness on his face has given way to one of deep sadness. Mrs. Vincent scans him with curious interest. She can not help respecting the firmness and strength of will which seem to underlie his calm, brown eyes. She does not like her niece's lover; he is not handsome; he has neither *l' air grand* nor *le grand air;* he is an uncompromising Catholic — as it ought to be—and at times he has told her some stern truths.

"You are going to hell," he said, gravely, once when she wanted to take Rose to hear a *risqué* opéra bouffe. "I can not prevent you from going, but Rose shall not go."

And Rose did not go to the opera that night. Mrs. Vincent never forgave him for this; she could forgive anything except being made uncomfortable, and he had caused her to feel uncomfortable.

"Well, my dear boy," says Mrs. Vincent, with a sprightly air that she much affected, "what is your pleasure?"

They have entered the cool, dark parlor. Before he answers, Mrs. Vincent notices that he wears a plain, gray business suit, and that he carries a portmanteau.

"I want to make an explanation," he answers. "If the matter were not urgent, I would not have intruded on your festivity of to-day. You have heard that the firm of Arlyn & Co. has failed?"

"No!"

"It is true. The crash occurred last week."

"And your prospects?"

"I have none." His eyes and lips are firm, but the involuntary gesture he makes is more pathetic than words. "In two more months I was to be a partner, but this crash has even overthrown the ladder that led to that—my clerkship."

There is a pause.

"Of course you will release Rose from her engagement?"

"If she wishes it—but that is impossible. Poverty with me will have no terror for Rose," he answers proudly. "I am not selfish, Mrs. Vincent. I will not ask her to sacrifice the brightest portion of her life, in order to keep her plight to me. Even if she were rich—"

"She is not, nor am I; yet all that she will have must come from me."

"Yes, I will release her. To my mother I owe a duty which I must perform, and for her sake and for Rose's sake, I must give up the one hope that has brightened my life. O God! 'Thy will be done!'"

All of a sudden his assumed stoicism has given way,

and Mrs. Vincent experiences an involuntary pang of sympathy. Instantly, however, he resumes his quiet, grave manner.

"Can I see her and tell her this?"

"You had better not," Mrs. Vincent replies, seeing at once the advantage of her position. "Rose is so warm-hearted and uncalculating that she would scorn the idea of your poverty making any difference."

"You are right," he returns gravely. "We should have a scene, which would unnerve Rose and probably weaken my resolution. My heart might prove stronger than my will."

"Write a note. Make no explanation. I will do the rest," said Mrs. Vincent aloud, and then within herself, "This man is a hero. He can bear the pain in store for him."

Alban Burns unsuspectingly falls into her trap.

"Yes," he answers, "I will write. If she loves me truly, she will trust, and while accepting the freedom I give her, still love and wait. But that is a delusive hope—"

"*Justement*," murmurs Mrs. Vincent.

"I will do my duty to my mother and her, and leave the rest to God," he says, half aloud.

He walks to the piano, tears a leaf from his note-book, and writes:

"I do not ask you to keep your promise, Rose; I release you from it. Mrs. Vincent will explain all.
"ALBAN BURNS."

This he gives to Mrs. Vincent. As he does so, he sees on the piano-cover a dainty pair of gloves and a half-withered rose. He knows that *she* has left them there.

"Rose is *so* careless," Mrs. Vincent observes.

He takes the rose.

"This is all that is left," he says, giving his hand to Mrs. Vincent. "Good-bye."

"*Au revoir!*" she responds, gayly. "Don't think too much of Rose. She is only a young, giddy girl, after all."

"She was everything good to me."

And he goes slowly through the garden, unconscious that Rose is watching from her window, and trying to take the tear-stains from her eyes in time to meet him.

Later: The moon has risen. On his way to the railroad-station Alban Burns has been thinking; now that he has given up Rose, a hundred reasons for not doing it present themselves to his mind:

"It is true that I could not drag her into poverty—I, without occupation, with small hope of any—and burdened with my father's debt; but I have been too hasty, and I have trusted Mrs. Vincent too implicitly. I will return and speak my last words to Rose."

Mrs. Vincent's lawn is deserted, but music of instrument and voice flows out through the lighted windows.

The Schuylkill ripples and murmurs in the moonlight, as it probably did on the same night a hundred years ago, beneath the keel of some Indian's canoe. The tree-leaves whisper soft words to one another and the wind; and Rose Vincent, white, tearless, sorrow-stricken, watches the leaves and the water.

"Gone! gone!" she murmurs, "without reason, without giving me a chance to explain anything that may have offended him! gone, and without a word except this miserable scrawl!"

There is a dark figure approaching. Hope whispers to

her: "It may be he returning"; but another voice also whispers:

"Miss Vincent!—Rose!"

It is Paul Bolton's voice.

"Rose," he continues, ardently, "Rose, to-day I told you that I loved you; to-night I ask you to be my wife."

Alban Burns pauses in the gloom cast by a huge sycamore. In that moment of suspense the agony of years is crowded. He waits for Rose's words.

Now is her time for revenge. Her guardian angel must have veiled his face when she placed her hand in that of Paul Bolton and murmured, "Yes."

II.

A ROSE IN SEPTEMBER.

"Alas! that we dream, and wake
To find the vision dead and dumb."
—*Miss Donnelly.*

A dingy brick house in a quarter of the city with which the street-contractors never meddle, in deference possibly to the wishes of the swarms of children that delight in mud-pies; a clean little room at the very top of this house, under the loft, with a spotless shrine of the Blessed Mother in one corner, a bed in another, a bright piece of carpet in the centre of the floor, three chairs, several sparkling cooking-utensils, and a wonderful mixture of wire and colored scraps of silk on a table.

Voila, mes amis, the home of Marie and Annette Deschapelles, flower-makers to the great public!

Marie lies on the white bed, and the pillow is not

whiter than her face. Her eyelids rest on her cheeks. A lily, half-made, has dropped from her nerveless fingers, which now clasp the beads of her rosary.

Annette sits near the table, her deft fingers busy among a spray of orange-blossoms which need only perfume to deceive a bee.

Annette's cheeks have the hue of rich damask roses, which they took from the pure air of her native Brittany, and of which the air of a foreign land has not yet robbed them. Her brown hair is hidden under a marvellously plaited cap—a cap that gives an air of demureness to the arch black eyes and smiling mouth. She hums a plaintive Breton ballad, and hopes that it may send her sister to sleep. But it does not produce that effect. Marie opens her eyes.

"You are making orange-blossoms, Annette? Orange-blossoms for a bride?" she asks, in a low, tremulous voice.

"Yes, *ma sœur*. Are they not of a beauty most striking?"

"Oh, they are well enough—the dear flowers, but they will fade in a day—in a day, I know, for I have worn them."

"*Petite bergere, je t' aime, je t' aime!*" sings Annette, breaking into a gay chanson all about "*l'amour,*" "*clair de la lune,*" and "*le rossignol.*" Her sister is not diverted, however.

"Annette, your songs are vain. There is sorrow in the world, child, and hymns would better befit your lips. But go, sing on until your heart breaks as mine has broken. Who is this poor bride?"

"Poor, *ma sœur!* Why, she is rich, and of a beauty most ravishing."

"Riches and beauty are not happiness. You have seen her, have you not?"

"Oh, yes. Madame Relvert, her modiste, sent her here yesterday when you were asleep, and I am to take these out to her this afternoon."

"And when is the wedding?"

"Next week."

"Have you seen the bridegroom?"

"No." Annette smiles, showing a pearly row of teeth. "You are better, my sister, for you desire to talk."

"A woman would gossip on her death-bed, and so would a man, for that matter," responds Marie, bitterly. "I know not why this marriage interests me. I pity all brides who love and hope; for I, too, have loved and trusted."

Marie's tone goes to her sister's heart.

"Have you seen the bouquet Monsieur Alban brought for you this morning? See! it is on the altar of Our Lady."

"I see—dahlias and flowers of Autumn. That is well. For me the Spring is past. Annette, you must not think of this Monsieur Alban."

"Think of Monsieur Alban?" cries Annette, a rosy glow mounting to the edge of her cap. "Why should I think of Monsieur Alban?"

"Why should maidens ever be foolish? Monsieur Alban thinks not of you. His heart is in the past. The other day, when you had to go away with flowers, madame, his mother, came in from her room below to make me some tisane. We talked of her son, and, after a time, she told me that he had loved a young lady, good and beautiful; that misfortune had come and swept away his means of subsistence; that his father had died leaving a debt which Monsieur Alban had promised to pay; and so, rather than allow her to share his poverty, or curtail his mother's means of living for the sake of his own happiness, he released her from her promise."

"And did she accept this release?"

"Yes."

"Then she was no true woman!"

"You are excited, Annette. I think that the girl was true enough, but she was very proud, and, instead of speaking to her himself, Monsieur Alban wrote. He gave her husks and not food—words on paper, not words warm from his heart."

"*You* are excited, Marie."

"It may be so. The young lady, however, has now another lover, and Monsieur Alban is sad. Oh, this is a sorrowful world!. I wish I were in Heaven!"

"I wish I were at home in Brittany; then I should feel as if I were on the road to Heaven; it seems hard to feel that way in a strange land."

"Why did I ever come here in search of *him?* He will hate me if he ever meets me."

"Do not think of *him, chère sœur*," says Annette, with an alarmed look on her face. "I am going now. I will call Madame Burns to keep you company while I am gone."

"Well, well. Give me that picture on the table. Madame Burns forgot it the other day, and it is necessary that I should return it to her."

"This photograph! Marie, Marie, it is Miss Vincent, the fiancée to whom I take these flowers!"

"*Eh bien*, I wish her joy!"

The sisters are silent until Mrs. Burns enters. Mrs. Burns is a pale, refined, fragile-looking woman, with an air of dependence about her—a woman who makes an assertion as if she were afraid of hearing the echo of her own voice. Her hair is gray, and lines of care are visible on her forehead. Her face lights up rarely when Marie thanks her for the flowers her son had brought.

"Alban is so thoughtful," she says, taking a seat beside the invalid. "What shall I read to-day?"

"You may read the Penitential Psalms in English," responds Marie, graciously. "I feel like doing penance, and it is a great penance to hear your harsh language, though *you* speak it softly. Bah, it is horrible!"

Carrying the box of orange-blossoms, Annette goes her way toward Mrs. Earle Vincent's house. The passengers in the horse-cars stare at her white cap, but she does not mind them. She is thinking of Rose Vincent and Alban Burns, and a thrill of pleasure fills her heart as she tells herself that the lady whom Alban loved is about to marry another.

Having reached Mrs. Vincent's stucco-decorated house, which, by the way, is in the American, or Harlequin, style of architecture, she is ushered into Rose's room.

Rose sits among silks and lace—the trousseau *en embryo*—and asks Annette to take a chair. Rose is paler, thinner. Her look of birdlike brightness has vanished. She is listless, and there are red circles around her eyes.

"They are pretty, very," she says, lifting the lid of the box, "and so natural. Your skill is wonderful."

Suddenly she casts the sprays away from her and covers her face with her hands. Annette rises.

"I forgot for an instant that you—but never mind. It is well that these blossoms are not real. I could not wear them. Anything sweet, fresh, and pure would be out of place in such a mockery. You are young, and you look sincere. Beware of pride, beware—but what right have I to teach *you?*"

Annette is touched. She pours out water and cologne with her deft fingers and bathes Rose's hot brow. For weeks Rose has been outwardly cold and calm. Now the restraint gives way before the French girl's sympathy. She tells her the story of that day in June. Annette listens, and then speaks of what Marie has lately told her.

"I see it all!" cries Rose. "It was my aunt's work. She explained nothing, and her hints and innuendoes drove me wild. And now it is too late! too late!"

Annette again feels an involuntary thrill of pleasure. It is, indeed, too late. When Rose is married may not Alban Burns seek for some one who can with her own hands help him in his poverty?

"I do not love this man, the man whom I am to marry. I do not even respect him, and yet in a week we are to receive a great sacrament. It is almost sacrilege, and I can not draw back, for I promised, with my eyes open, deliberately, to be his wife. Misfortunes, trials, are nothing, but the evils brought to us by our own perverseness are worse than serpents' stings!"

When Rose has grown calmer, Annette prepares to leave. Rose accompanies her to the garden. When they reach the lawn, a man enters through the little gate. He approaches, and, seeing them, lifts his hat.

"That is the man whom I am to marry," Rose says.

Paul Bolton takes a few steps forward, and then starts as if violently stricken by an unseen hand.

"Annette!"

"Monsieur Paul!"

Annette darts through the gate like a frightened deer, and is soon lost to sight among the trees.

Paul Bolton and Rose stand face to face—he trying not to seem startled and surprised; she looking the questions which she is too proud to ask.

Alban Burns has become three years older in the two months that have passed since June. Up to that time he had worked hard, sometimes far into the night, but he had rejoiced in his toil, for beyond the dust and struggle of the present there shone in the near future the sunlight of love. In a few days his life had changed completely. His hope was overthrown.

"It is just," he told himself. "I have made an idol for myself, and God has broken it."

And so he made his sacrifice—a sacrifice so great that my words can give you no idea of it. Had you known the man, you could have judged how great it was by the change it wrought in him. He was strong, self-contained, not easily moved by common things, and a change like that which had occurred seemed, as his mother expressed it, "to tear his life up by the very roots."

After the failure of Arlyn & Co. he endeavored to obtain employment in New York. He failed. Returning home, he secured after weeks of waiting a clerkship which involved much labor and little pay. He had his mother to work for and a debt to pay. The one sweetened his labor, the other oppressed him; but both spurred him on. He worked, and a man never knows how much he can do until he is forced to do it.

The debt consisted of five thousand dollars for which fraud on the part of another had made his father responsible; and at the side of that father's death-bed he had promised to pay it. Three thousand had been paid at the time of Arlyn's failure; two thousand still remained, and Alban is gradually diminishing this.

Strict economy is necessary, and the weight of it has all along rested on him, for he is determined that his mother shall not suffer. But she, too, saves in secret, and with womanly care and tact conceals it from him, smiling to think how easily he is deceived.

Mrs. Burns has never wholly forgiven Rose Vincent for releasing her son so easily. "You had a narrow escape, Alban," she often says. "That girl would never have been worthy of you."

He only answers, with a look of pain, "Mother, say anything but that."

Among those few relics which he holds most sacred there lies a rose. The bloom of June has departed from it; it is yellow and withered—a shadow in September of the season of roses—and yet I think he would die rather than let a rude hand touch it.

Annette runs along the bank of the river until she is breathless and panting. At last she stops and leans against a tree.

"I have found him—I have seen him with these eyes!" she murmurs, pushing back her cap to let the cool river-air play on her brow. "And he is the bridegroom!"

"Excuse me," Paul Bolton says to Rose, and immediately he is outside the gate and on Annette's track.

"Singular conduct!" Rose thinks. "This man has a secret. I will have two explanations—one from him and one from that French girl. They will probably contradict each other."

Paul Bolton's long strides enable him to reach Annette a few seconds after she has paused at the tree.

There being no chance to flee, Annette collects all her courage as soon as she sees him:

"*Bon jour*, Monsieur Bolton, my brother-in-law."

"*Bon jour*, Mademoiselle Deschapelles, my sister-in-law."

The latter phrase seems to stick in his throat.

"You have not asked for madame, your wife," responds Annette, with elaborate politeness.

"Marie?—she is well, I suppose?"

"Far from well. She is dying, monsieur."

"Dying?" Paul Bolton tries in vain to suppress the expression of relief that shows on his face.

"Yes, dying!" cries Annette, fiercely, in spite of the tears that fill her eyes. "And you have done it, Monsieur Paul. Oh, we two were so happy in the old house at Morlaix until you came! Marie was so beautiful, so well-educated, so superior to the other girls! Oh, Monsieur Paul, how could you have been so wicked?"

Paul Bolton's lips turn white, and he pulls nervously at his moustache.

"You married her," continues Annette, "and then in two weeks deserted her! Ah, if we had only listened to the *curé!* He warned her; but love is blind! She hoped for your return—she pined—sickened. I could not see her die, and so we came in search of you. I have found you, Monsieur Paul. I have made orange-blossoms for your second bride."

"Annette, keep my secret," Paul Bolton says, in a whisper. "What's the use of making a disturbance now? Marie will not live long, you say. Come now, be reasonable. I will pay you any sum you may name. Let me explain matters to Miss Vincent in my own way, and things will take their course."

"When Mademoiselle Vincent is married, Monsieur Alban must not think of her, and he will be free." This thought passes through Annette's mind like a flash of lightning. It is a temptation. She murmurs an *Ave* before answering him:

"You are a scoundrel, Monsieur Paul. I will save Miss Vincent if I can!"

She springs away from him. This time he does not follow her. Numbers of people are on the banks, and he is too well-bred to make himself unduly conspicuous.

"Marie! Marie!"

No answer. Marie lies white and still, with the black beads of the rosary clasped by her pallid fingers.

"Marie, I have found him!" Annette wails.

Mrs. Burns softly enters.

"You here, Annette?"

"Tell me, madame,—she is asleep?"

"She is dead, poor child."

Annette's grief is wild and incoherent; but from her broken exclamations Mrs. Burns soon gathers the sad story.

When Alban comes home at nightfall, Annette tells him all, and beseeches him to save Rose Vincent. She will not leave Marie's side.

"I will see her," Alban says, when the story is done; "it is my duty"; and to himself, "I will be cool, collected, unmoved."

He starts at once for Mrs. Earle Vincent's. He tries to feel that he is a martyr to duty; it is a very pleasant martyrdom. Rose meets him in the parlor, and stands near the piano, where he had stood to write that note. She greets him coldly.

"Paul Bolton has told me this already," she says, when he had finished. "We parted an hour ago."

A constrained silence. Suddenly Rose begins to cry.

"You are *so* changed!" This is her explanation. His coating of ice gives way; he reproaches her; she reproaches him. Storm; thunder; tears; and Rose sobs that she will wait for him, and never, never have anybody else.

They walk out into the porch. He shows her his withered rose, which looks pale and sad in the moonlight.

"You will give me a rose of September for my rose of June?"

"No," she murmurs; "God will give us heart's ease."

When God sends us anything good, He is generous: He does not do it grudgingly.

The next day, Alban received an eccentric note:

"*To the Son of my old Friend, greeting:*

"You have worked nobly. You have proved yourself worthy of your father, who was one of the best men that ever lived. You must forgive the way in which I have tested your honor; but I have lived in the world long enough to know that in many the virtue of honesty consists only in freedom from temptation. I have tried you sufficiently. I intended to send you the enclosed check long ago, before my departure for Europe, but somehow the thought slipped from my old head. When the villainy of another made your father responsible for this debt, I never intended to exact it from him, and when he died I watched you and waited. Come and see me. I have need of a man like you. In haste.

"BRYAN O'NEIL."

A check for all of the debt he has paid falls into Alban's hand. His heart is too full for coherent words of gratitude; but God knows.

Marie is gone; but Annette still sits before Our Lady's shrine and makes flowers. Like Alban and Rose, she has heart's ease—which is nourished by faith and love and hope—which may droop at times on earth, and which is perfect only in Heaven.

"My *dear* Mrs. Bolton," sweetly says Mrs. Earle Vincent, at her first garden-party after Rose's marriage. "I hear that your son is in business on some island."

"In business? Oh, no! Paul is at Monaco."

"Oh, yes, the gambling-place. I was sure a Bolton would never stoop to work."

THE JAWS OF DEATH.

THE room was small and scantily furnished, but in all its arrangements there were traces of womanly taste and thrift. The window was low and narrow, and looked into an uninviting court, but it was covered with a curtain of dainty white, through which a stray gleam of sunshine fell upon Nelly O'Connor's plants. These were a living sprig of green shamrock from the old soil, and a pet geranium, the gorgeous crimson blossoms of which shone out like rubies amid the emerald setting of its foliage, in spite of "winter and cold weather." It seemed as if the influence of Nelly O'Connor's loving heart had power to protect her silent pets from the blight of the fiercest frost, for while her neighbors' plants withered and died at the first touch of cold weather, hers throve well, and from their little window nodded defiance to sleet and snow.

On the neatly-papered walls of this little room hung three pictures—the Immaculate Conception, right above Nelly's head; St. Patrick and the Serpents, and Daniel O'Connell, whose "counterfeit presentment" was placed directly opposite old Mr. O'Connor's arm-chair.

Having told all I remember about the room, I shall try to describe Nelly herself.

She sat in her usual place by the window engaged in her usual occupation—sewing—for Nelly O'Connor had to work for her own living and for that of her father, too.

That pale gleam of winter sunshine lightly touched her smooth brown hair, and formed a halo around the head that bent over the work so intently. Imagine a graceful little woman clad in a dark dress with snowy collars and cuffs; imagine an oval face with less color in it than it possessed three months ago, when it looked its last on a certain green isle across the sea; a pair of dark blue eyes, serene, calm, yet bright, with at times a sparkle of laughter in their depth, and at others a shadow of sadness. Imagine—but what's the use of imagining at all?—anybody that never saw Nelly O'Connor can *not* imagine what a charming, modest Irish girl she was at this time.

After a while it became too dark to sew. Nelly rose and stirred the fire until it cast a red glow on the wall opposite. Then she flitted about the room silently and brought out the tea-things.

"Father's late this evening," she murmured, when the table was fully arranged. "If I hadn't so much confidence in Tip, I'd feel anxious."

And Nelly went to the door and looked into the gloomy court. There was nobody coming, so she lighted her lamp, and again the seldom-idle needle began its flight.

Five minutes later pattering steps became audible without, and there was a sound of scratching at the door. Nelly opened it, and a small, curly black dog bounded in and stood on his hind legs to receive the girl's caress.

Slower and heavier footsteps followed, and a tall, strongly-built old man entered the room. His hair was white as snow, his face was ruddy and unwrinkled; though old, he would have seemed perfectly hale and hearty, were it not for the strange indecision of his motions and the terrible expression of *blankness*—of some incompleteness—in his countenance.

That want of. something—that incompleteness—was real. For ten years Brian O'Connor had been blind. Light and darkness were the same to him.

"I was beginning to be anxious about you, father," she said, taking the old man's hat and overcoat.

"An' sure hadn't I Tip with me?" he answered in a cheery voice, as he stooped to pat the dog's curly head. "Faith, he's a raal Tip an' no mistake in his love of fightin'. If I hadn't held on to his string with all me strength, he'd have been the death of half a dozen curs to-day. But that's nayther here nor there. Let's have tay, Nelly jewel, an' I'll tell you something."

The meal over, Nelly gave him his pipe, and he sunk into his arm-chair, which was always placed in his favorite position, opposite the print of Daniel O'Connell. He could not see the picture; but as the great agitator often figured largely in his conversation, it gave him pleasure to emphasize his remarks by pointing with his pipe at the portrait of "ould Dan himself."

"Well, Nelly, mavourneen," he began, settling himself comfortably in his chair, "Tip and myself have had a long walk through the city, but there's no work stirrin' that a blind man can do." He spoke gravely, but without bitterness.

"An' what if there isn't, father?" said Nelly, hastily dropping her work. "Sure there's plenty for me to do."

The old man shook his head. "It isn't the likes o' you, mavourneen, that ought to be slavin' here from morn to night, wearin' your fingers to the bone for a worthless ould wreck that can do nothin' but eat and sleep."

"But you promised to tell me something, you know."

"Thrue for you. I've had as many advintures as the Seven Champions themselves the day. Who do you think I met first—from our place at home?"

"I'm not good at guessing, father." There was a look of expectation in her eyes.

"Faith, I knew very well who you'd name." And he chuckled. "But it was one of Dan Deagan's six daughters. She came across in the last steamer, and I knew her by her rough, harsh voice, jist like her father's. I didn't know her name, an' I didn't want to tell her I'd forgotten it, so I called her Kate, an' faith I hit the nail on the head." He laughed outright, and continued, pointing to the picture opposite, "For that's what they called a daughter of ould Dan's, and iver since the whole countryside has been swarmin' with Kates. She tells me that Father Kevan is stationed at a church outside the city. I've the name on a bit of paper."

"What! our own Father Kevan, from home?"

"The same, God bless him! A priest's a priest, anyhow, but it's a great comfort entirely to have one from our own place. I met Pierce Toole this afternoon." He paused for an instant.

Nelly involuntarily bent lower over her work, as if to hide the heightened color in her face. She forgot that the old man could not see.

"I was steppin' off the ferryboat whin I slipped betwixt it and the wharf, an' sure I'd have a cowld bed in the Delaware this same evenin' if it wasn't for a strong pair of arms that pulled me out, safe and sound, before I touched the wather. That pair of arms belongs to Pierce Toole. He's a fine, strappin' gossoon, sure enough, but, though he saved my life, I couldn't help noticin' that his breath smelt o' whisky."

Nelly's face flushed a deeper red.

"Sure, father, the best of men may take—"

"I know—I know," interrupted the old man, impatiently. "And I know Pierce Toole's nature. Sure he might have married you at home with me full consint, if it wasn't for his love for the liquor. I know him, I say: whin he gets a taste o' the stuff, he can't lave off drinkin'. Well, afther he had pulled me safe aboord, he asked me if I'd let him come and see me—*me!*" And he chuckled at the idea. "It's not me he wants, the spalpeen! I couldn't say yis, and I wouldn't say no, so I tould him I'd lave it all to you. He'll come to-night, and I'll tell him you'll not see him, if you want me to. I'll not stand between you and him any longer. You may choose for yourself."

Nelly made no answer, but she flitted across the room to the spot where a small looking-glass hung, and, with eyes and cheeks unusually brilliant, occupied herself in giving some extra touches to her hair.

Her father understood the movement. He smiled, half in sadness, half in mirth.

"Och ohone!" he said; "women are all alike. They'll lave their ould fathers any day, to take up with the first spalpeen that asks them!"

"An' sure didn't my mother take up with you?" murmured Nelly, with just a tinge of sauciness in her tone; and then changing to earnestness, "but I'll never leave you, father; don't be thinking of such a thing. As for Pierce, he has a good heart in spite of the whisky, and, father, I'll make him take the pledge."

"The pledge!" groaned the old man. "That's mighty well; but a man that don't kape his promise won't kape his pledge! Faith, what's the pledge to him, if he hasn't got the grace of God and the will to back it? Maybe I'm wrong, Nelly, but I've seen too many pledges taken and broken in my time—"

A knock at the door interrupted him. Nelly hastened to open it, and the subject of their conversation stood before them.

Pierce Toole was a handsome, stalwart young Irishman, with a frank, winning way about him that was apt to prepossess people in his favor. He had one great failing. He was intemperate in the use of intoxicating liquors. This failing had alone prevented his marriage to Nelly O'Connor. With Brian O'Connor's full consent, Nelly had said "Yes" when Pierce Toole had asked her to be his wife. But several times, in spite of promises given to old Brian, Pierce had "taken too much," and the justly-indignant father had withdrawn his consent to the marriage. Nelly was obedient; though Pierce Toole crossed the ocean in the same vessel with her and her father, she never during the voyage exchanged a word with him. Old Brian saw that his prohibition gave Nelly great pain, and probably his sympathizing, fatherly heart suffered as much as hers. It is a great mistake to think that hearts grow colder as they grow old; they may gain wisdom, but they do not lose their capacity of suffering.

And so, when Pierce Toole saved the old man's life that day on the ferryboat, the latter's heart softened, in spite of his better judgment; and here the prodigal stood, very near the door of the little house, looking extremely uncomfortable in his best suit, and twirling his hat nervously.

"Come in, Pierce, and shake hands," the old man said; and as Pierce Toole obeyed, he continued in a low tone: "Before we begin again on the old terms, I want you to take the pledge."

The young man's face reddened. "Let bygones be bygones. I'll not taste a drop o' the stuff. I'll give up drinking entirely."

"You've tould me that before. Will you take the pledge?"

"Sure me promise is equal to me pledge, any day."

"I hope not," said Brian, dryly.

"Well, I'll take the pledge, thin; but it's mighty hard—"

"You'll see Father Kevan about it next Sunday?"

"I will." And the young man, with a relieved look, turned away from Brian to Nelly, who, during this colloquy, had been trembling with apprehension.

The evening was a happy one to the two young people. The old man sat, smiling and sighing, among the shadows, thinking of the two to whom life just now seemed all joy and brightness.

"She's a changed girl," he muttered the next morning, as he heard Nelly carolling at her work like a lark. "Sure she hasn't sung for many a week. If I could only trust him—if I could only trust him!"

An expression of distress crossed the old man's face. He rose and went over to the windowsill, where the shamrock grew in the earthen flower-pot. He placed his hand tenderly among the leaves. This was his usual action when troubled; the touch of the soft leaves diverted his thoughts, and brought back to him the memory of bygone days and pleasant scenes in the fair land from which that sprig of shamrock came.

Weeks passed. Pierce Toole took the pledge, and kept it. One day Father Kevan married Nelly O'Connor to him, and nearly every soul in the city from the "old place at home" came to offer congratulations. The absence of "spirits" on the occasion was duly noticed by the guests; but the spirit of good-will was not wanting, and it was the general opinion that Pierce Toole had done well to marry old Brian's daughter. The old man removed with the happy couple to a neat little house. Pierce was earning good wages, and Nelly was no longer forced to dim her bright eyes by sewing at night. The future seemed cloudless, and, for a time, no sorrow marred their present.

But old Brian died on the same day that his grandson—a small Pierce Toole—came into the world. Bitterness and sweetness were equally mixed in Nelly's chalice just then.

Pierce grew more irregular in the performance of his religious duties, and, in consequence, his power of resisting temptation became weaker. He attended Mass, but merely from the force of habit. Nelly's remonstrances were met by smiles and evasive words. At last she discovered the consequence of all this. One night he came staggering home. He had broken the pledge.

Old Brian's words floated to Nelly's ears as she stood facing her husband—not angrily—but in bitter heart-breaking grief—

"What's the pledge to a man that has not got the grace of God to back it?"

From that night Pierce sunk lower and lower. A sad, heart-broken look never left Nelly's face. When little Pierce was able to walk, his father and mother were compelled to leave the home which had once seemed like Eden to Nelly. They went out to the suburbs—to a tumble-down barn which for a long time had been untenanted save by rats. Pierce Toole would not work, or rather, no one would employ a drunkard. Nelly's health failed, and she could not sew. Had it not been for the kindness of Father Kevan, she and the child would have starved.

Christmas Eve had come. The night was clear and cold; the biting frost had made the ground as hard as a miser's heart, and raised fairy forests and castles on those window-panes in the distant city, which were twinkling with a thousand happy lights on their happiest night of all the year.

Separated from the gaze of the watchful stars, one of which had cast its silvery ray on the path of the wise men long ago—separated from the gaze of the pitying stars and the blasts of the winter wind by a tottering fabric of frail boards, lay a pale, wan woman, wasted to a shadow of her former self. Near her was a child.

The wide, long interior of this barn was desolate and barren. The remains of a fire smouldered in a broken stove. On a chair stood a candle, but its dim, flickering light only served to make the darkness visible.

The woman who lay there sick, almost dying, was Nelly, Pierce Toole's wife. A red fever-flush burned in her cheeks, and her eyes shone with a terrible brilliance from the dark circles that surrounded them. Through her white, attenuated fingers she was rapidly passing a rosary—the one gift of her father she still retained.

Her head moved restlessly, and once or twice she attempted in vain to rise and approach the door.

"I am dying—dying," she moaned, "with none near me—no priest—no absolution—no—" She stopped abruptly, and bent her head in a listening attitude. "Oh, Blessed Mother, help me!" He voice became an appealing shriek. "Oh, Mother," she cried, "how often have I said, '*Pray for us now and at the hour of our death!*'"

A blast of wind made her shiver; a shower of snow-flakes was driven into the room.

"Pierce!" she said, half hopefully, raising herself on her elbow. "Pierce!"

"What! a human being here on this night!" said a voice that caused her heart to leap for joy. It was Father Kevan's!

"Poor child!—poor child!" he murmured, recognizing her. "And Pierce has brought you to this!"

"Sure he was weak, Father," she answered, willing that her last breath should be an excuse for him.

Father Kevan thanked God for the accident to his old gig which had led him and his sexton, Mick, to seek shelter for a time in this deserted place.

There was no blessed candle—none of those holy symbols which make the Catholic sick-room a vestibule of Heaven. Mick prayed reverently, holding his lantern where it would give the best light.

Nelly seemed to have forgotten everything but the Sacred Guest.

"Depart, Christian soul—"

It was over.

The priest raised the little child which, thin and pale, clung to its mother's empty breast. The child did not cry or move.

"Bring the light nearer, Mick!"

A figure had shuffled in at the door, and stood silent in the gloom.

The priest laid the child beside its mother, gently and reverently. Then he turned. The newcomer was Pierce

Toole. He seemed dazed by the picture before him. Father Kevan did not speak. Mick could not stand the silence.

"They're dead, Pierce—dead!"

"Hush!" said the priest.

Pierce Toole did not burst into sobs or cries. "I have brought the curse o' God on me."

"You rejected His grace," said the priest. "Pledge or promise is nothing without it."

Pierce Toole knelt beside his wife and child. His form shook and a big tear fell down his cheek.

Dead! Gone! He fell forward at the priest's feet.

. . . .

A gray-haired man, bowed down, yet not old, remarkable among his neighbors for his piety and humility, watches often all night in Father Kevan's church. By day he carries a hod, never murmuring in heat or cold, a helper of all that ask him. This man is Pierce Toole.

"Promise or pledge," he often repeats, when he has told his story, "is nothing without God's help. The drink is not bad. God made it. It's the forgetting of God that makes us misuse it. Mind that, boys."

CARMEL.

I.

"NON SUM DIGNUS."

LOOKING at the narrow, headstrong stream which Northerners might be tempted to call a creek, but which the people of San Antonio dignify with the name of a river, James Delaney, with a very dim reminiscence of Lafontaine, perhaps, thought of a country snake which had lost its way in a village. The San Antonio is serpentine in the strictest sense of the term; it runs through a pecan grove only to lose itself amid a crowd of bath-houses attached to the back gardens of the citizens. Making a sudden curve into a garden, it comes forth laden with the creamy petals of the camellia and the sunset-tinted leaves of the roses; then it darts behind a Mexican jacal and emerges, bearing the refuse of the family's mid-day meal. The sunlight makes it iridescent in one place and lime-like in another; it is a river of surprises, and it runs as wayward as black-eyed Dona Flora, who stands now, fan in hand, in the gallery of her house and looks anxiously at James Delaney.

James Delaney is thinking of the river, not of the lady, and his thoughts are not wholly sentimental. He is watching the velocity of the stream, and longing for the means to harness this powerful serpent. With capital, he could start a paper-mill in this lazy, half-Spanish town. He could turn the mud houses of the half-breeds into pleasant cottages, and make the vacant plazas crumble beneath the wear and tear of traffic. He does not know that all the capital in the world would not induce that lazy and happy Mexican to quit his beloved jacaleto, with its oven of black mud and its roof of sticks. He knows, however, only too well, that if improvements in San Antonio depend on *his* capital, that charming little place might remain lazy and beautiful until the end of time. He laughs a little as he wakens from his dream and remembers that a certain wallet in his left vest pocket holds exactly ninety-six dollars, and that sum is the lever with which he is to move San Antonio. It is all he has in the world, however.

This remembrance probably causes him to stretch out his arms, and to look complacently at the muscles which are vaguely indicated through his thin summer coat.

"Thank heaven," he said, "I have strength. That Delilah, hard study, has not destroyed my Irish vigor or made me less able to hew stone or draw water."

And he laughed again—a pleasant laugh, which made Dona Flora look at him.

James Delaney was not a particularly good-looking fellow nor a particularly ill-looking one. He had blue eyes, dark, deep, Irish eyes, which always smiled before his lips opened, a reddish moustache, hair a shade darker, and a tall, well-knit figure. His voice was delicious to the ear. There was a touch of the brogue in his speech which was very pleasant when heard amid the Southern twang or the nasal and drawling intonations of the Spaniards. He was what the French call an "*un homme manqué.*" He had been spoiled by a system of education which, unhappily, is very prevalent among Irish Americans. His parents, poor, but industrious persons, had come to New York with him, a little child, in the year '50. They worked hard night and day to give their only child a suitable education. The other children, girls, had died young. James was intended for the priesthood, for which he had neither vocation nor inclination.

His father and mother, kind-hearted and well-meaning souls in other things, could not understand why, after an expensive college course that left them almost penniless in their old age, he refused to enter the higher seminary. His confessor came to them and warned them that to force the young man would be almost a sacrilege; but the old people could not understand that. Sure his mother's cousin, Terence McMahon—God, rest his soul, the holy man—was as wild as a young colt before he went to Maynooth, and here was James—and a better son never lived—refusing to let his old parents have the comfort of seeing him celebrate Mass before they died. Dear old Mrs. Delaney's eyes filled with tears as she thought of this terrible disappointment. She could not bring herself to face it.

"Sure," she said, "your father and myself haven't had much time for prayin', we've been so busy workin' for you, James, and the only comfort we had was the thought that we'd have a holy priest of our own to help us make our souls. Oh, James, ma cushla, say that you'll not bring our gray hairs in sorrow to the grave."

His father did not say much. He sat in the evening in a little back room behind the shop, silent and grim; but his old pipe often went out, and the hand that held the paper, his favorite, trembled. That trembling, withered hand, in which the purple veins stood out from the sinews and wrinkled skin, troubled James' heart even more than his mother's pleading. Words spoken lose part of their force, but unspoken words touch a sensitive heart like red-hot steel.

James Delaney's heart was very generous and sensitive. He had never been taught to be demonstrative; the Delaneys were a silent family, and James had been long away; but he could not resist the impulse to take his father's hand in his, and cry out—

"I can't, father, I can't!"

"Who asked you to do anything against your will?" said the old man, his eyes twitching. "But don't say you can't; say you won't. I never thought that a grandson of Tom Delaney, who died for his religion and country, would come to this; but never mind," the old man's voice choked, "I'll say no more about it; remember this, James, I'll do no more for you."

Old Delaney was a man of few words. His son, with a feeling that was almost despair, understood that the iron had entered his heart.

"And sure," cried poor Mrs. Delaney, "what was the use of all the Latin and French, and them things with hard names, if you're not going to the seminary? We wouldn't have done amiss if we had kept you here in the shop, instead of slavin' hard to make you better than your neighbors. Ochone! I wish we'd kept you here."

"I wish to heaven you had, mother!" said James, kissing his mother's cheek and going quietly up to his room in the attic.

He threw himself on the bed, and burst forth into wild prayers.

He cried out the "Dominie non sum dignus," a score of times. He was not worthy of the highest and holiest calling on earth—he did not dare aspire to be one of those anointed men. He had been weighed and found wanting. He had not been called or chosen. You can imagine what struggles, what temptations, what hopelessness beset a young and generous heart like this, striving to do right, yet, in the eyes of those he loves, a reprobate, a contemner of holy things. Late in the night he wrote a long letter to the Jesuit father who had counselled him. After that, he fell asleep and dreamed that his dear old mother blessed him.

She loved him still in heart, but during the many days that followed, she made little sign of it. Old Delaney had commanded her to keep silence on the question at issue. Many times James caught her with a furtive tear in her eye, and sighs and ejaculations at intervals told him what was going on in his mother's mind. His father, always a silent man, seldom spoke to him now. James strove to help him in the shop; but there was little need for him there. His father's lips pressed themselves closely together, and one day they opened sarcastically, to say that "a *gentleman*, with his head full of Greek and Latin, was out of place among molasses and mackerel."

After this, James betook himself to Virgil and Homer in the attic. But the parts wearied him. Dido might mourn and Penelope spin, but the daily papers and daily life had more charm for our collegian; yet few were less fitted for the daily routine of life than he.

He dared not suggest to his parents that he should study law or medicine. This to them would have seemed like an insult; besides, he shuddered at the thought of longer remaining a burden to them. What could he do? The silent reproach that met him every hour at home drove him mad. He could teach; but few pupils cared to come to a corner grocery store in the Bowery for lessons; he looked out for a place in a school, and discovered, like the old Italian, who states the fact in his *ballata:*

> "The world with masters is so covered o'er
> There is no room for pupils any more."

He remembered, with some satisfaction, that he had three gold medals for essays on "The Future of America," the "Glories of Ancient Rome," and the "Use of the Cothurnate in Greek Tragedy." These three efforts had called down thunders of applause at as many commencements. He attacked the newspaper offices, with visions of glory filling his brain. Poor boy! He found that a man who can gather in advertisements or write comic paragraphs, was more valuable than he who could locate all the allusions in Horace or minutely describe the "properties" of the Greek plays. He seemed destined to have no place in the future of America, which he had settled so satisfactorily when he graduated.

Things went on in the same way at home. The place was clouded. Father, mother, and son were utterly miserable. The old man seldom spoke and his wife went about the house sadly as one heart-broken. James went to Mass with them, and poured forth his whole heart's grief and despondency before the Blessed Sacrament. And while he prayed, he felt that his father had looked on him as a pretender, a hypocrite.

It happened that the Congressman from the district in which the Delancys lived wanted a secretary—wanted one very badly indeed, for the learned legislator spelled even more erratically than he who called himself a "grater mán than old Grant." In order to conciliate the Irish vote he offered the place to James Delaney, who had made some friends, although he was not looked on with favor by the older neighbors. It was a great cross to the Delaneys to feel that their pride had fallen—that a certain vague and evil odor was attached to their son who had failed to be a priest.

James did not take kindly to the ways of politics. His early training had made him honest, if it had not made him practical. When the Honorable William E. Skinner had no further use for him, James had saved nearly three hundred dollars.

"Father," he said, one evening, "I have determined to go at last."

The old man dropped his paper and looked at his son with an eager, questioning glance.

"No, no!" said James, interpreting his father's thought—"I have determined to go South, to earn my living, and perhaps to come back—"

The old man put up his paper abruptly. His mother cried a great deal and kissed him; and the next day his trunk was packed and ready for him.

"God bless you," she said, and the touch of the wrinkled, toil-worn hand on his shoulder made his heart leap into his throat. "I thought—I thought, sure, that one day you'd be blessing your father and me."

The little room swam before his eyes. A groan forced itself from him as he kissed his mother for the last time. His father shook hands with him in silence. He never saw either of them again. He left them, with his heart full of parting benedictions.

. . . .

And so we find him watching the twisted San Antonio while Dona Flora gazes at him anxiously and rattles the sticks of her fan.

II.

CARMEL.

The roses cluster around the gallery of Dona Flora, for the whole town is a nest of roses at this time, pink, crimson, white, and gold. Just beyond that adobe house is an arching group of bananas, under which a dark-skinned Mexican, in sombrero and gray blanket, is selling the pecan candy which is so common an article of merchandise. The Angelus tolls from the cathedral, and the market people in the plaza cross themselves, while cabs rush past and the thrifty Germans hasten to dinner. A Mexican caballero, velvet-jacketed, with silver buttons flashing in the sun, dismounts, and passing contemptuously the signs which offer refreshment in the shape of St. Louis beer, enters El Globo Potosino, as the Mexican restaurant is named. Thriving German burghers enter the low houses, and a noonday stillness settles over the white expanse of the plaza.

James Delaney watches the San Antonio and murmurs the Angelus. Dona Flora has shaken down a great bunch of pale-tinted bells from a dagger-leaved plant, and left the gallery, to forget the stranger in her enjoyment of her beloved dish of *chile con carne*.

Delaney's arm is lightly touched. He turns, and sees two black, frightened eyes looking into his.

"Senor—" says a trembling voice. He takes off his hat, for it is a lady who addresses him. A young lady, clad in black, who, in stature, scarcely reaches his shoulder; she is agitated, and she pauses nervously in her speech.

"Senor, I beg that you will stay with my father. He is very ill, and I must go for a priest."

The young lady pointed to a *jacal* that stood a few yards from the river. Delaney hastened toward it. In order to enter he was forced to stoop. On a bed of dried leaves, hardly covered by a scanty blanket, lay an old man. He was evidently not a Mexican. His features were pinched and his complexion pallid. He opened his eyes as Delaney knelt near him, to feel his pulse.

"Where is Carmel?" he asked, feebly. "Has the priest come?"

"Not yet." Delaney gave him some water, and then began to recite the litany for the dying. The sick man responded almost inaudibly. Suddenly he asked:

"Your name? Tell me your name."

"James Delaney."

"An Irishman or an Irishman's son. I can trust you. I want my daughter to reach the North in safety. I had something, but these accursed Mexicans robbed me. See her safe out of this accursed place. Swear that you—"

The old man raised his arms in the air, as if to grasp the words he could not utter. He caught sight of the crucifix tattooed in blue ink on his arm and kissed it. There was silence. A few minutes afterward the priest entered. In half an hour, Carmel Boynton was alone in the world.

Her story was simple and short. Her father had been a miner in Mexico—a "boss." He had married a Spanish woman, and had adopted her religion. There had been a dispute over some land with his wife's relatives, after Mrs. Boynton's death, and Boynton and his daughter were compelled to leave the place, and they were going North when Boynton fell sick.

Carmel had sufficient funds to bury her father decently. Delaney went to the funeral, and accompanied her to the hut which she had never called home. He was struck with her gentleness and good sense. At this time he did not notice how beautiful Carmel was, for the grief surrounded her with such a halo that he thought as little of noticing the regularity of her features, or the splendor of her eyes, as he would have dreamed of criticising the looks of the angels in a picture by Murillo. He felt that she was very pure, and fair, and very much above him.

After he had said good-evening to Carmel on the afternoon of the funeral, a woman approached and addressed the girl.

"I have heard of your misfortune, my dear. I have seen you several times and taken a fancy to you. Come home with me, my dear."

The woman was not young, but she was painted to the eyelashes and dressed gayly, with banged hair, fluttering ribbons, and bangles. Delaney turned and looked at her. Her looks and her cracked voice made him sick. He went up to Carmel, who seemed surprised at the woman's kindness.

"Miss Boynton," he said, "let me decline this offer for you. You are under my protection."

The woman turned toward him.

"Oh," she said, with an equivocal laugh, "I did not know that this young woman had so soon found a friend."

"Miss Boynton," said Delaney, shuddering, as he thought of the dangers the girl might be thrown into, "you must leave San Antonio. Have you friends in the North?"

"Friends of my father's," she said. "Yes—many of them. They are in New York. But I can not leave. I must stay here and work."

"You must not stay here."

"Why not? There are persons here who will help me. This kind friends have promised. You have been very good, and even strangers, that American lady who spoke to me the moment ago, she will—"

"You must avoid her," interrupted Delaney, impatiently, for the simplicity of the girl exasperated him. "This is a lawless place, in many ways, you must learn."

"But I can not leave it, Senor. I am poor, and I can not beg. I must work," she answered, with a proud look in her eyes.

This girl ought not to remain, he thought. He reflected a moment.

"Senorita," he said, "your mother could tell you or a priest would tell you to go."

A faint tint of red colored Carmel's cheek, and a look of horror flashed into her eyes.

"You must go," he continued, "you will be safe among your friends in New York. I have some money that I can spare. Let me lend it to you. You can repay me." He took the wallet from his pocket and counted out all the money he possessed, with the exception of five dollars. She watched him thoughtfully; drew back her hand and then held it out again. She unlocked a little box which contained her belongings, and after a few moments' search, handed him a roll of parchment.

"Keep that, Senor, and if I should die or not be able to repay you, you can perhaps make that useful. It is the deed of my father's land in Mexico."

He refused it.

"No" he said, with a blush and a bow, "your word is enough."

She gazed at him with a thoughtful look in her large, dark eyes—a look that seemed to pierce his mind and hers, and measures the motives in one by the motives in the other.

"I do not know the English well," she said, timidly, "but I do know what the word gentleman means. I will take your money, and Our Lady of Mount Carmel will never forget you."

He heard her fasten the door of her little house, and he went away with a light heart to sup in a most frugal manner. He was almost penniless, yet was gayer than he had been for many a day. He did not seek shelter for that night, but lay down under the clear, bright sky, as many do in that happy clime. He went to sleep and dreamed that the woman he had seen was armed with the claws of a vulture and a terrible beak, and that she was about to pounce on a little white dove which had the eyes of Carmel. He awoke with a start. The San Antonio murmured softly, the scent of the roses came faintly to him, and he went to sleep again, for he could see the little nest in which the dove reposed peacefully.

It happened that some of the Ursuline Sisters were going North, and, through the influence of the priest who had administered the last sacraments to her father, Carmel was placed in their charge.

Delaney said good-bye with a strange feeling of weight on his heart.

"Adios, mi amigo," she said.

"Adios!"

Something fell into his hand. It was a pair of brown scapulars, with a little gold medal. Simple-hearted, generous fellow that he was, it never occurred to him to imagine that he had made a sacrifice. He was not inclined to give himself any credit for what he had done. He watched the flying train and an involuntary sigh escaped from him. The delicious air, the flower-scent, the novel sights, had no charm for him. Yesterday he was not unhappy. To-day he felt as if he had lost a friend. He made a rapid sketch in his note-book of the bearings of the land which Boynton had owned. He had asked Carmel about it. "Something may come of it," he thought.

Brain-work was not wanted in San Antonio, so our collegian, obeying Solomon's injunction to do what his hand found to do, tried brick-laying. He worked hard—that is, as hard as any man is expected to work in San Antonio—venison and turkey were cheap, so was good beef, and he lived well; but there was not much to hope for in a worldly way. He led a pure, simple life, making no friends—indeed the men who came his way, idlers and refugees, were not to his taste—and conning his old books.

If he had had a little money, he would have gone to Kimball county, and started a sheep ranch in a small way; but, as we all know, he had disposed of all his money. After a time, when brick-laying was scarce—and this came about just as he had become expert—he went out with a party of stockmen; and, after a time of probation, he became a ranchman, earning the munificent sum of twelve dollars a month and "found." "Found" expresses roughly the husks of the prodigal son. That's what it means when used in connection with cattle-drivers in Texas.

To Delaney this was a miserable life. There was no

one to whom he could speak his thoughts. All day he
was in the saddle; at night he lay under the stars and
tried to feel resigned. He prayed a great deal; and
thought very often, in a hopeless way, of Carmel.
Oh, why had he been brought up to hear and see things
which were unseen by other men? Every day, as he
looked on the exasperatingly unvaried prairie, he asked
this question. Why had he not been brought up to work
with his hands? Why had he been obliged to spend the
best part of his life over his Greek and Latin books, if
this was to be the end? If he had only been taught to
do something useful as well as it could be done, he might
have found a place in that busy, heartless New York.
He never, in his deepest despair, reproached anybody.
The thought of his father and mother was a weight upon
him; but that meeting was the only foundation for golden
castles such as he only whose blood is young and
Irish-tinctured can build; for all Irishmen are poets.

And thus his life went on. His fellows respected him
as one more learned than they. Despondency, warranted
by circumstances, and hope, warranted by none,
alternated with him; but hope always stayed the longest.

III.

THE MAN FROM TEXAS.

Carmel had found a welcome in New York from her
father's brother. Mr. and Mrs. Boynton were in what
is called "good" society, and, like "good" society itself,
they were of the earth, earthy. They were childless,
and Carmel's beauty and "distinguished air"—good so-

ciety loves a distinguished air—induced them to receive her cordially. They were not wealthy, but they had a fair income, so Carmel was allowed to consult dressmakers, and, by and by, those feeble-minded creatures, of unknown sex, the fashionable correspondents, gushed over her Spanish eyes and her general attractiveness.

At first Carmel was unwilling to live with her relatives. She wanted to work; but it became apparent that the old people had grown very fond of her, so she submitted to wear purple and fine linen, and go out a great deal.

"After a time," she said to her uncle, "I will pay you for these fine things, though I can never pay you for the kindness. In time I will sell the land of my father."

"Very well," said the old man, with a kind smile, "you can pay me when the land sells for a million."

"What does the child mean by talking of land?" Mrs. Boynton asked later. "I never heard that your brother left anything."

"Carmel's land is not worth anything. It's a wild jungle in Mexico, Robbs tells me; but don't tell the child. She likes to look forward to being an heiress some day."

It would be untrue to pretend that in this atmosphere, made up of the effluvia of stale feasts, the breath of flattery, and the vapid scent of plants that blossom only in the ball-room, Carmel did not lose some of her simplicity; and yet the bloom was not all rubbed off the peach. She was very earnest in her religious duties, and her meditations before the Blessed Sacrament kept a spring undefiled in her heart, and made her unconscious of certain influences that might have spoiled her.

She seldom uttered a prayer without a remembrance of a young man who had saved her from a fate worse than death. She never hoped to meet him again, though sometimes, when the excitement of a round of gaiety had left her wearied and disgusted, she longed to speak to him; for to her he was the representative of a purer and better life.

During Lent, while the Jesuits were preaching a mission, she was seized with a yearning for earnest life. It was so calm, so peaceful. There were no temptations in it. She was tired of the world and its vanities; she longed for peace. It is scarcely fair to confess that she tried on a nunlike costume and thought she would make a nice-looking sister. If she had found the dress unbecoming, she would not have given up her aspirations, she would only have sought out a new order with a more suitable dress. The Jesuit Father smiled when she told her story, her hopes, her longings, her disgust with the world.

"I have never thought of marriage," she exclaimed. "Never! There is no man in the world—" but here she paused and blushed. She thought of a certain young man who *might*—

"And where is *he*, my child?" asked the Director, translating her thought.

"There is no 'he,' Father," she answered, in confusion, "that is, I met him in Texas." And she told the episode.

The good Father made it plain to her that a disgust for the world and the knowledge that a certain habit became her, would not make a nun. *She* would never marry, she declared, *never*. Father Dalton smiled again.

As she went homeward that evening she met Mr. Robbs. Robbs—R. De Champagne Robbs—was a young man of the "best" society. He belonged to several clubs, occasionally drove a coach, and was reported to be a great swell, quite in the English style. He drank a little too much at times, but nobody minded *that*, as it was said he had great influence in Wall Street.

Lounging in the window of the Union Club that afternoon—it is *quite* in the English style to lounge in a club before dinner—R. De Champagne Robbs had made an exclamation.

"That little Carmel Boynton is a dashed fine gall," said his friend, Frederick Algernon Smythe. "Made a fine show ridin' with the hounds over on Long Island the other day. Pretty, by Jove! There she goes—goin' to church. Pious, by Jove—prayer-book and all. Pity she's so dashed poor!"

"*Poor!*" This was Robbs' exclamation. "She's one of the richest girls in the country, if this be true. Look here!" And Robbs read:

"Silver Mine near Santiago—mum—mum—mum—Tremendous excitement—mum—mum—two millions—mum—mum—daily working capacity—"

"What's the matter with you, dear boy?" demanded the languid Smythe, fingering the japonica in his coat. "Don't read in such an excited manner. What do I care about it? What does it all mean?"

"It means that Carmel Boynton owns a silver mine. Old Boynton showed me the deed, but the experts said it was no good. I'll just telephone to old Caudle in Wall Street."

"And propose to the little Mexican," said Smythe, ruefully. "It may be awfully jolly to you, but it's an awful sell on us other fellows."

Old Caudle's answer must have been satisfactory, for De Champagne Robbs made himself very agreeable to

Carmel on her way home; and when she reached her room she had entirely forgotten her dissatisfaction with the world.

In the meantime Robbs became master of the details relating to the Mexican mines. He was so well contented that he proposed to old Boynton for Carmel.

"She is such a child," De Champagne said, ingeniously, "that I thought it best to come to you first; besides, I prefer the European fashion in most things."

"I have no money to give her," said Boynton, knowing that the European fashion demanded a dowry.

Tears forced themselves into the disinterested young man's eyes.

"You do not intend to insult me, I am sure," he said, gently. "I am very sensitive. Money and love are, with me, incompatible."

Mr. Boynton was much affected, and the matter was arranged. The old people congratulated themselves as having made a good sale of Carmel. People said young Robbs was fast, to be sure; but then, people also said that Robbs was rich.

But why prolong a story which would consist now in the recital of the nothings that "good" society uttered apropos of this sale. It was concluded by everybody that Carmel was engaged. A letter from Mr. Robbs will explain what did happen much better than a mere observer could do it. It was written to his dear English friend, Mr. Harcourt Vane, whom he had met during his travels abroad:

"I have been 'left' again, dear boy—left again. I told you of the San José heiress. You know the vile American custom of letting girls have opinions of their own. Well, Carmel has opinions of her own. I saw the old man and made it right with him. He told me she was a Romanist, but I didn't mind that, there are some really nice Romanists, you know. And I don't care much about my wife's religion, provided she doesn't interfere with the children. Well, I sent her an immense bouquet on a cotillion night—a regular stunner, cost me five pounds. And then I asked her, and told her the old fellow was willing. She hesitated. We were at De Stacy Robinson's ball. I was in the act of seeing her to her carriage. I felt her hand tremble on my arm. There was a slight murmur—ye gods! I saw myself master of the San José mines.

"The Robinsons—awfully crude Americans, you know —had a calcium light in front of their house, and just as we reached the sidewalk a man fell in front of us. I thought he was drunk, so I gave him a kick. Carmel screamed and called out something. In an instant she was kneeling beside the tramp, her satin dress trailing in the mud.

"He wasn't drunk. He is a certain young Irish-American, James Delaney. He was sick. He had known Carmel in some wild cow-boy district. And as I kicked, his coat flew open, and she saw a medal or a scapulary or something she had given him.

"Well, she recognized him, and he recognized her. He had come all the way from Texas to tell her that she was the greatest heiress in America. His pocket-book had nothing in it but papers on the San José mines. She had him taken to Mr. Boynton's, and she and a Sister of Charity nursed him.

"Everybody said she'd marry the fellow. But she did not. He has gone down South as manager of the San José mines, on an *immense* commission, they say, and taken his aged parents—some low people, I believe, with him.

"Carmel has put a lot of money into some institution for the education of young girls. Isn't it too bad? They say she goes to Mass every morning, and that this fellow attributes all the good that has come to him to his having been true to some Papistical rules of which that scapulary was the badge. Queer idea! I'd become a Romanist to-morrow if it would bring me such good luck. I said this to Carmel, but she said it wouldn't do."

www.ingramcontent.com/pod-product-compliance
Lightning Source LLC
Chambersburg PA
CBHW030553300426
44111CB00009B/965